THE COASTWATCHERS

THE COASTWATCHERS

ERIC A. FELDT

The Coastwatchers by Eric A. Feldt.

Published by The War Vault, 2019.

FIRST PRINTING, 2019.

ISBN: 9781708714512.

CONTENTS

1

THIS IS THE STORY OF THE MEN OF FERDINAND, and of FERDINAND itself. It is the story of a secret and highly unorthodox military unit which, out of the foresight of the Australian Navy and the determination of a handful of enemy-surrounded planters, missionaries, government officers, and miners, grew into the organization that supplied information from the heart of Japanese-occupied tropical islands in the Southwest Pacific, to the two Allied Headquarters of the Pacific Theater.

It is a story of damp, dimly lighted jungle camps, of hidden treetop lookouts; of silent submarines landing a few intrepid men on hostile beaches, in the dead of night; of American airmen mysteriously rescued from enemy-held islands surrounded by enemy-dominated seas. It is the story of how Allied coastwatchers managed, in strange and devious ways, not only to exist under the noses of the Japanese, but also to radio out vital military information. It is the story, too, of the bravery, the loyalty, and the ingenuity of many tropical natives, and of the perfidy or weakness of others.

FERDINAND was a small organization. All told, it numbered only a few hundred officers and men, both in the field and at its bases handling administrative work, supply, and communication. Yet it wove an intelligence network over more than half a million square miles of island and ocean. So secret was this organization of coastwatchers behind enemy lines that not even its existence was admitted during the war. Few knew that when the first landing waves of United States Marines hit the bitterly contested beaches of the Solomons, back in the jungles were Allies who were still 'older inhabitants' of Guadalcanal or New Georgia or Bougainville, coastwatchers who were eyes and ears for the invasion forces.

The coastwatchers' codename, FERDINAND, was chosen from the child's storybook, Ferdinand the Bull, but with no frivolous purpose. Besides serving as one of its cloaks of secrecy, this name was an order to the coastwatchers; a definition of their job. It was a reminder to them that it was not their duty to fight, and thus draw attention to themselves; like Disney's bull, who just sat under a tree and smelled the flowers, it was their duty to sit, circumspectly and unobtrusively, and gather information. Of course, like Ferdinand, they could fight if they were stung.

Harried by the Japanese, sometimes betrayed as well as helped by natives, the lonely coastwatchers often did have to fight, with fleetness and improvisation taking the place of force.

But even when they were unobtrusive and circumspect, their effectiveness was tremendous. For example, when the Japanese attempted their first air attack on our landing forces at Guadalcanal, 23 of the 24 enemy torpedo bombers engaged in the raid were brought down and no damage was done to our invasion force. The defeat of this particular air force and of many that followed was made possible by the warnings by radio of a coastwatcher, hidden 300 miles away, between the great Japanese air and naval base of Rabaul and the battleground of Guadalcanal. At Guadalcanal and at many other battles of the New Guinea-Solomons area, the work of the coastwatchers gave the Allies a considerable, even a decisive, advantage.

Neither FERDINAND nor the Australian coastwatching system out of which it grew sprang up full-blown with the emergency of war. The story of its origin goes back to 1919 and to the problem of protecting Australia's long, undefended coastline.

The island continent, its population of seven million largely concentrated in its southeast corner, presents large areas where, in wartime, an enemy might operate without hindrance and, in fact, without anyone's being aware of it. Pondering this problem after the last war, the Navy hit on a scheme of appointing selected civilians in the coastal areas as coastwatchers, their duty being to report any enemy activity, suspicious event, or subversive behavior in time of war.

On the greater part of the Australian coast, the watchers appointed by the Navy were generally postmasters, harbormasters, schoolteachers, police, or railway officials; people who had at hand the means of passing information by telegraph. The General Post Office agreed to send their reports over the telegraph lines of the Commonwealth to the Navy Office at Melbourne. The watchers themselves were supplied with printed instructions on what to report and how to report it.

The north and northwest coasts of Australia, the least inhabited parts, presented a more difficult problem. Before the 1930's, the few scattered missionaries and managers of cattle stations in these areas had no means of swift communication. Then the invention of the pedal radio gave them a link with the outside world, and Naval Intelligence was quick to enroll all missionaries and cattlemen owning these instruments.

Frugality was the governing factor in the design of the system, for the Navy had little money in peacetime. The coastwatchers were unpaid, and it was not possible for the Navy to supply them with radio equipment. It was a case of making the most of the personnel and the material available.

The most important addition to the scheme was made when government administrative officers at coastal stations in Papua, New Guinea, and the Solomon Islands were enrolled as watchers. Unfortunately, the geographical positions of the stations were determined by civil government needs and not by strategical requirements. The Navy partly remedied this defect, as time went on, by appointing selected planters to the organization.

Some of the patrol and district officers in the islands had radio communication and could use the code of the islands' administrations. Others had neither. Six government officers in the area had both radio communications and high-grade codes.

The arrangements for organizing this pre-war network, simple as it was, were necessarily protracted. State governments, boards of missions, territory governments, all had to be consulted and their co-operation sought in lengthy and voluminous correspondence.

But by September 1939, the coastwatchers were eight hundred strong, the great majority of them, of course, on the Australian mainland. In Australia's island screen, where FERDINAND was eventually to operate, the system was still very thin and spotty, but at least a nucleus existed, and funds were available. Upon the outbreak of war with Germany, the Navy directed the organization, such as it was, to commence functioning.

It was at this point that my connection with the organization began. I had been a naval officer before I became an islander. After joining one of the first terms of cadets to enter the Royal Australian Naval College, I had gone to the Grand Fleet in 1917 as a midshipman. In 1922, I had retired with the rank of Lieutenant, and the following year had gone to New Guinea, in the government service. When war broke, I was warden of Wau Goldfield in New Guinea. I was on the emergency list of Royal Australian Naval officers, with the rank of lieutenant commander. So, in September 1939, I rejoined the Navy.

I was directed to report to Commander R. B. M. Long, Director of Naval Intelligence. Long had been a term mate of mine at the Royal Australian Naval College and we knew each other well. On him had fallen much of the burden of building up the Naval Intelligence Division, and it had been a thankless task, calling for patience and equanimity. Lack of funds had prevented him from carrying out his ideas in full, and now he had to work against time to fill in the blanks.

He was a leader rather than a driver, and, if anything, over-indulgent of the faults of his juniors. Years of secretive work had developed in him an indirect, oblique approach to problems, a habit which he sometimes carried to extremes. Experience had given him a wide knowledge, and he combined a capacity for working long hours with an unfailing good humor. Above all his other virtues was his ability to let anything alone if it functioned properly.

Under Long, I was appointed Staff Officer (Intelligence) at Port Moresby, in charge of the intelligence organization in Papua, New Guinea, and the Solomon Islands. Long and his civil assistant, W. H. Brooksbank, who had also borne the long struggle to build up the coastwatching organization, provided me with all the information—a considerable amount—which would be of use to me.

It was to be my duty, first, to ensure the proper functioning of the organization in the islands, as it then stood; and second, to expand it so that it would cover all our needs. Long knew what he wanted, but because of his lack of knowledge of island conditions, did not know quite how to get it.

So he left that part to me, together with the problem of dealing with those difficult people, the islanders. None of us then knew, of course, that the organization we were building would eventually operate in hostile territory, its posts surrounded by the enemy.

Recruitment poster for the Australian Imperial Force

2

To Americans, the islands where FERDINAND operated are known as the Southwest Pacific. To Australians, from the perspective of their still more southwesterly position, they are the Northeast Area, a chain screening the island continent. In the Navy, we thought of them somewhat as a fence, but a fence with several gates; the straits between the islands. In the period between the declaration of war on Germany and the invasion of the Japanese, my job was to make the fence as effective as possible.

On 21 September 1939, with the war sixteen days old, I set out with a sheaf of printed coastwatcher instructions to visit every man in the islands who had a teleradio. My travels took me by ship, motorboat, canoe, bicycle, airplane, and boot throughout the Solomons, the New Hebrides, Papua, New Guinea, New Britain, New Ireland, and their satellite specks of land. I saw nearly everybody and nearly everybody saw me. I already knew more than half of those I met, and all were helpful.

By December 1939, I had enrolled all existing teleradio operators, taught them how to code, what to report, and that speed in reporting was the prime essential. With an eye to the future, I also instructed about a hundred others in reporting, although most of these had no means by which a message could be passed to us except by runner to the nearest teleradio; often a matter of days.

When I returned to Port Moresby, I proposed to Long that we depart from the Australian scheme of using only coastwatchers with communications equipment already at hand, and lend additional teleradios to selected persons at strategic points.

At this time, the war with Germany was of course receiving first priority, and a proposal such as this, meaning diversion of effort to the Pacific, represented one more strain on inadequate resources. But Long, imbued with the belief that Japan would one day enter the war, pressed hard and carried the plan. Its prompt approval made all the future possible. The governments of the islands and the Royal Australian Air Force eagerly assisted us in distributing the teleradios to their strategic positions. But even under the pressure at which everyone worked, it was August 1940 before the instruments were all placed in the far-flung ports and lonely plantations.

Still one more move was needed to close the gates in the fence. The principal gap in the chain is that between New Ireland and

Buka, with the tiny Anir (Feni) and Nissan Islands from which the sea lanes can be watched. A plantation manager manned a Navy-supplied teleradio on Nissan, but as navigators usually prefer the route near Anir, it was vital that Anir, too, have a watcher.

For this desolate point, we selected Chief Yeoman of Signals S. Lamont, an old sailor, as Irish as Paddy's pig. He was a complete stranger to conditions of life on an isolated island, but a resourceful and dependable man. While the news was coming through of the debacle in France and the capitulation of Belgium, he was landed and placed in a temporary camp, and then was left to shift for himself. His first few months on Anir must have been acute misery but, as we expected, he adjusted himself and carried on his watch ably.

While we were choosing watchers and placing teleradios, we were also working out a method for integrating men and instruments into a unique communications system. Taking the materials at hand as our basis, we fitted each teleradio in the area, whether naval or privately owned, with a crystal cut to give a special frequency, known as 'X.' Loudspeakers kept constantly switched on at key stations in Rabaul, Tulagi Harbour, Port Moresby, and Thursday Island, could receive any signal sent on X frequency at any hour. Previously the small stations in the area had communicated with key points at fixed times; 'skeds,' as they were called.

We had no trouble in enlisting co-operation for our plan, for in the Solomons, radio was managed by the Government, and in Papua and New Guinea it was in the hands of Amalgamated Wireless of Australia, a company in which the Commonwealth Government held 51 percent of the shares. Until the Japanese attacked, Amalgamated Wireless was in charge of maintaining our teleradios, while the Navy paid it for this service and for the watch kept on X frequency.

The teleradios themselves had been developed by Amalgamated Wireless. They were grand instruments, standing up to heat, wet, and amateur handling, with a range up to 400 miles on voice and 600 miles if keys were used to transmit Morse. The model we used, the '3B,' produced in 1939, consisted of a transmitter, receiver, and loudspeaker, with four alternative transmission frequencies which could be tuned to complete accuracy. All parts were enclosed in three metal boxes, each about a foot deep, a foot wide, and two feet long. Power was supplied by batteries like those a car uses, which were charged by a small gasoline engine weighing about 70 pounds, the heaviest part of the set.

The instrument had one serious disadvantage. It was difficult to carry, requiring twelve to sixteen porters. Foreseeing that the time might come when this would be a serious handicap, Naval

Intelligence drew up requirements for a portable teleradio and placed orders. An error crept into the manufacturing and after many months we were supplied not with the type we wanted, but with a radio similar to the 3B, only not quite as good. The Air Forces developed what we wanted independently, and eventually we were able to obtain it and even to supply it by parachute to coastwatchers. In the meantime, however, the 3B was our mainstay.

In this grim game of watching and reporting, part of the value of the signal would be lost if the enemy knew he had been reported and could take countermeasures, so a code was an absolute necessity.

'Playfair,' a simple cipher known to most schoolboys, had been chosen in peacetime when the coastwatchers were first appointed by the Navy. It has the virtue that it needs no documents other than a list of agreed-on keywords, but it has the disadvantage of being low grade. I devised a variation known as 'Playfair Feldt Method'—one by which the bigrams were broken—which was a little more secure than the original. Eventually, after the watchers had amply proved themselves, the Navy supplied us with really good codes.

Long before the war, the Navy had pondered the problem of reliability of coastwatchers and had devised a scale to take into account both its faith in the individual informant and the likelihood of the occurrence he reported. This grading system was carefully used from 1939 until Japan entered the war. But when coastwatchers came fully into the picture, with war on their doorsteps, they established such a gilt-edged reputation that their reports were automatically accepted, qualified only by any doubts which the watcher himself expressed.

In December 1940, the coastwatchers had a first tangle with the enemy when two German raiders chose the small island of Emirau, north of Kavieng, to land prisoners from ships they had sunk. This gave the watchers some real practice. A boat from the island reached Kavieng where the District Officer, who was the coastwatcher there, signaled its arrival and the position of the prisoners. Arrangements were promptly made to pick up the marooned passengers and crews. Soon the officers dispatched, more than busy collecting information concerning the appearance of the raiders, their armament, their methods, and for the reconstruction of the routes they had followed. With the arrival of the refugees in an Australian port, the coastwatchers settled down to waiting again, now with a feeling that they had a real role to play.

The presence of the raiders, however, added indirectly to one of our minor but annoying troubles; the patriotic fervor of loudmouthed flag-wavers. These nuisances had nothing much to do, so they engaged in a heresy hunt. They were not so much security-mad. In New Guinea some of the Germans, even some Lutheran missionaries, were Nazis, and after their internment suspicion of all Germans, including anyone with a German-sounding name, burned to incandescence.

The surveillance of subversive activity was the duty of Military Intelligence, so I took little part in it, but at times found my way beset with difficulties. For instance, when I proposed making an Australian Lutheran missionary a coastwatcher, a high civil official said, horror in every syllable, 'But he spells his name F-r-e-u-n-d!'

I could only reply, weakly, by spelling my own.

Another who was held in deep suspicion by the ultra-patriotic was Ken Frank, manager of the Amalgamated Wireless station at Port Moresby. Frank's advice and expert assistance to us were beyond price but he was a cynic who derided the Empire; consequently, while he worked day and night to save the country, he was amusingly enough dubbed a Fifth Columnist. Later, when disaster was near, Frank sat at a receiver with the bombs falling around him, still wisecracking about Old School Ties and Strategic Retreats, his accusers long since having sugared off to safety.

During our period of waiting, the lesson from Europe had been the need for co-operation among the Armed Services. So, in Melbourne the Chiefs of Staff of Australian Army, Navy, and Air Force pooled their authority and exercised command as the 'Combined War Room' overall forces.

Our coastwatcher reports, which obviously concerned the three services, were available instantly to all. Coastwatchers were under general supervision of the civil government in the islands, but experience had shown us that in times of even minor stress civil officials were so busy at their own affairs they had no time to attend to ours. To remedy this, the Navy appointed intelligence officers to Port Moresby, Thursday Island, Rabaul, Tulagi, and Vila, each to control coastwatchers in his own area and to transmit intelligence to Melbourne and to Area Combined Headquarters in Townsville.

Through this arrangement, I lost my assistant Hugh Mackenzie, who was appointed to Rabaul. Mackenzie had been in the same term as I at Naval College. He had spent most of the years between the two wars in New Guinea and Papua, first as a rolling stone and later as a planter. He was conscientious and thorough in an unsystematic way, occasionally doing something quite illogical. The coastwatching service was lucky the day it got Mackenzie, for this man, who completely lacked the qualities of salesmanship and showmanship, was to fill brilliantly one of the most dramatic and responsible assignments of the battle for Guadalcanal.

Mackenzie and each of the other four Naval Intelligence Officers assigned to coastwatcher control kept a plot of ships in his area. Should Lamont on Anir sight a ship, for instance, he would immediately code a signal and call Rabaul on X frequency. Amalgamated Wireless at Rabaul would telephone the signal over a direct wire to Mackenzie, who would decode it. If no ship on his plot corresponded to that reported, his office would pass Lamont's signal to the Air Force and would then code a signal in high-grade cypher for Melbourne and Townsville. The Air Force's Rabaul Advanced Operational Base would send out an aircraft to intercept and examine the ship.

If the sighting were of aircraft instead of a ship, the signal from the coastwatcher had to be sent in plain language. Experience had shown us that by the time the signal was decoded, aircraft information was cold.

As far as could be done, the intelligence position was sewn up. As far as could be done...

There was one grave weakness in our position. We had insufficient force to back up and hold our intelligence screen. Australia's sea forces, somewhere to the south, were not adequate in any case to deal with more than a squadron of light cruisers. The Air Force had some Catalinas, a few Hudson bombers, and half a dozen Wirraways. The Army had little more than a battalion in Port Moresby, about the same force at Rabaul, and still smaller forces at five other points in the vast territory. In terms of war, we had merely token forces.

It was obvious that if the enemy came on anything more serious than a raid, any of our key coastwatcher points might be occupied and our chain broken.

So we were increasingly haunted by the specter of enemy occupation, and by the anomalous position of the coastwatchers. Under international law, coastwatchers, as civilians, had no real right to transmit intelligence once their area was effectively occupied. Should they continue reporting they would be absolutely unprotected, their position that of spies.

No policy was laid down on this disturbing possibility until late in 1941, when Long made the decision that civilian coastwatchers were to cease reporting in the event of enemy occupation. Bound as he was by international law and by the limitation that civilians could not be ordered to remain in invaded territory, he could take no other stand. Unofficially, however, we all hoped that in case of invasion some civilians would remain and report enemy movements.

So, in practice, we left things pretty much in the air. Watchers were informed that they were not ordered to remain. However, we took care not to give a definite order that they cease reporting and we did give them careful instructions on how to contact another radio station should their own control station fail to reply.

Thus, when Japan struck, the decision was really in the hands of the watchers themselves. A civilian coastwatcher could remain, at his own risk and in the hope he would get recognition and support. But there was no promise, even an implied promise, that he would get either. All he had was the promise of certain peril.

3

WHEN, A MONTH AFTER PEARL HARBOR, the hurricane of war struck at the Northeast Area, it worked havoc with our island intelligence chain. Here and there, parts of the chain were left freakishly intact; in other places it was destroyed, or its links dislocated.

There was, for instance, C. C. Jervis, planter and retired Navy telegraphist on Nissan Island, who watched an enemy ship move toward the lagoon entrance of his low, undefended atoll; he calmly coded and sent a report of its presence, and was never heard of again.

There was J. Daymond, assistant district officer at Gasmata, a noisome, marshy native prison island off the south coast of New Britain, who warned Port Moresby of its first air raid, giving the town ample time to prepare, and then was betrayed, unwittingly, by his countrymen: the news was broadcast in Australia that enemy aircraft had been sighted over Gasmata, direct information to the Japanese that we had a reporting station at that point. Promptly the enemy bombed and gunned Gasmata station. For the nonce, Daymond and his staff were saved, having wisely moved with their teleradio across to the mainland.

Unsatisfied, the Japanese landed a force at Gasmata two weeks after the fall of Rabaul. According to the story that percolated through, they asked the first native they saw where the kiap was, and were led, in innocent simplicity, to Daymond and his assistant, who had returned to the island. A third member of the staff radioed the bare facts of their capture, and that was the last heard from him, too. We did not even receive an acknowledgment of our reply to his desperate message.

There was, on the other hand, L. G. Vial, a young assistant district officer evacuated by the Air Force from Rabaul, who was swiftly commissioned an Air Force Pilot Officer, supplied within a week with teleradio, codes, food, and instruction, and flown to Salamaua on the New Guinea coast a few days before the Japanese moved in. Hidden in the hills above Salamaua airfield, for six months, in his quiet unhurried voice, he reported aircraft on the way, their types, numbers, course, and height. His was the voice most listened for at Port Moresby, and at last a correspondent dubbed him 'The Golden Voice,' a title which embarrassed him considerably. At the end of his watch, he was awarded the American Distinguished Service Cross.

There was D. G. N. Chambers on Emirau Island, north of Kavieng, who made a remarkable escape by launch, passing enemy-held Rabaul at night. Next morning, driven ashore by an enemy destroyer, his launch wrecked, he managed to find a party of other refugees and to make his escape with them. His experience was typical of a number of the watchers who were forced to flee their posts but who survived to serve FERDINAND another day.

There were W. L. Tupling on Ningo and J. H. McColl on Wuvulu, small coral islands in the Admiralty Group, 250 miles northwest of Rabaul. When the radio station at Rabaul was silenced, they tried desperately to raise Port Moresby on their teleradios, but distance and the intervening mountain ranges were too much. So, uninstructed, they remained at their lonely posts to warn a small detachment of Commandos in the islands of approaching ships, to help in destroying everything of use to the Japanese, and finally to aid in evacuating the soldiers. At last one of their signals was picked up, they were instructed to evacuate, and in a plantation launch they made their way, like Chambers, to safety and to future service.

And there was Cornelius Lyons Page, watcher on Tabar Island, east of New Ireland, the outer perimeter of our coastwatcher defense. In many ways, Page's story epitomizes the frustration, the improvisation and, in the light of what was happening, the almost unreasonable faith which were the themes of coastwatcher existence in the six months after January 1942. It exemplifies, also, both the magnificent and the maddening aspects of the island backgrounds of our watchers.

Although Page was only thirty years old when Japan entered the war, he was already a confirmed and seasoned islander. Brought up in a Sydney suburb, he had come to the islands with his parents at the age of nineteen. In Rabaul, 'metropolis' of the Northeast Area, he was given a job behind a counter in a store. But his eyes ranged far away beyond the hills that fringed the harbor. He met men who lived untrammeled lives (or so it seemed to him); recruiters, miners, planters. The glamor of far places in the islands called him insistently, whispering of white beaches and palms in moonlight and of hot, still jungle, but not of loneliness and melancholy.

So, Page left his job in Rabaul and settled on Mussau Island, northwest of Kavieng. He took up land and commenced to plant it with coconuts, trading with the natives to pay his way. Personal freedom, complete freedom was his. His dream was realized. Now he had only to five it, unspurred by further ambition.

Days, unmarked, drifted to months, and months to years. Having no European neighbors, Page talked to natives, growing from a stranger to a familiar with them. Their thoughts impinged upon his, slowly at first, but shaping his ideas as time went by, as two stones rubbing together shape themselves to each other. He came, imperceptibly, to regard Massau, Kavieng, and the nearby islands as his country, indeed as his world, to feel that other places were nebulous and far away.

Big and virile, he enjoyed his life. And yet, under the overlay of his contentment, his heritage of energy, will, and pride, unchanneled toward a goal, was at odds with his environment. Aimlessly goaded to further adventure, at length he sold his plantation on Massau and went to Tabar, where traces of gold had been found. He tried prospecting, then took jobs here and there in the New Ireland area, never staying long in any.

Familiarity had bred an acceptance of the natives in a higher status, a place closer to himself, than the European generally concedes, and on Tabar, Page took a young native girl, Ansin Bulu, to live with him. This was more than an outlet for excess sexual vitality. Through companionship the relation between the two developed into something much deeper than is usual in such liaisons.

When war broke out with Germany, Page felt the urge to fight, but it all seemed far away and not of his world and, undecided and restless, he let the days drift by. Then, when copra became all but unsaleable, a planter who decided to go after ready money gave him a job as manager of his plantation, Pigibut, on Simberi, one of three small islands in the Tabar group. Earlier a teleradio had been lent to this planter by the Navy, and so with his plantation duties Page also undertook the coastwatching duties of his predecessor.

The island group was a small world of its own, its only connection with the outside world an unreliable twenty-mile canoe journey to the nearest point on the New Ireland shore, and the occasional visits of copra ships. It was a backwater, a little group of land specks of no importance whatever.

On Simberi, in addition to the plantation which Page managed, there was one other plantation, managed by 'Sailor' Herterich. On Tatau Island, three miles to the south, a plantation was owned and managed by Jack Talmage. Talmage was an elderly veteran of World War I, a quiet man, respected by his neighbors. A sailor, Herterich was not. He had settled in New Guinea when it was a German colony, but when the war was lost to Germany, he became not so much German as the husband of a native woman; and so escaped deportation. In the years since, he had managed plantations, a lazy, unreliable man, who drifted along with the tide of life.

The other four plantations in the island group were owned by a firm and run by a succession of managers, transients who came, stayed awhile, and left. The only other inhabitants were the natives, who had the reputation of being idle, quarrelsome, and lacking in character.

With the outbreak of war with Japan, the Tabar group was immediately jolted from its inconsequential position in the outer nebula of New Guinea. Those who navigate aircraft differ little in their methods from the navigators of ships. After a long trip over open ocean, the navigator likes to make a landfall to fix his position. For Japanese pilots, flying from Truk to bomb Rabaul, the usual landfall was Tabar.

In the month that preceded the fall of Rabaul, Page kept watch for these planes, reporting them day and night. It is interesting to speculate on the possible difference this might have made in the course of the war, had there been a squadron of modern fighter aircraft at Rabaul instead of the antiquated Wirraways. Page's warnings would have given them time to reach altitude, intercept the unescorted bombers, and shoot them down like ducks. The enemy losses would have disorganized the Japanese capacity for long-range attack and reconnaissance.

Perhaps Japan would have paused, given us time to move our forces to the area, and smash the enemy convoy when at last it moved, so that there would have been no campaign in the Southwest and South Pacific. All a might have been, but if it had happened so, what fame would have been Page's!

While Page watched and signaled, Sailor Herterich considered his position. The Japanese would come, and then what would happen to Sailor? He had best be a German again, an ally of Japan. Busily he spread word among the natives that the Japanese would come and were to be treated as friends.

Page heard the whispers being passed around, and countered them. The Japanese would not come, he said, and if they did would soon be driven off. He, Page, was staying. The natives, hearing both opinions, uneasily reserved their decision.

Page's radio signals had not escaped the notice of the Japanese, and with the fall of Rabaul and Kavieng he became a hunted man. Once they were established in the area, the Japanese promptly sent a warship to raid the plantation. Page had already moved his teleradio to a hut in the jungle, however, and he was not discovered. When the ship had gone, he signaled over his teleradio, reporting its departure.

At our headquarters in Townsville, Page's position appeared untenable. I signaled, 'You have done magnificent work. Your position is now dangerous if you continue reporting and under present circumstances your reports are of little value. You are to bury your teleradio and may join either party on New Ireland or take other measures for safety. Good luck.'

Page took no notice of the signal. He was on Simberi, a master who had told the natives he would stay. This was his world, his only frame of reference. He was fighting the war, but it was the Tabar War, his own war.

He continued to send signals concerning the extent of the Japanese occupation at Kavieng, the names of Europeans in the area who had been captured, enemy guns and defense positions.

In Townsville, we knew nothing of his local problems or his state of mind, but it was obvious that he had no intention of leaving. This being the case, the best course was to try to keep him quiet until a time came when his information would be of greatest use. A sudden complete silence might lead the Japanese to think he had gone. So we sent another signal, 'Your reports appreciated, but it is more important to keep yourself free. Do not transmit except in extreme emergency. You will be ordered to make reports when they will be of greatest value.'

Finally, as he still came on the air, we ordered him to cease transmission altogether, until ordered to recommence. Even this did little good. Such disobedience, inconceivable in any other wartime operation, was not too surprising in an islander. We had to accept it, interwoven as it was with other traits so valuable to us.

Meantime, extremely worried over the civilian status of men in Page's position, we were making recommendations that Page and others be given naval rank. Possibly rank would be no protection against a brutal enemy but, even so, every aid was needed. Aside from its dubious advantages of personal safety, rank would permit us to pay the watchers and to provide for their dependents.

At long last, in March 1942, the red tape was cut, and Page, unseen by authorities or doctors and without signing any forms, was commissioned a sub-lieutenant, Royal Australian Naval Volunteer Reserve, probably a happening without precedent.

On Tabar, as the natives watched events, they slowly began to lean toward Herterich and the Japanese, although Talmage supported Page to his utmost. Ironically, Page, the man who had been so close to native life and native thinking, was losing his influence and with it his control. In March, renegade natives from Kavieng, possibly encouraged by Herterich, looted the plantation and threatened to report Page's whereabouts to the Japanese.

Shortly after this event, Hans Pettersen, a half-caste, fat, sly swine of a man who had been in disrepute since boyhood, came to live with Herterich. He too preached acceptance of the Japanese and gradually the natives' attitude toward Page drifted from uncertainty to positive opposition.

In view of these developments, it was problematical that Page's whereabouts could be kept secret even should we be able to impress upon him the need for discretion. So we advised him to make for Buka, northernmost island of the Solomons, which was still clear of the enemy. Beset by an obstinacy which was aggravated by his dislike of Herterich and Pettersen, Page rejected the suggestion. His reply was to send a further list of captured Europeans and to warn that Namatani airfield on New Ireland was mined, information he had obtained by careful questioning of runaway natives.

Other radios were also on the air, and coastwatchers were listening to each other to glean any news they could. Page and a watcher on Bougainville were accustomed to chatter to each other in Kavieng dialect which both knew, and which was as safe as any code.

Once teleradio eavesdroppers heard two missionaries in Papua talking to each other when Page wanted to send an urgent signal. The missionaries were depressed as they discussed their prospects, and Page listened with growing impatience while one said, 'I will pray for you, Brother.'

The other replied, 'And I will pray for you, Brother.'

At this point, Page was heard to break in, 'Get off the ruddy air and I will pray for both of you.'

For his signals to headquarters, Page obtained new code key-words during communication with his mother in Australia, through names of persons and places woven into the conversation.

By the end of March, Page was a dot in a Japanese-held ocean. Every surrounding key point had been occupied and even thought of escape was futile, unless it could be managed by outside aid. Supply, too, was becoming impossible for him locally, with fewer and fewer natives supporting him. His plantation supplies were nearly consumed, and he had no arms whatever to defend himself. He moved into caves, and at one time only Ansin Bulu, his native wife, stood by him.

To drop supplies from an aircraft was the only solution, but our few aircraft were overworked, and each trip threatened a loss that could ill be spared, while parachutes were rare as diamonds.

So, it was late in May before a drop could be made ready. Cap and badges of rank, food, a rifle, and ammunition were included in the supply packets. The pack containing the rifle jammed in the bomb-bay doors, during the drop, and had to be returned to Port Moresby in that position; just one of those things that happened. The other supplies, fortunately, were successfully dropped and found by Page.

Shortly afterward his radio developed a fault in the voice transmission, and he had to send his signals laboriously by Morse, touching two wires together in place of a key. The signals were hardly readable. Ken Frank, the cynical Amalgamated Wireless man at Port Moresby who had appeared so sinister to the super-patriotic, guessed the fault as a broken lead-in, and the whole part was dropped to Page by parachute, rectifying the fault; a fine feat of remote diagnosis.

The supplies, indicating outside support for Page, restored his prestige a little with the natives. But when he signaled that the Japanese were enrolling native police, we knew that he could evade the enemy for very little longer. We decided to attempt to evacuate him.

Several United States submarines had recently arrived in Australia, and, with the help of the U.S. Naval Liaison Officer, a rescue trip and a rendezvous were arranged. Page at last agreed to take our advice and to make his escape on the vessel.

For three nights, Page kept the rendezvous, flashing the agreed signals from a torch in a small boat. Every flash must have seemed an invitation to unseen enemies. Every ripple of the water must have made his heart leap with hope of friend or fear of foe. Those three nights must have been a fairly complete catalog of hope, desperation, and triumph over panic.

But no submarine came. Later, we learned the vessel had developed a serious mechanical defect and had been hard put to limp back to port. These were old submarines, which had already taken a beating in the Philippines and were not to be compared with the models of efficiency which later operated in the South and Southwestern Pacific.

We made distracted attempts to get another submarine to undertake the mission, but there were other tasks of urgent strategical value and the Navy regretfully decided it could do no more.

In the meantime, Page signaled that a ship with Japanese, natives, and dogs was due on a certain day to hunt him. One of our aircraft, searching for the ship, could not find it, but during its hurried run bombed an old wreck to impress the natives with the fact that Page still had support.

When next we called Page on the radio, no answer came. The Air Force, in spite of the risk entailed, then sent a Catalina with a crew of nine on a last rescue attempt. The pilot flying low around the island and searching carefully, saw only natives sitting stolidly on the beach, unmoving and giving no sign.

Two years later, a young Australian Naval Officer, attached to U.S. Naval Headquarters at Emirau, put in at Tabar by PT boat. From an ex-schoolboy of the Rabaul native school who, with a sense of history, had written an account of the happenings on the island, the officer obtained the brief story of Page's capture and death.

Ansin Bulu was first picked up by the searching Japanese, and held in Kavieng jail. A week later, the jungle hiding place of Page and his planter friend, Talmage, was discovered by a hostile native. On 16 June 1942, the Japanese were guided to the spot, and the two men were captured as they slept in their hut.

They were taken to Kavieng jail, and after a few weeks Ansin Bulu was released, while Page and Talmage were taken to a small island by a party of Japanese who returned without them.

After Page and Talmage were executed, the Japanese made Hans Pettersen Kiap of the Tabar group, with the special task of growing food for Japanese troops. This he did, flogging and ill-treating the natives and robbing them of the little money and goods they had.

From one point of view, Page was just a young man of no particular learning, certainly no strategist, who had left himself no retreat. From another, he had been the source of information of very great value, among it the important negative information of what the Japanese were not doing in the New Ireland area. Four of his five months in enemy-occupied territory were on borrowed time; a less skillful man would have been caught much earlier, a less courageous one would have retired in the first month.

Thus Page's epitaph. His story has one sequel. On the Australian officer's second PT boat trip to the island, an emaciated and aged-looking native woman came forward to meet him. Simply, she handed him a piece of toilet paper, dirty and crumpled. In faint pencil, it read,

To CO. Allied Forces for Lieut-Co. E. A. Feldt R.A.N. from Sub-Lieut C. L. Page, R.A.N.V.R. 9th July.

Re: The female Ansin Bulu, Nakapur Village, Simberi Island, Tabar.

THIS FEMALE HAS BEEN IN MY SERVICE 7 YEARS. HAS BEEN OF GREAT VALUE TO ME SINCE JAN. JAPS LOOTED ALL SHE OWNED VALUE £50 PUT HER IN PRISON AND GOD KNOWS WHAT ELSE. HER CRIME WAS SHE STUCK. SIR, PLEASE DO YOUR BEST.

SUB-LIEUT C. L. PAGE

A two-man AIF light machine-gun unit

4

ISLANDERS LIKE PAGE WERE THE CORE OF FERDINAND. Without them, coastwatching would have been an impractical Boy Scout adventure. More than most enterprises, FERDINAND was the creature of its environment, completely dependent on the vices and virtues of the white islanders and the natives, the relation of the native and the European to each other, the advantages and disadvantages of terrain and climate.

The Allies' armed forces learned, by hard experience, what it means to cope with the mountains of the Northeast Area, the jungle, the rain, and mud, the burning sun on open grass plains, the flat, soggy swamps and water-logged beaches, the fever and dysentery and tropical ulcers and scrub typhus, and the summation of all these, which saps the energy and endurance and is a constant brake on human endeavor.

After the first Allied landings had been made in this area, any staff officer could foretell the conditions troops would encounter and eventually could make arrangements to minimize their worst effects. But when Japan struck in the Pacific, not many men knew these things.

Natives had considerable knowledge, but they could not very well convey it to others or use it in warfare themselves, except in a very limited way. The Asiatics, who formed a social group between the Europeans and the natives, had little of the needed lore or much drive to use it. In general, they had been content merely to trade and accumulate what wealth they could, and by and large they expressed no political or organizational aspirations, although most of them, Cantonese, belonged to the Kuomintang.

There were a few Europeans who had that lore, acquired from their island vocations, and it was on these men we depended.

Perhaps foremost among them were island administrative officers. Each territory in the Northeast Area is divided into districts, each of which was administered by a district officer responsible to the territorial administrator. The system was the same throughout the area, although in Papua the districts were called divisions and the district officers were called resident magistrates, while in the Solomons the administrator's title was resident commissioner. Australia governed Papua and Mandated New Guinea, which includes New Britain and New Ireland. Britain governed the Solomons.

The district officer was a real power in his district, responsible for all forms of governmental activity save for public health and occasional exceptional affairs. Of course, he was subject to the law and there was machinery for appeal from his decisions; but appeals are long and costly affairs in which the average man does not indulge. So, the district officer, with considerable authority, exercised his functions of magistrate, chief of police, head jailer, coroner, licensing authority, collector of customs, inspector of labor, land purchaser, and local treasurer. His duties brought him into contact with all phases of life. One district officer, who knew better, said to me with a twinkle in his eye, 'I have to be, like Caesar's wife, all things to all men.'

In particular, the district officer was arbiter of the relation between Europeans and natives. To him the native came with any complaint of ill treatment. He was the kiap, who had power to settle all matters. An able and tactful district officer kept the wheels of the machinery of everyday life running smoothly, but an incompetent one invariably set section against section, and had a constant turmoil on his hands.

On the district officer's staff were cadets, patrol officers, and assistant district officers, rising in rank in that order. Young men were selected as cadets, sent to a district for training and experience under the tutelage of an experienced officer, and then promoted to patrol officer after a term of about two years.

As a patrol officer, the young man, accompanied by native police, traveled from village to village, maintaining law and order. Since there were natives in all degrees of control, from those near the settlements who led an ordered existence, to those in recently explored country who lived in primitive savagery, the patrol officer acquired a knowledge of native life in all its facets.

In constant company of native police, he grew to know these men particularly well, to know under what circumstances they would be courageous and when, as the native puts it, their bellies are water. With this experience came the habit of command.

A patrol officer was called on to settle all manner of disputes. Today the issue might be the value of taro damaged by an intruding pig in a garden; tomorrow it might be the peace terms between two villages which had been at war with each other so long that the mind of man ran not to the contrary. Constant use gave him a good command of pidgin English, a more unusual accomplishment than is generally supposed, for although all Europeans in the islands use pidgin, a very few speak it well.

So the patrol officer got experience, and with it, exercise. As his work led him from village to village, sometimes it was on a passable walking track, sometimes he 'broke bush' through jungle. But his trail always led up one steep slope and down another, or through humid swamp or over hot *kunai* (coarse grass) plain, or on the soft sand of beaches. He lived on the food he carried, supplemented by game or field fruits from native gardens, fruits which for the most part are unappetizing and unattractive. His life was hard, but he could not allow it to be too hard or his health would break. He invariably had malaria germs in his body, and a period of malnutrition was an invitation to them to hold carnival in his bloodstream while he racked and sweated under a palm thatch roof, far from help or comfort. Continued malaria held the threat of the dreaded and often fatal blackwater fever.

Promoted to assistant district officer, he led much the same life, but with added responsibilities, either as assistant to a district officer in one of the larger settlements or as supervisor of part of a district. He still walked from village to village. Indeed, he could not look to any surcease from this duty even after his promotion to district officer. For any district officer who did not go on patrol himself was soon branded an office kiap, or verandah king, who did not know what went on in his own district.

The planters were often as versatile as administrative officers. Almost invariably they started as junior employees on large company-owned plantations, learned the work, and then either launched out for themselves or became managers of company plantations.

The planter directed the work of his 'line' of native laborers. He himself had to know how copra should be dried and bagged, how to repair or even construct a drier, how to recognize and counter any of the diseases or pests of his crops and stock. He had to know how to kill and cut up cattle and corn the meat. If the plantation used bullock carts, it was his task to break in the bullocks; if a motor truck was used, he was his own mechanic. Many plantations had their own motor launches, so he was often somewhat of a seaman as well.

Then there were all those things which a white man, living alone, must do for his own comfort. He was his own plumber, carpenter, and if he wanted to hear the news, radio mechanic. Most planters were cooks also, for cook-boys are trained, not born. So the planter was a man of many parts, able to look after himself in any circumstances.

If the planter was versatile, the alluvial miner was equally so. The underground miner and the dredge crews worked in large organizations, but the alluvial gold miner of New Guinea was the world's most marked individualist. When he was prospecting, he had all the disadvantages of the life of a patrol officer, but without the advantages of the officer's prestige as a government official.

When he settled to mining his holding, which he took up by right and not by permission of any man, he built his home, directed his natives in their work of digging water races, installing pipes and nozzles, planting gardens, tempering tools and sharpening them, moving boulders, and washing gravel. Independence was his second nature, and he asked only that he clean up enough gold to pay his way.

The oil prospector was, in many respects, like the gold prospector. Though he was often a highly qualified geologist or surveyor in the employ of a company, he met the same problems as the patrol officer and the miner.

The missionaries formed a checkerboard of sects and nationalities. In Papua they were British or Australian, except for one group of French Catholics. On the Mandated New Guinea mainland there were German, Austrian, and American Lutherans, German and Dutch Catholics, and Seventh Day Adventists. In New Britain were German, Dutch, and Polish Catholics and Australian Methodists. French and American Catholics and Australian Methodists shared New Ireland, Buka, and Bougainville. Anglicans and Catholics, Methodists and Seventh Day Adventists were all to be found in the other Solomon Islands.

In most villages, a native mission teacher lived and taught the rudiments of his faith under the direction of the nearest missionary. Some missions, besides conducting churches, schools, and hospitals, owned and managed extensive plantations, employing labor in the same way as any other employer. But, in general, the missionary's point of view tended to become that of the village native, whereas the planter and miner looked at native matters from the perspective of native labor.

Lacking, in general, a common meeting ground with the rest of the Europeans, the missionaries tended to draw apart. This was most marked in the Mandated Territory, where barriers of language and nationality also intervened; it was least noticeable in Papua, where the missionaries taught the natives cricket and where a mission produced a native team which sometimes beat the Europeans.

The natives were all Stone Age men less than a hundred years ago, and many still are. Contact with Europeans has altered the basic elements of their lives surprisingly little, though knives and axes have replaced stone tools, and cloth has replaced grass or bark garments. The villages, with an average population between 100 and 200 persons, look and sound much the same as they did in the remote, isolated past. The village coconut grove is larger, having been planted under government directions, but there is still a yearly time of scarce rations. The number of malignant spirits still haunting evil places depends on the individual's degree of belief in mission teaching.

But there are changes, apart from the knives and cloth. The villager, except in the far interior, does not live in fear of a raid from his neighbors, since most tribal fighting has long since been stamped out. If a man thinks himself wronged, he can go before the government-appointed native chief, and if he is dissatisfied with the decision he can go to court, where a patrol officer will determine his case. If he is sick, he can go to the government hospital, and in the village, he is given preventive treatment for yaws and hookworm. Where formerly there was a different language every twenty miles or so, there is now pidgin, in which communication can be had with all manner of strangers. There is money and things to buy with it, and the native, like the rest of us, likes making and spending it.

When a native hired out to work, he usually entered into a contract for one, two, or three years, its conditions set by law to include food, housing, clothing, and tobacco. His wages were low. Usually, some of his pay was deferred, to be drawn at the end of the contract. Then there was an orgy of buying and a triumphant return to the village with a box full of knives, cloth, beads, fishhooks and lines, flashlight, scented powder, or whatever else the eye fancied. Ten shillings was retained to meet next year's head tax, for, with the other concomitants of civilization, the native has taxation.

The effect on the native of contact with whites has been the subject of earnest study by anthropologists, who have written many weighty volumes on the subject. But the reverse influence, the effect of the contact on whites, has hardly been noted, and that only by novelists. As coastwatchers were all conditioned by their association with natives, it is necessary to sketch this effect to complete the picture.

Generally speaking, a man was not a true islander until he had lived four or five years in one of the territories. Before that lapse of time, he was apt to return to civilization and bore his friends and acquaintances with bad pidgin and untrue tales. If he stayed for as long as five years, however, he was sure to be more at home in the islands than anywhere else.

Constant dealing with and authority over natives gave the islander a habit of command, but no habit of obedience. With this went a sense of responsibility toward the natives, not of the kind that coddles but that takes into account the impact of any project on native life.

As a corollary, the islander rarely thought of any undertaking without counting on the help of the natives. He acquired a distaste for doing those things a native usually did for a European; menial tasks or work requiring little intelligence. But if an islander expected a native to take a risk, he almost invariably shared it with him.

Individual Europeans varied considerably in their opinions about native rights, but each was usually consistent to his conception of them, so that a native rarely encountered capricious treatment.

The islander was, in fact, something of a seigneur, with the saving experience that he went on leave about every two years, to ride on trams and be jostled about in crowds.

Most islanders were in an economic position somewhat above the average; well-paid and reasonably secure. This too encouraged an independence of mind, even a certain arrogance, on which the garment of discipline fitted only where it touched. Their own knowledge and experience had taught them that order and system were necessary to carry through any undertaking, but not that discipline was necessary for its own sake. Of course natives had to be automatically obedient; but to apply such a rule to themselves? No!

Let it be admitted that, apart from missionaries (who had their own peculiar deficiencies) the islanders in general drank to excess, their speech was coarse, some loved widely and illicitly. They would bicker among themselves but would show a clannishly united front to outsiders, to whom they seemed kittle-cattle, difficult to deal with.

A characteristic of the best islanders was the capacity for deep friendships between individuals, friendships of years' standing, where all was known and forgiven, where mutual loyalty transcended all other considerations. When an islander of this type called another islander his friend, he was describing a relationship uncolored by illusions, unbreakable by circumstance.

In spite of all the knowledge and skills he possessed, it was impossible for even the most experienced islander to pass himself off as a native. So, of necessity, all FERDINAND's men in enemy-occupied areas openly retained the appearance of Europeans and, in their relations with the natives, the status of Europeans.

Without the natives and without help from FERDINAND headquarters, the coastwatchers could never have existed in the enemy-held islands, let alone have done their dangerous work. For no one can live in the jungle without aid. The jungle is, in effect, a desert. Game is scarce.

In emergency, the heart of the top of any palm tree can be eaten but it is not sustaining. The sago palm grows wild in many places, but to extract the edible starch is a lengthy process, forcing the worker to remain in one place and leave ample evidence of his presence.

At its best, the food the jungle can supply is only enough to sustain life, and under a prolonged diet of jungle food, mental and physical vigor decline until there is no ability left to do more than barely support life itself. Even natives cannot live indefinitely on jungle products only, but rely on cultivated foods.

So the coastwatchers, like any other force, had to have a supply system; local organizations improvised by the watchers themselves in the field, backed up by a basic FERDINAND supply system.

Eventually, there were others besides islanders who were to become FERDINAND men, at first mainly on the staff, later in the field. Some of these were Australian Navy officers and men, and many were soldiers from the Independent Companies, Australia's Commandos. Some were from the United States Army and Marine Corps. A few learned their trade so well that at the end they were hardly distinguishable from islanders.

These outsiders were especially valuable for the youthful energy they supplied. For the islanders, as a body, were rather old for the strenuous duty they performed. Nevertheless, in spite of age and of singular hardships, they stood up well, and although individualism was the pivot of their personalities, each one, as will be seen, put his duty and his identification with the Allied cause first, himself last.

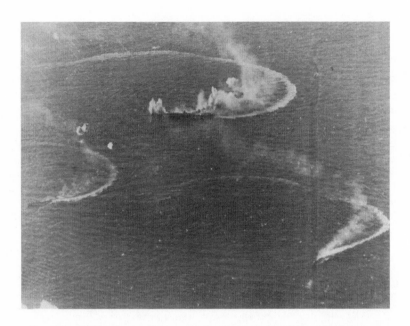

Carrier *Zuikaku* and her destroyers under bombardment

5

IF EVER A MAN WAS GIVEN A DIFFICULT ASSIGNMENT, it was the mission on which I sent Keith McCarthy during the desperate days when Japan was ripping into our defenses.

With the fall of Rabaul, silence had closed over that town. We knew nothing of the fate of our forces there or of the coastwatchers in the vicinity. It was urgent that we ascertain our position and the extent of Japanese penetration so, two days after Rabaul had been taken, I signaled McCarthy, coastwatcher at Talasea toward the western end of New Britain, to take his teleradio to the vicinity of Toma, near Rabaul, and report on our situation.

This was a tall order. To carry it out, McCarthy had a trip of 200 miles along the coast, then a trek through practically unknown jungle to find people whose whereabouts he did not know, and then, probably, to lead them out and transport them to New Guinea by means which were not apparent.

Actually, I had no right to give McCarthy orders, for he was a civilian. But he had served with me as assistant district officer some years earlier, we knew each other well, and I knew he was the appropriate man for the job. A tall, red-headed man of Irish descent, he was no cool, premeditating type. His affections and emotions governed him, but when his fine, free carelessness had landed him in trouble, he could extricate himself, logic guiding his Celtic fervor until the danger was past. He had shown this capacity when ambushed in the heart of New Guinea by natives, coming safely out although wounded by three arrows, one of which he described as having ruined the beautiful symmetry of his navel. I could only hope that his long practice at improvising ways of escape from diverse and unorthodox difficulties had fitted him for coping with what lay ahead.

On receipt of my signal, McCarthy called together the several Europeans at Talasea. Two planters, named Marsland and Douglas, volunteered to assist him. The others agreed to take a schooner and make their way out.

Leaving Douglas to hold the base, McCarthy and Marsland, accompanied by a few native police and McCarthy's seventeen-year-old native teleradio operator, set out in a launch. They radioed their departure, then kept silence for two weeks, for they knew that a radio signal, even in code, is a shout that all may hear.

Meantime, with the assistance of the Australian New Guinea Administrative Unit (Angau), a hastily formed military administration for the territory, we were arranging for all small craft possible to be collected from the New Guinea coast for ferrying the New Britain troops and refugees whom we anticipated McCarthy would collect.

An officer was delegated by Angau to take charge of the flotilla. When he gave reasons, which may have been valid, why he should remain in comparative safety, no more time was wasted on him and Angau appointed G. C. Harris to take command.

Harris, a big, fleshy young man with a bald head surrounded by a fringe of fiery red hair, had a hard face and a soft, lisping voice, a truculent disposition and a courteous manner, little sense of humor but a generous good nature. In short, he was a collection of contradictions. His only quality not offset by another almost the opposite was his courage. Being red-haired, he was, following the Australian custom, called 'Blue.'

He had been a patrol officer at Lae when Rabaul fell, and when Lae was abandoned by the civilian population he had determined to join the coastwatchers. His first action was to take possession of all the funds left behind in the abandoned offices; he knew cash would be useful.

After appointment as head of our evacuation flotilla, he journeyed by launch to Finschafen, across the straits from New Britain, where he picked up a mission launch and three missionaries who were determined to join our forces. One of these was the Reverend A. P. H. Freund, whose name had so horrified a civil administrator during the days when we were organizing our coastwatcher chain.

These three, with Harris and a planter, journeyed to Rooke Island in the straits, where they were joined by the remainder of the flotilla; two more launches and five islanders from Madang, farther up the New Guinea coast.

It would have been hard to find a more pathetic task force than this haphazard little group of launches. But unarmed, its fastest boat capable of only eight knots speed, the 'Harris Navy' set out toward Talasea to do what it could to rescue our retreating troops and aid McCarthy.

McCarthy, meanwhile, made his way to Pondo plantation, 50 miles southwest of Rabaul. Here he found his first Rabaul refugees; some of the troops of the Australian battalion which had been stationed at the port. Led by an able young officer who later distinguished himself in action, this small party was still fairly fit: troops, not rabble.

The officer signaled over McCarthy's teleradio that he had valuable information on Japanese tactics which he wished to bring out without delay. His General's reply was to place McCarthy in charge of all evacuation operations and decisions, with the rank of captain. Here McCarthy showed unexpected shrewdness. He refused the rank so that as a civilian he would not be placed under orders of any senior officer.

McCarthy disagreed with the young officer's contention that he must get back to base and report what he had seen as quickly as possible. Instead, McCarthy dispatched him with his men in his, McCarthy's, own launch, with instructions to take charge of the Talasea section of the coast. It was a sensible plan, but the officer and his men continued past Talasea without stopping, and made their way to the New Guinea mainland, escaping through Salamaua just before the Japanese occupied it, incidentally depriving McCarthy of their aid and the boat, both of which he badly needed. There was no lack of courage in this officer, as both his earlier and later career proved. It was just an ill-judged action, part of the pattern of confusion and retreat.

Collecting two timber men and a planter at Pondo, McCarthy put one of them to work with Marsland, repairing a launch damaged by a Japanese landing party which had called a few days before at the plantation. He dispatched one of the timbermen, a tall, thin, dour man named Holland, to the south coast to collect whatever troops he might find there, and he himself set out to collect troops from neighboring plantations.

With every step, he wondered if the next would land him in the clutches of a Japanese patrol. And at every plantation stop he found small bodies of our troops, dispirited and helpless, suffering from malaria and tropical sores. They had escaped the Japanese, but they could not escape another enemy, their own ignorance of the country. One group McCarthy found had thought it was near starvation when actually there was a large field of tapioca alongside the house in which they were camped.

McCarthy bullied, threatened, and cajoled the ill and languid men, forcing them against their own demoralized wills to move back to Pondo. He himself turned back only when assured by natives that there were no more Australians between him and the Japanese.

Holland, for his part, walked day and night to cross to the south coast of the island. Here he found that a large body of troops had been intercepted by the enemy and massacred in cold blood, while others had passed by and were now blocked to the westward by the Japanese occupation of Gasmata. He also learned that Mackenzie was in the rear with his Rabaul coastwatcher party. Holland sent word to him, by native runner, of the evacuation and thus a new tributary joined McCarthy's stream of refugees.

At Rabaul, Mackenzie had been kept apprised by Page on Tabar of enemy air attacks from Truk, and of the approaching enemy landing. On the day the enemy convoy was expected to arrive, he had sent two of his assistants to Toma to establish a new radio reporting post. Then, knowing that a fugitive life lay before him, he had burned his confidential books and codes.

That night the Japanese had landed, opposed by Australian troops on the western beaches of the harbor, unopposed elsewhere. When daylight showed the formidable array of Japanese ships, the order had been given, 'Every man for himself.' Some hardy men fought it out to the last in the gullies near the airfield, but the majority streamed from the coast in any direction, provided it was away from the Japanese.

Mackenzie had offered his small naval staff for the fighting, but they had not been used, so when the retreat began, he had collected his men into a truck and set off for the newly established radio post at Toma. On his arrival, he found a host of vehicles, abandoned by troops who had already driven thus far to the end of the road, and then struck off into the jungle. As an observation post, it was patent the position would not do. Reluctantly, Mackenzie ordered destruction of the teleradio and gave his men the choice of retreating with the troops or staying under his command. Without hesitation, they elected to stay with him.

Which route to take to the westward was a dilemma. If they took to the northern coast, miles of trackless jungle would have to be traversed and then 300 miles would lie between them and the western end of the island. The route to the south coast, also, lay over jungle-clad mountains, but Mackenzie felt that if they could pick up a boat, once they reached the coast, there was a fair chance that it might be sailed to the Trobriands.

Linking up with a small military party, which included a military intelligence officer named Peter Figgis and the superintendent of the Rabaul police, Mackenzie and his men therefore struck south, following a primitive native track. Sodden with perspiration, they carried their packs up the mountain slopes, their wet boots, encased in thick mud and dead leaves, making every step leaden.

When Holland's message reached them, Mackenzie decided to send his men to join McCarthy while he and Figgis remained to do what they could to rescue those on the south coast, too far away to join McCarthy's evacuation.

So, turning about, Mackenzie's men plodded northward toward McCarthy. On the way, dysentery broke out among them. Two were too sick to go further, and Chief Yeoman Lamont, who had stood the lonely watch at Anir and had been relieved to Rabaul just before its fall, decided to stay and care for them. Sorrowfully the others bade the three goodbye and struggled on to join McCarthy west of Pondo.

McCarthy's scheme was working, thanks to his driving personality and the devotion of his planter and timbermen assistants. Once started, the troops kept moving, but at all times there was something for McCarthy's attention; canoes, to help them over the worst stretches, to be found and paid for; a party of stragglers to be picked up; directions to be given the few officers who retained initiative enough to command. Food was scarce and unpalatable, malaria was taking its toll, strength was failing.

And, as far as these dispirited men knew, here was the prospect before them: Talasea was miles away, the western end of New Britain 150 miles farther. Then there were the straits to be crossed. This done, no one knew how, they could look forward to a walk of another 200 miles with broken boots and weakening, rotting bodies, to an inland airfield from which those who survived might be flown out to Port Moresby; that is, if Port Moresby itself had not been captured in the meantime.

These men were not only retreating, they were utterly defeated in body and spirit. But red-headed, energetic McCarthy drove them on.

As soon as he had got the troops moving, McCarthy had signaled to us his whereabouts and his plans, and we in turn informed the 'Harris Navy' of where to reach him. The arrival of the little flotilla gave some new hope to the troops and, inadequate though it was, ferried them over the more difficult stretches.

Keywords for McCarthy's messages to us became a problem. Of the two agreed-upon code words with which he had started, one was compromised by capture, and the only hope we had of our schoolboy cypher remaining inviolate was in continually changing the key.

So we fell back on mutual knowledge, and I would signal, 'Use as keyword the Christian and surname of the tall thin officer who was formerly chief of police,' and he would send his signals coded with 'John Walstab,' until told to use the name of 'the fat officer who lives on fowls and ice cream.'

We rapidly ran through our list of mutual acquaintances who could be identified in a short sentence and were hard put to get changes toward the end. Luckily, McCarthy had been taught the 'Playfair Feldt Method' and this allowed us to use a keyword a little longer than would otherwise have been possible.

When his party reached the center of the north coast, it had a great stroke of luck, for here McCarthy learned that the Lakatoi, a motor ship of about 300 tons, was at Witu, a small island a good many miles offshore. She had been loading copra from the nearby plantations when the enemy invaded the area, and the captain, lacking nerve to run out, had remained in harbor, waiting for the first Japanese to whom he could surrender.

McCarthy dispatched an armed party in one of the 'Harris' launches to seize the ship. Boarding her with a tommy gun at the ready, McCarthy's men found that the nervous skipper was willing to agree to anything, provided someone else would take the responsibility. The entire party of troops was ferried across to Witu by the 'Harris Navy,' with only one tense moment when two Japanese aircraft dipped low but failed to see the small, packed craft.

The Lakatoi's hold was full of copra, light and bulky. To make room and to lessen the risk of fire, it was thrown overboard, sacrilege in the eyes of the firm that owned the ship.

When everything had been made ready, the men were aboard, and the Lakatoi was about to cast off, an unexpected addition turned up; a widow, Mrs. Gladys Baker, who managed her own plantation on Witu. She earned her passage if anyone did, spending all her waking hours dressing sores for the duration of the voyage.

Bell, Douglas, and Olander, three of the islanders who had helped McCarthy, had decided to remain, Douglas and Olander to return to their plantations near Talasea with a teleradio, Bell, also with a teleradio, to go eastward to Open Bay. The 'Harris Navy,' its job now done, left for Medang on the New Guinea mainland.

The Lakatoi cast anchor soon after darkness fell. We were signaled that she had left, then radio silence was maintained. With 212 persons aboard, she cleared the reefs and set her course westward, doing a steady ten knots. As dawn lightened the sky, she slid into harbor at Rooke Island, anchoring as close to shore as possible. Small boats scurried to shore, and soon the ship was covered with branches from the jungle. With nightfall, the Lakatoi came to life again beneath her leafy covering.

On this second night, she had to run the gauntlet of Vitiaz Straits. The engineer gave the engine all the speed it could safely stand. McCarthy, his goal in sight, was afraid the skipper might lose his nerve, so he and one of his men kept watch to see there was no deviation from the course.

In the engine room, his tireless assistant, Marsland, kept watch. Beside the radio, ready to send a signal should they be attacked, stood an army corporal. The cabins were filled with the sickest of the men. Others slept in the hold or on deck, lying wherever they could find space to stretch out.

Slowly the night passed with nothing to mark its passage except the neutral stars rolling impersonally across the sky, and the Lakatoi moved onto safety.

Near China Straits, at the eastern end of Papua, it was met with supplies of food and medicines, but we could spare no ships to transfer the Lakatoi's packed and wretched human cargo. So the Lakatoi continued on her voyage, entering Cairns harbor in North Queensland on 28 March 1942, nine weeks after the fall of Rabaul.

As the ship touched the wharf, McCarthy, who had carried the burden so long, drooped and wilted in complete mental and nervous exhaustion. With never a quip or joke, he found nothing now of interest or value. Ashore, he sat at a table, a dead cigarette between his lips, an untasted glass of beer before him, and answered questions with grunts and monosyllables.

Of all on board, only six were fit men. All the rest were sick, debilitated by poor and insufficient food, weakened by malaria and exposure. Most had sores, the beginnings of tropical ulcers, covered by dirty bandages. Their faces were the dirty gray of malaria victims, their clothes in rags and stinking of stale sweat. They were wrecks, but they were safe, and some—among them McCarthy—would fight again.

6

BACK ON NEW BRITAIN, MACKENZIE LEARNED from natives that more than a hundred of our soldiers were still huddled on the south coast. While he made his way toward them, he signaled to us that help would be needed.

Taking a teleradio, an Angau lieutenant slipped across from the Trobriands in a fast launch and, after a little searching, found the troops and reported the area clear of the enemy. Immediately the evacuation ship we had borrowed, the Laurabada, formerly the Papuan Administrator's yacht, scooted across on a fast night-time trip.

At dawn, it hauled in near shore, was camouflaged by her crew, and against odds remained undiscovered by searching enemy planes. At dusk, Mackenzie, Figgis, and the troops were brought on board; 153 evacuees in all. The Laurabada arrived in Australia late in April.

One small party had been left behind, however, because news of the Laurabada's arrival had failed to reach it. Luckily this group could hardly have been better equipped for striking out for itself. It was led by D. A. Laws, government radio superintendent at Rabaul, who was later to become one of our watchers, and it had a teleradio and ample food.

The fact that they had no boat and that enemy parties might arrive at any time did not particularly daunt Laws and his men. Scouring around, they found an old boat hull and a truck engine, both abandoned at plantations.

For a month, they worked with these unpromising materials, until they had a vessel that would run and that would keep out the water, about the best that could be said for it. In this they set out for Buna on the northern New Guinea mainland.

Excellent mechanic and radioman that Laws was, he was no navigator, and he shared the simple landsman's faith that if you point a boat toward a spot, that's where you will land. The southeast monsoon was blowing hard, however, and when Laws and his group made land, they found themselves 200 miles northwest of their destination, with the enemy between them and Buna.

Without the teleradio for signaling their position, they would have been in a very serious fix, for the ample food supplies of a month before were now reduced to starvation rations. We were able to drop them supplies, luckily, and thus fortified they were able to manage the arduous jungle and mountain trek to Bena Bena, from where they were flown to Port Moresby.

After Laws' departure, only three teleradio equipped watchers remained on New Britain—Bell, Douglas, and Olander, the three islanders who, after assisting McCarthy, had decided to remain. There was no point in attempting to evacuate them, at least for the time being. It was probable that they could take care of themselves for a good while, and chances were we should need them there, on the spot.

Our role was the collection of intelligence, and at first sight it seemed we had got little from our New Britain operations up to this time. Actually, we had a mass of negative intelligence, which is as valuable in its way as positive information. We knew, for instance, that the Japanese held Rabaul and Gasmata as posts only, and that they had not spread themselves to occupy the remainder of the island.

We had also verified our expectations regarding the native reaction to invasion—that natives in general would be sympathetic to us, but not to a degree to endanger themselves. It was apparent that the natives would be loyal, by and large, wherever the control of our Government continued, and that police and personal boys could be relied on to stand all but the harshest strains.

We were also aware that there was no reason to be optimistic about native help where the control and influence of our Government were completely shattered.

One curious and unexpected element to our distinct disadvantage had been injected into the pattern of native attitudes. This was the recrudescence of a semi-religious belief that the ships that came to New Britain were sent at the behest of the ancestors of the living natives.

From time to time in the past, self-appointed prophets had arisen with news of revelations of this nature. The Europeans, said these prophets, intercepted the ships with their cargoes of rice, tinned meat, fish, cloth, and all the other fine things prepared by the ancestors, and then made the natives work and pay for their own property.

Naturally this was an attractive theory, and a few clever knaves had little trouble reviving it now with the new twist that the Japanese invasion was a judgment on the Europeans for their thievery. The leading exponent of this idea was Butari, an often-convicted criminal, who was not without force of character and was gathering many followers.

Still more surprising to us, however, was the behavior of some of the Europeans in New Britain. Many made no attempt to escape at all. Their reasons appeared to be various. Some were elderly and soft, and would not face the obvious hardships which escape entailed. Some had spent most of their lives creating a plantation from the jungle, and to them their life's work had become life itself.

Some, secure so long, could not grasp the idea that the whole structure about them was being dismantled; they could no more understand this disintegration than the cheese mites can understand the knife which cuts their world in two.

Some, no doubt, were swayed by their responsibilities to their native laborers, many of whom were far from their villages. Some, managers of company-owned plantations, awaited orders from their head offices, orders which never came.

It must be confessed, also, that there were some who remembered that in World War I the German planters had been allowed to live on their plantations under Australian occupation, continuing to produce copra and to be paid for it. These hoped to do the equivalent, to live comfortably in their plantation houses, waited on by native servants, making money while others fought the war.

Of course there were many among the Europeans who rose admirably to the occasion, among them those who had assisted in our New Britain evacuations. Others escaped independently, and among these were several who were to serve FERDINAND later. Throughout the islands, most of the younger men joined the Australian New Guinea Administrative Unit.

In New Britain we had at least got most of our men out and were feeling fairly secure about the three who remained. In New Ireland it was a different story.

New Ireland, 200 miles long, lies athwart the northern end of New Britain, its nearest point only 40 miles from Rabaul. For two-thirds of its length it is narrow and only a few hundred feet in height, territory in which it is virtually impossible to hide. In its southern third, it bulges to a width of 40 miles and carries a steep range running from north to south.

On the east side of the island, just where the coast begins to bulge, stands Namatani, headquarters of the government sub-district. Namatani was not a town, only a settlement of a few bungalows and Chinese stores, quarters for native laborers and police, a hospital, and the government office. It was the center to which planters came to sign on native labor, to obtain gun and trading licenses, and for an occasional court case. A small bay provided anchorage for local craft, and a desultory attempt had been made to construct an airfield.

In a way, Namatani was a cross-section of agricultural New Guinea. It was a doldrum, but a pleasant doldrum, whose inhabitants led quiet lives, going about their task of turning coconuts into copra.

A. F. Kyle was assistant district officer, and G. M. Benham was patrol officer at Namatani. Their wives had been evacuated, and they were living in Namatani in bachelor state when Rabaul was attacked.

Bill Kyle was a very short, rather plump man who had served in World War I as a youth and had been in the islands for fourteen years. Despite his size and shape, he was a good athlete, a first-rate cricket player. His personality was a mixture of idealism and worldliness. He was apt to take strong dislikes to people and not trouble to conceal it, but he also formed deep friendships to which he gave fanatical loyalty.

Greg Benham was a tall young man with a slouchy gait, his tact and unvarying good nature carrying him through a pleasantly frictionless life.

The two remained at Namatani until they saw the Japanese convoy arrive off Rabaul. Then they set off down the east coast, collecting planters and missionaries on the way. In a week they reached within a few miles of Cape St. George, the southern tip of the island. From here Kyle signaled that he had a boat and a party of ten, and asked for directions.

Owing to an error, his question was not referred to our headquarters at Townsville. Instead, a reply was sent from Port Moresby, asking Kyle to remain. Kyle, thinking the signal was from me, his closest friend, immediately acceded. He urged Benham, who was sick at the time, to leave, but Benham refused to abandon his friend.

So, with no more question, they dispatched the others, leaving themselves without means of escape. They were no residents of a fool's paradise. They were intelligent men who knew how black the outlook was and they stayed in the full knowledge of the risks.

As soon as I realized what had happened, we sent them a signal advising that they make a post inland, in the uninhabited mountains, and hole up there. We hoped that if they kept quiet, they might remain unnoticed for a long time. In the meantime, they reported warships in St. George's Channel.

Our advice posed a dilemma for the two men. It was true that if they could establish themselves deep in the mountains, their position known only to loyal natives, they might last indefinitely. On the other hand, it was improbable that their position actually could be kept this secret, and the move would mean letting go their hold on the bulk of the native population, many of whom might turn against them once the threads of control were broken.

As a compromise, they made camp on a ridge near the cape, from which they could see St. George's Channel. From here they hoped both to retain their control over the natives and to be able to make a getaway to the mountains if necessary.

Soon more complications arose. Four weeks after the fall of Rabaul, they were joined by ten refugee soldiers who had tried to make their escape from New Britain by boat, but had been driven ashore near Cape St. George. As soon as we heard this news, we realized that if Kyle fed them, his and Benham's supplies would be used up in a few weeks and all would be lost. We signaled that we would drop food from a plane, but directly after this message was sent Kyle reported his receiver out of order. Doubting that he had received our promise of help, we went ahead with our plans, arranging to drop a receiver along with the food.

This was the first attempt to drop supplies by parachute in the entire Southwest Pacific Area, for at this point we had not yet attempted to get supplies to Page. Like all pioneering efforts, it had its difficulties. We had had some experience in dropping supplies without parachute in New Guinea in peacetime and knew, for instance, that a half-filled bag of flour landed well, whereas a full bag burst like a bomb. To attempt to drop a radio receiver without a parachute would, of course, have been madness.

We turned for help to the Air Force. In peacetime that service had devised two pieces of supply-dropping equipment; one, a harness of webbing in which a packing case could be lashed; the other, a cylinder for dropping liquid. There was only one of each in all Australia, but the Air Force let us have them both. The radio receiver was packed in a case and lashed in the webbing, and the other supplies were fixed to condemned personnel parachutes. The liquid container was found to be unusable.

The Air Force arranged to use a Hudson bomber to drop the radio in daylight and a Catalina to drop the other supplies at night. No, they did not want me to go in either aircraft to guide it to the dropping point; that would only be one more killed if the plane did not return. A good sketch would do.

In the meantime, we had no word from the two coastwatchers. The Hudson pilot reported he had dropped the radio at the correct spot, but that three Japanese destroyers, which had fired at him, were anchored offshore. The Catalina pilot reported on his return that the ships had gone, but that he had seen no sign of life ashore.

For six weeks, only silence responded to our efforts to get through to Kyle and Benham, and our hearts were heavy with the thought that two good men had been sacrificed to no purpose. And then one day we were pleasantly shocked to hear Kyle on the air again. The report he gave us, stripped to the bare facts, was brief but harrowing.

Just before we had dropped the supplies, a party of Japanese had been led by a native to the hidden station on the ridge. Kyle was in the hut at the time, and the Japanese got within twenty feet of him. Hurtling his plump body through the side of the hut, he dove down the mountain, the hut protecting him from the enemy's shots. He was joined by Benham, who had been in the jungle nearby, and the two fled up the west coast. Crossing over to Namatani, they found their houses had been burned. Then they circled down the east coast.

At one point, on this trip, they had stopped at a plantation house, and while they were within it, eighty Japanese in cars and trucks arrived. Kyle and Benham walked out the back steps as the Japanese came in the front. That night the Japanese got within thirty yards of them as they hid among trees, but again they made a getaway.

The soldiers, who had been camped near the coastwatcher station, had not been discovered by the Japanese, nor had the enemy patrol found the teleradio, hidden in the jungle. Once Kyle and Benham had established themselves at a new spot on the eastern coast of the island bulge, they sent a trusted native for the soldiers, who arrived not only with the teleradio, but with the receiver and some of the other supplies we had dropped.

A little grim comedy was injected by the fact that the soldiers had found, among the supplies, a letter I intended only for Kyle. It told him that if any more refugee soldiers arrived, he was to let them starve rather than jeopardize his own safety. The letter apparently hurt the feelings of the soldiers, but the two bottles of whiskey in the supplies may have salved their sensibilities.

At their new post, Kyle, Benham, and the soldiers were soon joined by a group of civilians, led by J. H. McDonald, our coastwatcher from Kavieng, at the northern tip of New Ireland. McDonald, district officer at Kavieng, had moved most of the town's civilians to a camp in the jungle when he saw that invasion was imminent, and had left the town to a Commando detachment.

The officer in charge of the Commandos had decided it was useless to fight, and had embarked his force in a small motor vessel. Setting off down the coast by night, the Commandos put into a bay at dawn to hide, and finding themselves under the guns of a Japanese destroyer, surrendered. It is not a bright paragraph in our history, but these men had been placed in a position where only the best of troops under inspiring leadership would have fought.

A few civilians who attempted to escape independently from Kavieng were also captured, but McDonald and his party made their way safely down the west coast. Among them was the Kavieng Amalgamated Wireless operator, who repaired some slight damage which Kyle's receiver had sustained in its descent.

The first information we sent to Kyle and Benham over their repaired radio was the news that Kyle had been appointed a lieutenant and Benham a sub-lieutenant in the Naval Reserve, and that allotments had been arranged for their wives.

Before long, Kyle managed to obtain a plantation boat into which twenty-three persons, the entire party, could just fit. Again Kyle asked for instructions.

At this time, Allied forces were moving into position for the Battle of the Coral Sea, and a watcher on eastern New Ireland might provide vital information for this engagement. I had been encouraged to believe, also, that other forces from the New Hebrides would soon move forward and attack Rabaul, another operation which would bring the New Ireland watchers into a key position and would soon afterwards release them from danger. Therefore, I simply instructed them to come out if they considered the position untenable. They replied they would stay, and once again they watched others move away to safety.

Although Kyle now had a good receiver, his transmitter had become weak. When he was unable to communicate directly with us, Page on Tabar would relay his signals. Through this channel, we learned that the coastwatcher station on Anir Island had been burned, but that our man there, a Navy telegraphist named Woodroffe, who had replaced Lamont just before the fall of Rabaul, was still free. Since Anir was a wooded, hilly island, we hoped Woodroffe might hold out indefinitely. We dropped him food and a teleradio, but heard nothing from him.

All went well with Kyle and Benham until the end of May, when Kyle reported to us that the Japanese were about to commence civil administration at Namatani. This was disturbing news. It would end the authority which the coastwatchers, up to this time, had succeeded in keeping over the natives. Should the natives actually assist the Japanese, there was little hope our men would evade capture.

And, as we feared, they soon signaled that they had been betrayed by natives and Chinese.

We had no time to lose. We speedily arranged for a submarine to pick them up, and gave them rendezvous instructions for the night of 30 May. They did not come on the air that morning, but we did not regard this as alarming, assuming that they had moved to the rendezvous.

We heard no news from the submarine until she was four days overdue. Then she reported that she had engine trouble and would make port next morning. When she arrived, there were no coast-watchers aboard. After our high hopes, the shock of the bad news was like a kick in the guts, for Kyle was my closest friend.

For two nights, the submarine had kept the rendezvous, and no one had appeared. But we could not give up all hope, and with it, all effort. There was one more chance; we might actually land a man on the island to seek out the watchers.

Pilot Officer Cecil John Mason, a planter with experience in both New Guinea and the Solomons, was available. If another submarine could be obtained, he could land on New Ireland, and, on the same trip, could try to pick up Woodroffe from Anir. We would have liked to send him to Page, also, but that was too risky. Page, we knew, had by this time almost certainly been captured.

Mason made his preparations while I went to Brisbane to make a personal appeal to the Admiral in command of submarines. The Admiral saw me with his entire staff in attendance, and I soon sensed that I had an uphill road ahead.

I could not wonder at this. I was a naval officer myself, and I knew that submarines could not vary their duty of sinking ships except for very good reasons. The submarine command had already gone out of its way to attempt one New Ireland rescue. In vain, I pleaded that the area was a shipping route and that the submarine could hunt on it by day. The Admiral was adamant.

At last I played my trump card; a letter from Kyle which had been sent out with the last party to escape. It told of his and Benham's escapes up to that time, reported on Japanese garrisons and armament in the area, and, in a matter-of-fact way, described his and Benham's prospects.

We may get chased out again any time [he wrote], and will probably lose the wireless. It is so dicky I am afraid to move it again; I think it would be the end of it. It is hidden in the bush, but not too far away; and the natives may give it away...

Don't worry about us. With extra food and medicine we can last for some months unless there is more patrol activity than there has been up to date. However, I hope you can eventually get us out or we counterattack, as they seem to murder anyone they find with teleradios...

Look, Eric, if our radio goes bung, as it well may, we will stay here so you can always drop instructions. If we are chased, we will try to leave a boy here and later circle back to him. Should not be any time away, not more than a few days. If our transmitter goes, tell Page to send messages twice at our sked times; our receiver should last out. If any time you are dropping something, could you drop two coats and the appropriate rank-rings? We have only trade shorts and shirts and it might make a difference if we should get grabbed...

The Chief of Staff read Kyle's letter first, then handed it to the Admiral, and sat back with the face of a man whose mind is made up. Even before the Admiral had finished reading, the Chief of Staff, who knew his boss, said to me, 'When will your man be ready to start?'

Mason left on 3 July in a U.S. submarine. Armed with a rifle, he went ashore at night in a collapsible canoe close to the point where Kyle and Benham had established their second post, hid his canoe, and carefully scouted toward the nearest native village.

Speaking to the first native he encountered, he saw, too late, that he was wearing an armband with a rising sun emblem. The native answered his questions sulkily, denying all knowledge of Kyle and Benham and refusing to answer or evading other questions. He did reveal, however, that there was now a Japanese post at Muliama, where Kyle and Benham had been established. As soon as darkness fell the next night, Mason retrieved his canoe and returned to the submarine.

That same night, he landed on Anir. Here he quickly found a friendly native who told him Woodroffe was alive and in the bush. Mason gave the native a note to be taken to him, arranging a meeting at midnight the next night. Then he returned to the submarine.

A few hours later, at four o'clock in the morning, the submarine look-out noticed a steady light, as from a lamp, ashore. It may have been Woodroffe, but by this time Mason was physically spent. He had had no sleep for thirty-six hours and daylight was near, so it was decided to leave the rendezvous to the next night, as arranged in the note. The submarine drew off and dived for the day, away from the prying eyes of aircraft.

On the following night, 2 July, Mason landed at about ten o'clock, having arranged to be picked up by the submarine two hours later. At midnight, as the submarine prepared to move in toward shore, a Japanese patrol boat was sighted and the submarine hastily dived. At two o'clock, when the coast was again clear, the submarine returned, but could find no sign of Mason. The captain waited until daylight was dangerously close, then stood off. For the four succeeding nights, he doggedly returned to the meeting place, each time to find nothing.

To this day, we are not sure what happened. A captured Japanese document later revealed to us that Mason and Woodroffe had been taken, but how was not related. Did they, in the darkness, mistake the Japanese patrol boat for the submarine and approach it, possibly even hail it, so that escape was impossible? Did the native to whom the note was given betray them? One thing we did know; they gave the enemy no indication of the presence of the submarine in the vicinity.

More than a year later, we found that Kyle and Benham had been captured just eighteen hours before they were to have been picked up by the first submarine. That the submarine had not been attacked at the rendezvous shows that they had kept silence in the face of questioning—doubtless savage questioning.

While the tension was at its worst, during these and other rescue attempts, I received an official reprimand from Melbourne for using slang in official correspondence. I had used the word 'sked,' coined from 'schedule' to denote an agreed-upon time of radio transmission, and this, apparently, was most offensive. The thought that some senior officer, charged with the defense of Australia, had nothing better to do while the country's existence hung by a thread, cured me of any tendency to use slang for the next half-hour. I used only old Anglo-Saxon four-letter words or their derivatives.

Guadalcanal: Marines on the Ground

7

IN THE SOLOMON ISLANDS, OUR COASTWATCHER network was holding intact to a remarkable degree. From Buka at the north to Guadalcanal in the south, our key men were outwitting the Japanese. And if it were possible to designate the men who contributed most to Pacific victory, the names of Jack Read and Paul Mason on Bougainville and Buka would surely stand high on the list.

Jack Read had taken on the duties of assistant district officer and coastwatcher at Buka Passage, the 300-yard-wide strip of swift indigo water between the two northernmost islands, only a month before Japan entered the war. He had never before been in Bougainville, but he had lived in New Guinea for twelve years and had had experience in other parts of the islands. Although war was upon him before he could learn all the details of the local situation, the natives and the jungle presented to him no really new problems.

He was a wiry fellow, with dark hair, clear gray eyes, and a thin straight gash of a mouth above a long, firm chin. His voice was deep and a little harsh, his laugh explosive. His manner was blunt and straightforward, rather firm than tactful.

Read's headquarters was set in the Passage itself, on Sohana, a small island containing two bungalows, an office, quarters for native police and laborers, a jail, a native hospital, and a storehouse. To the north lay Buka, 30 miles long and 10 miles wide, a flat island with low hills near its western shore. To the south was the flat, mangrove-fringed shore of Bougainville, stretching away to high mountains in the blue distance.

Narrow, dazzling white beaches separated the reefs of the Passage from the green of the jungle or the duller green of statuesque plantation coconut palms. Here and there a callophyllum tree, reaching for light, leaned horizontally over the water. On the northern shore stood a native village of thatched huts, their brown roofs in lines as straight as could be made by men unable to measure.

Peaceful folk lived in the houses, cultivating taro, banana, and sweet potato, drying a little copra for ready money to spend at the Chinese trade stores, and building their fragile but speedy outrigger-less canoes. Cannibals once, they now attended a mission church. Their skins are the blackest of all Melanesians. Fully half the black dogs and black cats in the Northeast Area are named 'Buka.'

To the west of the village, a small huddle of Chinese stores and dwellings was dignified by the title of Chinatown. Here Cantonese and their descendants sold cloth, knives, peroxide, lamps, and such items to the natives, and in return bought copra and ivory nuts.

By day there was little movement in the drowsy Passage. Sometimes a motor schooner passed through with a muffled throb of engines and a white moustache of wave beneath its bow. By night, an occasional canoe stole past the reefs, its dozen paddlers stroking in cadence to a six-note chant, the mature voices topped on the higher notes by a young boy's soprano.

It was a lotus land, where a man might live a large part of his life away, peacefully going about his daily tasks, and find with surprise, years later, that so much of his mortal span had gone.

But now the inhabitants of Buka Passage tensely watched war approach. Twenty-five soldiers of the Australian Imperial Forces, under the command of Lieutenant J. H. Mackie, had been stationed at the Passage to guard a partly completed airfield and its fuel and bomb stores.

At Soraken, a plantation ten miles to the west, two of our Catalinas were temporarily based for carrying out daily searches to the north. Mackie's men were members of the 1st Independent Company, trained as Commandos, hard-bitten men, most of them older than their officer, which made his command no easier.

The first sign of the Japanese was their reconnaissance aircraft, lazily circling over the two islands from time to time. On 21 January 1942, the crews of our two Catalinas took off suddenly, carrying with them the bits of personal gear normally left ashore. This was an ominous sign, not lost on Read and Mackie.

Read, determining that he would not be tamely caught when the enemy arrived, took advice from those who knew the local geography and selected a place called Aravia as a retreat. To reach it, it was necessary to travel twenty miles eastward along the Bougainville coast and then to walk inland for two hours, climbing a thousand feet. Mackie also decided to put in supplies at this retreat and behind Soraken plantation.

Read urged the other Europeans to make preparations along the same lines, but they were a refractory bunch, resentful of any interference from the Government, and they declined to do so on the ground that it would be derogatory to their prestige with the natives. The Chinese, well aware that a corpse has no dignity, followed his advice.

The night after word reached Read and Mackie of the fall of Rabaul, they set their natives to work. In the darkness, surefootedly picking their way along the familiar paths to the beach, the workers carried rice, tinned meat, clothing, benzine, cooking utensils, and trade goods, and loaded them into boats that made trip after trip to the Bougainville shore of the Passage. There other natives unloaded the boats, and began transporting the supplies to Baniu, farther along the coast. Read set off for Baniu by launch, taking with him a native crew, two police-boys, cash, office records, and the teleradio.

He had made his preparations only in the nick of time. It was daylight when he started for Baniu in the launch, and he had gone about a mile when he sighted a plane at great height. As he headed for shore, the plane turned and pointed low toward the defenseless launch. Machine guns stuttered and a crop of white splashes jumped on the water. Then the plane banked, disappeared for a moment over Buka Passage, and reappeared leading a formation of five. Bombs dropped over Read's headquarters, Chinatown, and the airfield, and machine guns strafed the native houses.

At the airfield, Mackie's men turned their machine guns on the planes and apparently brought one down in the sea. Then the guards blew up the fuel and bombs and left for the Bougainville shore.

Read continued on to Aravia, where, with the help of two other Europeans in the government service, he set up camp. It was not difficult for such experienced men. Houses can be run up quickly, thatched with palm-leaf or kunai grass; wood and water were abundant. Natives brought field fruits to supplement the rice and tinned meat. And the teleradio brought news of war; bad news, most of it.

Locally, the news was bad too. At Kieta, midway down the long eastern shore of Bougainville, a panic had seized the Europeans. It was touched off when a native police boy on watch on a hill above the town reported a Japanese flying boat had alighted just outside the harbor. Although the report was soon demonstrated to be erroneous, the district officer and his staff, some of the missionaries and planters, piled on a small schooner and departed in haste. Unforgivably, they took with them the teleradio assigned to Tom Ebery, our coastwatcher at Toimonapu, south of Kieta, while Ebery himself, an old man, remained.

From native scouts, Read learned of these events and heard also that the natives had looted Kieta after the hasty evacuation, and that Dr. Kroening, a district officer of the old German administration, had set himself up in authority.

Read immediately set off for Kieta, traveling by launch at night, and arrived to find the white flag of surrender flying from the public buildings. Dr. Kroening bustled up to him, arrogant and boastful, to be coldly and firmly informed by Read that he himself was now in charge.

Finding Sergeant Yauwika and Corporal Sali of the native police, both of whom had served with Read in other parts of the territory, Read set them to work recovering most of the food which had been carried away by the natives. Having no illusions about the probability of a Japanese occupation in the near future, he transported it to inland dumps. This took time, and it was near the end of February before he returned to his camp at Aravia. Mackie in the meantime had withdrawn his men inland.

Under the influence of Drummond Thomson, a highly respected and intelligent planter, many of the refractory Europeans in the vicinity of the Passage were now persuaded to leave, although quite a number, among them three women and a group of missionaries, remained. Dr. Kroening and his wife, internment awaiting them in Australia, were hustled off with the departing Europeans.

During this time, Angau had been formed at Port Moresby, and Read was appointed a sergeant. The appointment would place him under Mackie's command, and although Read recognized Mackie's good qualities he felt he could not surrender his initiative. He shut his rat-trap mouth firmly and signaled a refusal, adding that he would prefer to go to Australia and enlist there. I signaled Read that if he would remain for six months, I should try to have him commissioned into the Navy. The six months was a pure guess on my part; I trusted something would have happened by that time to resolve the whole question of coastwatching. Read had been a patrol officer under me in Madang District, so we knew each other well, and the personal influence turned the scale. He promised to stick it out, no matter what his position might be.

Read and Mackie now decided to set up watching stations, each with a teleradio: at Kieta; at Numa, which was on the east coast north of Kieta; at Buin, on the southern shore of Bougainville; at the Aravia camp; and at the northern tip of Buka Island. This would cover the two islands except for the undeveloped west coast of Bougainville, which was unlikely to be visited by the enemy first.

Four of Mackie's men were sent to man the station at Buin, and another four were sent to Numa. Read himself manned Aravia.

Percy Good, a coastwatcher planter, was already at Kessa near the northern tip of Buka. He was a man of fifty or more who, before he became a plantation owner, had been a radio mechanic for Amalgamated Wireless. Because of his age, it had been expected that he would evacuate, and we had instructed him from coastwatcher headquarters to cease reporting.

He felt this decision keenly and, remaining in spite of it, offered his services to Read. Read arranged that his teleradio should be moved to high land near Cape Henpan, at the very tip of the island, above Good's low, exposed plantation, and he sent four of Mackie soldiers to man it. Good was hurt by this decision but acquiesced and remained at his plantation, leaving his offer of service still open.

To Kieta, Read and Mackie assigned Paul Edward Mason. Mason was another planter who had long since determined to stay and see it out as a coastwatcher, whatever happened. He was a short, fair man, over forty, who gazed benignly through his spectacles and spoke slowly, generally pausing thoughtfully before replying even to a casual remark. He had been in the islands for more than twenty years, but looked less like a 'tough guy' than any other man on Bougainville, missionaries not excepted. Those who knew him well, however, realized that his serene expression was the product of modest but complete self-confidence.

Radio had been one of his hobbies, and he had taught himself all that was to be known of frequencies, condensers, inductions, and circuits. He could wind his own coils, make his own repairs, send and receive in Morse. He had maintained communication with Port Moresby and Tulagi when others in his vicinity were unable to do so, and while Read was in Kieta he had sent and received all signals for Bougainville. It was he who gave Tulagi warning of its first bombing.

He had been appointed a coastwatcher in 1939 and had made up his mind then to the course he would take if the war came to Bougainville. While other planters remained to care for their property, or in the blissful faith that whatever happened to anyone else, nothing unpleasant would happen to them, Mason realized that he was giving up any hope of escape other than his own ability to evade the enemy.

By 6 March, all parties were in position and were maintaining communication both with Port Moresby and the south Solomons.

At this point, Read suddenly remembered there was a dump of 20,000 gallons of aviation fuel at Soraken, where the two Catalinas had been based. He dispatched a demolition squad of two soldiers, who pierced each drum and capsized it, an arduous, lengthy job but the only method they had. On the morning of 8 March, six Japanese cruisers and two destroyers anchored in Carola Haven, near Kessa, and a Japanese landing party debarked at Good's plantation. For the time being, they put Good on parole.

News of this reached Read by native runner, and he immediately signaled it to Port Moresby. He was mystified about why he had not received a radio message from the party of soldiers stationed at Cape Henpan, and when he could not make contact with them through his teleradio, he set off to find out what had happened.

When he reached Buka Passage, he met the soldiers, who were on their way to the Aravia camp. For some reason they had been unable to work the radio properly and, upon being warned by natives that some Japanese were approaching, had dismantled and hidden it and then left the post. Natives were sent to retrieve the radio and the party was reinstalled near its original place, with hopes that it would do better next time.

Our news broadcasts now took a hand, and announced that Japanese warships had been seen off Cape Henpan. The Japanese, listening in, rubbed their eyes. They knew none of our aircraft had seen the ships. Their presence, they reasoned, must have been reported by Good, the man who apparently had no workable radio but did have a room full of radio bits and pieces. Two days after the broadcast, the Japanese ships returned to Kessa. A party landed, killed Good, then marched up the coast, took a missionary prisoner, and carried him off on board ship. Once again, someone in ignorance had effectively betrayed a coastwatcher.

At least the wretched incident served to blow some of the red tape loose. At last, when Good's death was reported, the authorities were jarred into giving coastwatchers military status. Within two weeks, Read was appointed a lieutenant and Mason a petty officer in the Navy, and watchers in other places, such as Page, Kyle, and Benham, were given status. Mrs. Good was paid a pension as if her husband had been a member of the armed forces.

So far, Read, Mason, and Mackie had not had to cope with actual enemy occupation of the islands. But on the evening of 30 March, while Read was passing close to Buka Passage in his launch, he was warned by his alert native police-boy, Corporal Sali, of a ship off Sohana Island, Read's former headquarters. Read stopped the launch, and in silent uncertainty allowed it to drift. He could see nothing and was about to go on, when suddenly the two men heard the note of a high-speed engine. Turning about, Read sped away, to discover later that he had nearly blundered into the Japanese, who had landed to occupy Buka Passage.

Since they had little fuel with them, Read and Sali hid the launch near the Passage and then took a canoe to a Catholic mission a few miles south. While Read ate breakfast with the missionaries, he was told that the mission had been visited and looted by the Japanese the day before, but that the priests and nuns had withdrawn to a hideout in the jungle, returning after the Japanese left.

Even while they were telling him this story, a small ship, full of Japanese, approached the mission. Again the missionaries, with Read, successfully withdrew to the hiding place. Read attempted to persuade them to accompany him to the east coast of the island, but they refused to leave their native flock, and soon afterwards passed under Japanese control.

Mackie, during this time, was on a visit to the Cape Henpan party of soldiers, attempting to get them off to a good second start. Read's primary concern was to warn him and the men that Buka Passage was occupied, and their retreat cut off. He wrote them a note, and sent it off by a native police corporal, Auna.

Bravely, Auna passed through the area in which Japanese picket boats were patrolling, delivered the note, and then unaccountably gave himself up to the Japanese, without revealing his recent errand. This inconsistent behavior was probably occasioned by the fact that he had been mixed up in looting, and perhaps he thought he could escape punishment only by deserting.

Before taking any measures to escape, Mackie signaled the arrival of more Japanese warships off Cape Henpan. He and his four men were in a very serious position. Their retreat through the island was blocked at Buka Passage, and the coastal waters were patrolled by enemy picket boats. In this extremity, a Fijian missionary, the Reverend Usaia Sotutu, came to their aid. He provided them with canoes and guides and slipped them through the patrolled waters by night, until they reached Bougainville.

Read, accompanied by Sali, in the meantime walked across Bougainville to the east coast. Crouched in the mangroves by the shore, the two men watched hundreds of Japanese troops being disembarked by launches and landing barges from a transport and destroyers. As they watched two cruisers head in from the east, they knew that this was no mere raid, but a permanent occupation.

To the south, below Bougainville, the Japanese meantime occupied Faisi in the Shortland Islands. The Buin party of soldiers reported the landing but, in spite of warnings from headquarters, remained in their house near the beach.

Within a week, the Japanese landed at Buin. The soldiers escaped with only their lives, losing their supplies and teleradio. This was sheer carelessness, neglect of the most elementary precautions. This experience, coupled with the previous one at Cape Henpan, showed us that soldiers, if left to themselves without experienced islanders, were apt to be useless as coastwatchers.

At about the same time Buka Passage and Faisi were occupied, a Japanese raiding party visited Kieta and was promptly reported by Mason. Two of his soldiers, who had lingered in the town in spite of his warnings, barely escaped.

Accompanying this raiding force was Tashira, a Japanese who had lived in Kieta in peacetime. Collecting the natives, he told them that for them the war was over, the Japanese were in complete possession, and the few Europeans who were left did not matter. Unfortunately, the missionaries who were still at Kieta stupidly repeated this propaganda, seeming to take it seriously themselves, and the natives began to look askance at Mason, who was still undiscovered by the Japanese. Mason immediately sent off a note to the Bishop of the mission, a man of good sense, who had remained at another mission post on the island. The Bishop rebuked the Kieta missionaries, who thereupon were at some pains to try to correct the impression they had created, and Mason's position with the natives improved for the time being.

For greater security, however, he decided to move to a supply dump farther down the coast. On his arrival there, he was laid up for several days by a severe attack of malaria. The soldiers who had been with him at Kieta had moved on to the Aravia camp, and he was alone except for two native

houseboys. After a few days, however, he was joined by the four hungry and bedraggled soldiers who had fled Buin. Fortunately, his fever abated until, as he said, he 'could eat nearly as much as the soldiers,' this being, in his experience, the ultra in superlatives.

Realizing that Buin should be covered, he applied to coast-watcher headquarters for permission to move his station there. Air reconnaissance had shown us that the Japanese landing in the Shortland Islands was a permanent occupation, so his request was quickly approved. Two of Mackie's soldiers and two native police were added to his own natives to make up the party.

On the night of their arrival in Buin, Mason and his party heard the welcome sound of bombs being dropped by our aircraft on enemy ships at anchor. This was the first concrete demonstration that any of these men had that there was anyone else on their side in the war.

For his observation post, Mason selected Malabita Hill, from which he could see the whole area enclosed by the Shortland Islands, Fauro Island, and Bougainville—an area which was to become a principal anchorage for a large part of the Navy of Japan. A few miles inland from his observation post, in very rough country, he set up his camp.

Read, meanwhile, was searching for an observation post from which to keep watch on Buka Passage. He first tentatively selected a mountain from which he could see the whole of Buka Island and the sea to east and west in fine weather, but from which nothing was visible when the clouds descended in a damp, gray mist.

Further search disclosed a better site, named Porapora, not so high and closer to the Passage. Knowing that his location could not long be kept secret from the natives, Read, with foresight that was part of his nature, did not use this second location but reserved it for the future. His principal nightmare at this time was the thought of a teleradio breakdown. Mason, the only technician, was more than a hundred miles to the south. So Read developed a mild phobia about the care of his set. No royal child ever received the solicitude that he lavished on his radio.

From their bases at Buka Passage and in the Shortlands, the Japanese now began to send ships to examine the east coast of Bougainville. Enemy parties went ashore at all the small ports and plantations to interrogate anyone they found. At one place they encountered Father Lebel, an American missionary who was nobody's fool. Lebel met the Japanese in full canonicals, acted the pompous ecclesiastic, and in reply to a question about his parish, indicated all Bougainville with a wave of his hand. The Japanese, impressed, paroled him on condition he did not leave the island.

In another harbor, they took away a Methodist missionary, but did not molest two Australian widows. An Austrian-born planter, a naturalized British subject, was questioned and then released.

The pieces were now set on the board; the Japanese at their bases with their ships visiting the coast; Read and Mason at their observation posts; Mackie and most of his men in their camp near Aravia; the planters and missionaries at their homes; the natives in their villages. For the moment, the position was one of balanced equilibrium but with two unstable factors; supplies, and the attitude of the natives. The native is a realist in matters of race. Since he first came in contact with other peoples, he has been subject to them and has developed the habit of looking to whoever is the most potent for direction. At Buka Passage itself, the natives gave immediate obedience to the Japanese. They had to live there, and the Japanese were there in force. That settled the question. On Buka, some natives resisted the Japanese demands and were summarily executed. Distrust and fear spread among the remainder on the island.

Near one village, Read had hidden some supplies, which were looted by the natives. Hearing rumors of this, he sent a native sergeant and constable to investigate. The village natives, driven by guilty consciences, attacked the two police, wounding one and killing the other. This was a bad affair, for it left that village permanently on the side of the Japanese. Through most of north Bougainville, however, the natives remained loyal and helpful. Read was particularly fortunate in having Sergeant Yauwika, whom he had picked up in Kieta. He was the best type of native non-commissioned officer, a frictionless link between Read and the native police, and through them, to the natives generally.

In addition to the natives from the Bougainville and Buka villages, the area contained a good many natives from other parts of the territory, who had been working on plantations. They were much lighter colored than the indigenous natives, their brown bodies appearing positively blonde beside the local blacks, and were called 'Redskins.'

For them, the outlook was gloomy. They felt they had little chance of ever seeing their homes again, and to a native, an eventual return to his home village is an essential of life. The 'Redskins' felt their only chance was to stick to the Europeans, and when their employers ceased production they rallied to Read, who paid them, fed them, housed them, used them as carriers, and prevented them from becoming a rabble of homeless outcasts.

Fortunately, money still held its value, as the natives used it among themselves even when there were no trade articles to buy. Read had not only saved the Government's cash at Buka Passage, but on his second visit to Kieta had called a miner to his aid to dynamite the office safe there and had added those funds to his money for carriers and food.

Read was also extremely fortunate in having Usaia Sotutu, the Fijian missionary who had helped Mackie and his men escape from Cape Henpan. Usaia had been offered a safe conduct for himself and his family by the Japanese if he would join them. When he did not reply to this overture, he was marked down for capture, but he moved his wife and children to a safe place and continued to assist Read, taking no payment for his services until, a year later, he was enrolled in the Fijian forces. Before the invasion, Usaia had supervised the work of native mission teachers in the Bougainville and Buka villages.

Although the mission teaching had been stopped by the Japanese, who started their own school at Buka Passage (which taught nothing but when to bow), the native teachers remained in the villages. They were the most intelligent among the natives. Usaia, assisted by a half-caste, Anton Jostin, organized them as a spy service. From one to another, they passed their information until it reached Usaia or Anton, who passed it on to Read. In addition, Usaia sometimes managed to infiltrate friendly natives into Buka Passage.

In spite of encouraging signs in the native attitude, however, it was obvious to anyone of experience that time would bring deterioration. It was a question of how much time would elapse before native loyalty cracked, and what would have happened in that time elsewhere.

Read and Mackie, owing to their foresight, had plentiful supplies in northern Bougainville, but Mason had only what he carried with him. In answer to a signal from him, a plane was dispatched to make a moonlight drop, but through an error the supplies were released seventy miles from Mason's position. Informed of this fact by teleradio, Mason walked, then borrowed a bicycle and rode, then walked again, to the place where the drop had been made. Then, unable to find the supplies, he made a weary and empty-handed journey back to his post.

During his absence, the Japanese landed a patrol to search for his party, but, warned by natives, the men had withdrawn and hidden.

A second drop to Mason, including a petty officer's cap and arm badge, was more successful, while a successful drop for Read was also made. These supply drops were not made to provide food and trade articles alone. They were the only means of communication, other than radio, so they included key words for the code, maps, and personal letters. They were good morale builders; not only for the coastwatchers but for the loyal natives who were encouraged by the sight of an aircraft from their own side.

Dropping radios was still risky because of lack of proper parachute equipment. So when Read, in spite of his solicitude, developed a defect in his radio transmitter, he sent Usaia on the hundred-mile trip to Mason to have it repaired. Because of his ability to live on native food, Usaia made the trip much more quickly than even the most experienced European could have traveled. A short while afterwards, Usaia moved a large quantity of supplies from the hinterland of Kieta to Read's lookout by native carriers, a great feat since, under the propaganda ministrations of Tashira, the natives about Kieta were turning pro-Japanese.

The planters of northern Bougainville, who had remained against Read's advice, now began making demands on him that supplies should be dropped to them. Read forwarded their request, which met a hostile reception from the Air Forces. The planters grumbled and did not make Read's life any easier.

One planter, the Austrian-born fellow who had been questioned by the Japanese but allowed to remain free, became a real source of danger. No one knew exactly what had transpired at his interview with the Japanese, but it became known that he had written to the Japanese commandant at Buka Passage and it was suspected that he proposed to sell the enemy his produce. This development would gravely endanger the coastwatchers and soldiers, for if a European treated with the enemy, the natives would soon follow suit and would gradually pass completely under Japanese domination.

Worried, Read reported the circumstances and asked for instructions. I replied, 'Take any measures you consider necessary for your own safety. There will be no inquest.'

Extreme measures were not needed, however. Read and Mackie haled the planter before them and placed him on parole. He agreed to remain on his plantation, to seek no further contact with the enemy and to avoid any which the Japanese should seek with him. He observed these conditions and, as a result, still lives.

All this time, Mason and Read had been reporting the arrivals and departures of ships, the position of Japanese supplies and troop barracks, and the building of installations. This information was passed on to the Air Force to guide its bombers. Sometimes, after one of our air raids on Buka Passage, Read would signal back to us the results of our strikes, information which had been passed on to him by Usaia's scouts.

The Japanese, of course, were not ignoring the presence of the coastwatchers during this period. The enemy knew they were in the jungle, but not exactly where. The presence of Mackie's soldiers, even though they had made many blunders and had not yet adapted themselves to conditions, also gave our watchers a distinct advantage. Simply because of the numbers on the coastwatchers' side, the Japanese commander knew that if he sent out a patrol to kill or capture our men, it would need to be a strong one. The larger the patrol, the more slowly it would move, and the less likelihood it would have of catching our men. In the meantime, the commander had his bases to build up and defend, and he could not spare a large patrol for any length of time.

That Japanese commander must later have realized that his toleration of Read and Mason was the most serious blunder he could have made. At coastwatcher headquarters, we already knew that before the summer was out Read and Mason would be filling a vital niche in the Allies' plans. We could not even hint of this to our two men, of course, but we knew that up to now they had filled in the blanks themselves and that they had allowed no consideration to divert them from their intelligence role. So, without any portentous insinuations of what was to come, we simply continued to depend on them. Ferdinand himself could not have been more self-effacing than they.

The demise of the *USS Wasp*

8

Soon after General MacArthur assumed supreme command in the Southwest Pacific in March 1942, Long called a conference in Melbourne and outlined a scheme for the formation of an intelligence unit for carrying out activities behind the enemy lines, its men to be drawn from all the armed services of the Allies, its funds to be contributed by all the countries concerned, with the resources of each service and country available to all.

We in the coastwatching organization particularly felt the need for such a plan. We already had a set-up for supplying all the armed services with coastwatcher information, but there was still nothing to prevent each service from sending in its own coastwatchers independently. One pair of eyes can see just as much as any number of pairs, of course, but it is surprising how often this simple fact is forgotten.

Another aspect of the future that disturbed us was the fact that although our watchers had finally been given naval status, no provision had been made for enrolling additional personnel to provide more parties. Not so many of the inhabitants of New Guinea and the Solomons were fitted by experience, physical fitness, and character for coastwatching, and of those that were, aside from those already enrolled as watchers, most had joined the Army or Air Force, where entry was easier than in the Navy.

Supply as well as personnel was a thorny problem. We had only the Naval Board as an approved source for such unorthodox items as trade articles for natives; twist tobacco, knives, calico, and beads. The Navy supply system was designed to protect the taxpayers' pockets in peacetime, and the first such items we had asked for took four months to arrive. Long before they came, we had had to obtain them by irregular methods. Items such as parachutes—obtainable only from other services—and aircraft and submarines, for supplying, rescuing, or placing coastwatchers, had been provided us only through personal negotiation with commanders. We had felt that the fate of our parties depended on the vagaries of local command. The larger and older the office, the heavier its infestation of red tape.

Long's plan was adopted by the Allied Command, and as a result the Allied Intelligence Bureau was formed, with the coastwatching organization of the Northeast Area as a part of it.

The coastwatcher situation was still somewhat complicated by the fact that the watchers in the unoccupied South Pacific Area remained part of Australian Naval Intelligence, rather than the new Allied Intelligence Bureau. I was put in charge of the watchers in both areas, and was responsible to the Controller of the Allied Intelligence Bureau for the one, to the Director of Naval Intelligence for the other. These divisions of authority were not strictly adhered to, but as success crowned our efforts, no one raised academic questions of control.

It was at this point that our organization in the Northeast Area, the portion under the Allied Intelligence Bureau, became FERDINAND. In choosing the name, I was motivated by the fact that proposals founded on the more improbable types of spy fiction were being suggested and seriously considered. It was an inevitable conclusion that too many senior officers had read adventure stories and believed them. Some officers seemed to imagine that intelligence work necessarily involved beautiful females who handed papers from their bosoms to men in false black beards. FERDINAND was meant to lead the mind of the coastwatcher away from these romancings and to remind him of his job of un-histrionic watching.

Soon after FERDINAND was named, we were confronted with a serious proposal that coastwatchers combine their training and operations with those of an organization designed to carry out sabotage work at enemy bases. This was quite against FERDINAND principles; sabotage would certainly draw enemy attention, which would soon terminate any intelligence activity. We managed to resist this threat successfully.

FERDINAND at once became a portmanteau word, including in its meaning not only the coastwatchers of the Northeast Area and their activities, but also the supply and base organizations on which they depended.

As soon as the Allied Intelligence Bureau was formed, we applied for and obtained islanders from the other services.

Some of these were old coastwatchers, like McCarthy, who had received an Army commission; he was delighted to transfer to FERDINAND and, as he put it, to reality.

I did not want these recruits to FERDINAND to obey orders, even my own, without thinking about them. Alone in the jungle, they would be the only competent judges of their own conditions. From the start, they must think for themselves, all the time. They would have to know, as well as or better than their superiors, what they were there for, what information was of value, and how it would be used.

To the military mind, they needed discipline and needed a lot of it, urgently. In our view, they already had the bulk of the training they needed. They knew how to live in the jungle, how to handle natives, how to fend for themselves. The training they lacked was in code and radio work, in recognition of ships, aircraft, and defense installations.

Above all, they needed to be protected from having the habit of independent thought drilled out of them. An iconoclastic idea, this, applicable only to a small body of selected officers; volunteers subject only to the punishment of being returned to their original military units.

So we had no camp and no formal training. Our recruits lived in pubs, where their virgin indiscipline could not be violated. Each day they came to the office, where they read all the signals that had been exchanged with parties already in the field and saw what happened to information when it was received. Their reading showed them the trend natives were taking, what pitfalls there were, how necessary a code was, and that, without a teleradio, a coastwatcher was doomed and useless. So, knowing their lives depended on it, they learned how to code and decode, how to operate a teleradio and effect simple repairs to it.

FERDINAND headquarters looked like a slice of chaos with all these men milling about in it, jostling, reading, arguing, appealing for decisions above the hubbub. But they were learning their jobs the best way, by teaching themselves and by sharpening each other's wits in the apparent anarchy. Paddy Murray, my clerk, carrying on his office work in their midst, did not go mad, but nearly.

Of all the benefits the formation of the Allied Intelligence Bureau conferred on us, one of the most important was its facilities for informing us in advance of all projected Allied operations. This made it possible for us to place our parties in the best positions in time to be of maximum assistance.

We turned to the Solomons, where things were about to happen.

9

IN THE SOUTHERN SOLOMONS, AS IN THE NORTH, our coastwatchers had a grandstand view of the Japanese occupation.

When the expected bombing commenced, soon after the fall of Rabaul, our naval intelligence officer for the area, Lieutenant D. S. Macfarlan, was located at Tulagi, where the Resident Commissioner of the Solomons, W. S. Marchant, also maintained his headquarters.

Most civilians had been evacuated, leaving only a skeleton civil staff, a few planters and missionaries, a small Australian Army and Air Force group on Tanambogo Island in Tulagi Harbor, and a scattering of our coastwatchers, spread through the area like a cricket team.

Fortunately the Japanese bombers concentrated on the radio station at Tulagi, a creation of such imposing latticework that it appeared a center of high-powered communication. But it was a fraud; the radio equipment was old and almost useless, so much so that Sexton, the operator, had earlier pleaded, 'If the Japs come here and ask me where the radio station is and I show them this, they will shoot me for concealing the real one.'

On Tanambogo, virtually undisturbed by the Japanese bombers, was the unobtrusively placed Air Force station, which did the real work.

Warned by Mason on Bougainville of enemy air raids, Macfarlan, Marchant, and the few other Europeans on Tulagi sat uneasily in their slit trenches while the enemy aircraft leisurely made their bombing runs. When the raids became frequent, and it was evident that there was nothing to prevent a Japanese advance, Marchant decided to move to Malaita Island, northeast of Guadalcanal, establish himself at an inland post, and hold control over the natives as long as possible.

Taking radio operator Sexton, the district officer, an Anglican missionary, and a teleradio with him, he attempted to get Macfarlan to accompany him also. This was a situation that had been foreseen when Macfarlan was appointed to Tulagi—the civil authority, intent on its own duties, treating Naval Intelligence as a secondary consideration. Macfarlan, remembering his instructions to go to Guadalcanal when invasion seemed imminent, stood firm.

Marchant at first declined to lend him a teleradio, although five of those under his control had been lent the Solomons Government by the Navy specifically for coastwatching. To break the impasse, we ordered Macfarlan to go to San Cristobal and take possession of the Navy teleradio there, but in the meantime, he won his point.

He landed on Guadalcanal near Lunga, later to become the scene of heavy fighting. Here he found K. D. Hay, an extremely obese planter and a veteran of World War I, who had decided to remain. Hay had removed large quantities of supplies from Tulagi and was busy transporting them inland.

The two men pooled their supplies, which included even a refrigerator, and set up a station on Gold Ridge, a mining camp 4,000 feet above sea level in the hills south of Lunga. There they were joined by A. M. Andressen, a miner who had been in the Solomons for twenty-five years. Macfarlan, who was inexperienced in island jungle life, wisely took advice from his two companions and made out well.

Anticipating the importance of Guadalcanal, we had still two other watchers on the island. One of these was District Officer Martin Clemens, a tall, engaging, ambitious young man, who was established at Aola on the north coast, about forty miles east of Lunga. With his native police, he was maintaining as much authority as he could over the restive village natives.

The other Guadalcanal watcher was F. A. (Snowy) Rhoades, a dour, silent man who, alone of all our coastwatchers, really looked the part. His unruly hair, deeply lined face, cold blue eyes peering out beneath bushy brows, and a mannerism of hanging his head like a prizefighter protecting his chin made him almost a caricature of the complete jungle fighter. He was as tough as he looked and, where Japanese were concerned, bloodthirsty. He had been appointed a coastwatcher in the early days, and when civilians had been evacuated had chosen to remain. His post was at Lavoro, a company-owned plantation of which he was manager, on the western end of Guadalcanal.

A few miles to the north and west of Lunga, opposite the western end of Guadalcanal, lies Savo, a small volcanic island commanding the western approaches to Tulagi. Here L. Schroeder, old, frail, and in ill health, kept a trade store. He too had decided to remain and had been given a teleradio made up of bits and pieces.

To the north, on long, narrow Santa Isabel Island, our watcher was District Officer D. G. Kennedy, a New Zealander who had spent most of his life in the islands. A determined, dominant man of middle age, he was one of those to whom command comes naturally, and at last he had found himself in a position where he could really use his talents.

After the Japanese took Rabaul, he hid his motor vessel in a creek and made camp in the jungled hills, warning the natives that if the Japanese came, they were to have no dealings with them whatsoever.

Feeling that some effort should be made, also, to keep watch on islands to the northwest, he dispatched a half-caste to the Shortland Islands with a teleradio and instructions to report. Since he feared that approval would be withheld by the resident commissioner, he made this move on his own responsibility. When the Shortland Islands were occupied, at the end of March, his watcher was unfortunately captured.

In radio, as in other walks of life, the professional operator is far ahead of the amateur. Sexton, with the resident commissioner's group on Malaita, could transmit and receive signals from Vila, key station in the New Hebrides, when no one else in the southern Solomons could. So it was arranged that all coastwatching signals should be sent to Marchant, who now held the command of Lieutenant Colonel in the British Solomon Islands Protectorate Defense Force. At Malaita, our men's signals could be recoded into the high-grade cipher held by Marchant and passed on to the Naval Intelligence Officer at Vila.

When transmission to Vila became more difficult than usual, Vanikoro, an island 300 miles southeast of Malaita, acted as link. The radio there was operated by Mrs. Boye, wife of the manager of a timber company. Unperturbed by the events in the Solomons, Mrs. Boye remained on Vanikoro all through the fighting and was later, deservedly, appointed Honorary Third Officer, Women's Royal Australian Naval Service, and awarded the British Empire Medal.

On 1 May 1942, Japanese aircraft made a particularly savage raid on Tanambogo, strafing and sinking the Air Force's motorboat and causing considerable damage ashore. All but a skeleton staff of our Air Force was thereupon withdrawn to Florida Island.

Next day, Kennedy reported two enemy ships at anchor in Thousand Ships Bay at the southern end of Isabel. Enemy occupation was obviously near. The last of the Air Force men left Tanambogo for Florida Island. From there, the troops voyaged to the southern end of Guadalcanal in a small vessel concealed for just this eventuality, and thence to Vila. It was an able retreat, made at the last possible moment, a credit to the junior officers who organized and carried it out. Three days later, when the enemy occupied Tulagi, there was a welcome awaiting, thanks to coastwatcher information. Two of our aircraft carriers, guided by Kennedy's information, steamed into position south of Guadalcanal, and their planes sank nine of the enemy's convoy ships. Schroeder, on Savo Island, had a perfect view of the battle and his reports were the most accurate and complete tally of the enemy's casualties. Macfarlan also reported what he could see of the action. Rhoades and Clemens, being on the lowlands, saw little.

Because the enemy occupation of Tulagi was only part of a general move south from Rabaul, our carriers then had to hurry off to meet and help defeat the forces moving to attack Port Moresby, at the Battle of the Coral Sea.

For the present, the Solomons were left to the Japanese and to our coastwatchers. The occupation of Tulagi, our coastwatchers were aware, left only one way out for them—Allied reconquest of the Solomons. Some had small vessels but did not intend to use them. Others had no means whatever of leaving. None of them knew or was in a position to judge when our counterattack would take place. So far, the Japanese advance had gone unchecked. They continued to send intelligence with only the faith that the Allies would one day strike back; if soon, to save them; if not soon, well, that would be bad luck.

During the next few weeks, the Japanese, working night and day, reinforced Tulagi, Tanambogo, and Gavutu. A seaplane base was established in the harbor, and the enemy's aircraft ranged over the surrounding seas on reconnaissance flights daily. Our watchers' reports of these aircraft movements gave the Allied Naval staffs some idea of the pattern of search which the Japanese followed.

Ten days after the Japanese occupied Tulagi, Clemens, from his post at Aola, found the crew of a U.S. plane which had made a forced landing; the first of many airmen that the coastwatchers were to save. The Japanese wasted no time before sallying forth from their bases. Within a fortnight of the Tulagi occupation, one party visited Savo, where Schroeder evaded them by hiding in the jungle. However, on Savo they captured an educated native medical practitioner, took him to Tulagi, and broke him down until he led the Japanese to the creek on Isabel Island where Kennedy's boat was hidden. Warned of the enemy's approach, Kennedy hid in the jungle, but his boat was burned. When the Japanese had left, he took another boat from a plantation and at night moved his police and supplies across the wide channel to Segi, on the southern shore of New Georgia.

The selection of this spot, across a narrow strait from Vangunu Island, was a stroke of genius. The waters here were unsurveyed, unknown even to the Japanese fishermen who had surreptitiously charted as they searched for trochas shell in the Solomons in peacetime. On charts, the surrounding shores were shown only as dotted lines and the only hydrographic information given was a warning to mariners to avoid the strait and its reefs. Only local natives, who Kennedy felt could be kept loyal, knew these channels.

Kennedy, with his proclivity for organization and command, still continued to keep a watch on Isabel also. He repaired a radio which had been partly destroyed by an earlier evacuee to prevent it from being of use to the Japanese, and gave it to Geoffrey Kuper, a half-caste, who had been trained as a medical practitioner. Stationed at the southern end of Isabel, Kuper remained happily undisturbed.

Meantime Schroeder, who was standing up to the hardships well in spite of his age and frailty, decided that even though he had once escaped the Japanese on Savo, that small speck of land provided too little scope for continued evasion. By night, he crossed in a canoe to Guadalcanal and joined Rhoades.

Rhoades was now reporting that Japanese reconnaissance parties were examining the grass plains of Guadalcanal and the nearby coast. One party visited a mission, uncomfortably close to Rhoades and Schroeder, who thereupon moved inland. From their positions, Macfarlan and Clemens confirmed these reports of Japanese activity. Macfarlan, from his height at Gold Ridge, could also see Tulagi clearly, except when clouds blocked his view, and he reported enemy ships bringing in supplies. As Allied aircraft from Port Moresby and the New Hebrides raided this shipping and the Tulagi base, Macfarlan signaled the results. When the Japanese began construction of an airstrip near Lunga, Macfarlan and Rhoades gave detailed reports of progress.

The Japanese now paid the coastwatchers the compliment of organizing a propaganda campaign against them among the natives. A Japanese who had lived in the Solomons and who had been a barber in Fiji headed the enemy's Native Department. The native medical practitioner who had been captured on Savo, and who was now completely intimidated, made translations of propaganda into a native tongue.

The natives were told, through pamphlets, that the British rule was finished, the Japanese firmly established, and that the whereabouts of the remaining Europeans must be reported. Not one native responded to either the blandishments or the threats, and the Japanese were left to search for the watchers without native assistance.

Rhoades, from his post to the west, also sent natives to work at the Japanese airfield and to barter food. To estimate numbers, he asked his scouts for comparisons with villages whose populations he knew. Later Rhoades and Macfarlan grew quite heated about the merits of their respective systems.

Farther east, Clemens sent his police, dressed as village natives, to Florida Island, to learn what they could of Japanese forces and fortifications on Tulagi, Gavutu, and Tanambogo. The information he could glean in this way was not very extensive, since the Japanese discouraged native visits to these islands.

Things were going well for the coastwatchers, but not monotonously so. In July, Macfarlan broke a bone in his foot while scouting near Lunga. A native medical practitioner strapped it so effectively that in a month it was entirely healed. Rhoades and Schroeder were forced by Japanese patrols to move further westward, then to the south. Their food was running low, and they depended more and more on the products of native gardens.

South and east of the Solomons, U.S. forces were gathering for the attack. In the Tonga Islands, the First U.S. Marine Division, under General Vandegrift, was rehearsing the landing. Battleships, carriers, cruisers, and destroyers were concentrated into a task force to cover the attack.

To FERDINAND headquarters in Townsville came two Marine officers to learn what we, could tell them of the enemy. Thanks to information sent by Macfarlan, Rhoades, Kennedy, and the others, supplemented by Air Force photographs and reports, we were able to hand them neat maps of Lunga, Tulagi, and Gavutu, with the positions of guns, defense works, other installations, and the approximate number of troops at each point.

Realizing that the attacking forces would continue to need all the information they could get, we had already sent Mackenzie to Vila to receive and interpret information from the Solomons watchers and to disseminate it immediately to the U.S. forces engaged in the action. Part of his job, also, was to guide and restrain any ill-conceived proposals for extension of FERDINAND activity into such fields as sabotage. As D.S.I.O. (Deputy Supervising Intelligence Officer), Mackenzie was to become well known to the South Pacific forces, though it is doubtful if any of the Americans, trained in alphabetical titles, ever inquired what the letters stood for.

Airstrikes against our invasion forces would, we knew, come from Rabaul and Kavieng, the only Japanese bases yet capable of being used by bombers. The air route from Rabaul to Guadalcanal passed over Buin, that from Kavieng over Buka Passage. Enemy fighters could take off from Buka Passage. To ensure the safety of Read and Mason at these posts, we decided in July that any information they might send us in the interim should be sacrificed. They were instructed to move from their posts, clear of any danger, and to maintain radio silence until instructed to resume reporting.

Two days before our invasion, Read and Mason were alerted. Mason moved back to Malabite Hill, overlooking Buin, and Read made for the site overlooking Buka Passage, on Porapora, which he had kept in reserve for just such an occasion as this. The two men could only surmise what their orders meant, but they knew some extraordinarily important movement was afoot. The U.S. forces were told of the frequency on which Read's and Mason's reports would be sent, so that the signals might be received direct by the fighting ships. As a safeguard against any possible fumbling, Marchant on Malaita was instructed to transmit the signals to Vila, where Mackenzie could pass them on to the fighting forces. Still another channel was arranged through Port Moresby, Townsville, and Canberra to pass the warnings to Pearl Harbor, where a powerful transmitter was to broadcast them throughout the Pacific.

To confuse the listening Japanese, new call signals were designed for the two watchers. And to ensure that even if the Japanese decoded the signal ordering this change, they would not be able to understand its import, Read was told to use the initials of his daughter and Mason the first three letters of his sister's surname. Thus little Judy Read came into history with the call sign JER, and Mrs. John Stokie with the call STO.

Marchant, as the attack drew near, had been instructed to send weather reports daily from Malaita. These, added to meteorological information from other Pacific areas, made possible a weather forecast some days ahead. Thus it was that our convoy, covered by low clouds and rain, approached the Solomons unseen by the enemy.

10

OUR INVASION OF GUADALCANAL AND TULAGI at dawn on 7 August came as a complete surprise to the Japanese. As the first light streaked the sky, dive bombers from carriers attacked Tulagi, Gavutu, and Tanambogo, while warships bombarded gun positions ashore and on Guadalcanal, and transports moved into both areas. So complete was the surprise that enemy seaplanes near Gavutu were sunk at their moorings by gunfire from ships.

But surprise is a short-lived advantage, and it was now that our coastwatchers came truly into their own. Four hours after our attack began, Mason, in his jungle lookout on Malabite Hill, 400 miles away, heard the roar of enemy bombers. Immediately he flashed the message to the Allied invasion forces, 'From STO. Twenty-four torpedo bombers headed yours.'

Twenty-five minutes later, Pearl Harbor broadcast the warning through the whole Pacific.

With two and a quarter hours' warning of the attack, there was time for our ships to disperse in readiness, for carrier-borne aircraft to be refueled and re-ammunitioned and to lie in wait at high altitude; time for all preparations to be made without haste and without undue interruption to the task of unloading the supplies.

On board H.M.A.S. Canberra, one of two Australian warships engaged in the invasion, there was time, for example, for the bos'n's mate to pipe over the loudspeakers, 'The ship will be attacked at noon by twenty-four torpedo bombers. All hands will pipe to dinner at eleven o'clock.'

When the torpedo bombers arrived, they were met by fighters and guns at the ready. Those enemy planes that escaped the fighters were shot down by gunfire. Only one Japanese aircraft survived to return to Rabaul. No damage was done to our ships.

Next morning at 8:40 o'clock, Read and his natives heard the drone of many aircraft approaching, changing to a roar as 45 dive bombers from Kavieng passed overhead. Before the sound had died away, Read was on the air with the signal, 'From JER, forty-five dive bombers going southeast.' At 9:10, Pearl Harbor broadcast it for all to hear.

Two hours later, Read tuned in to the aircraft carriers' wavelength and heard the preparations being made to receive the enemy aircraft. A little later, he heard an excited voice, 'Boys, they're shooting them down like flies, one, two, three... I can see eight of them coming down in the sea now!'

Read, on lonely Porapora, felt the glow that was justly his.

That afternoon, Mason reported more aircraft. Again the fighters met them, again the Japanese attack was smashed, and Mason, listening in to the fighter control, knew like Read that his long wait was justified.

Next day, the Japanese attacked again, were reported, and again suffered heavy losses. Crippled by the casualties and unable to mount more attacks until reinforcements were flown in from the Carolines, the enemy had to hold his hand for the next few days.

The Japanese were told nothing of the part the coastwatchers were playing in their defeat. All reference to coastwatching was censored from the news, and there were no indiscreet releases as there had been in the past. Of course, the Japanese should have realized how the radioed warnings were causing the defeat of their Air Force, but apparently, they did not understand what was going on, until later.

The Marines, after heavy fighting, had overrun Tulagi in a few hours. Gavutu was taken, but not wholly subdued, on the first day. On Guadalcanal there was no initial resistance; the Japanese there, mainly members of construction units, left their hot breakfasts and fled. On Tanambogo, the Japanese held out for four days, sweeping with deadly fire the causeway which connected it with Gavutu, and turning tanks over with their bare hands.

Landing with the first wave of Marines on Tulagi were Dick Horton and Henry Josselyn, two young district officers from the Solomons who had been picked up by Mackenzie in Vila and enrolled in FERDINAND. Assigned to the Marines as landing guides, they were each awarded the Silver Star for their part in the beachhead fighting.

On Tulagi, Gavutu, and Tanambogo, the Marines settled, digging trenches, emplacing guns, and preparing for the counterattack which everyone expected. On Guadalcanal, they formed a defensive perimeter of about two miles' radius around the airfield.

Within it they toiled in the dank heat, preparing positions, transporting supplies, equipment, and ammunition, eating and sleeping when and where they could. Seabees, those diligent, indefatigable men, unloaded ships, made and repaired roads, and dragged machinery ashore to put the airfield in order. While they worked, fighting blazed along the perimeter where the Japanese were rallying.

At sea, luck was with the Japanese. On the night of 9 August, Japanese surface forces attacked the transports' screen of cruisers, sinking one Australian and three U.S. warships. The transports hurried their unloading and departed to avoid air and submarine attacks, leaving the Marines to hold what they had taken. When the airfield was useable and ships could be given air cover, they would return.

To the Marines, it was the beginning of the campaign. To the coastwatchers, who had waited in the jungle since the Japanese invasion, it was the passing over the crest of the hill. At last, they could feel that it was not a one-way war. They could tell the natives, even in faraway Bougainville, that the Japanese had been pushed out of Tulagi and Guadalcanal, and that we were coming back.

Macfarlan, Hay, and Andressen had had a grandstand view of our landing from their post at Gold Ridge. They had heard the roar of our aircraft and had seen the ships bombarding the shore. They had seen the first air battles and had watched the Japanese aircraft shot down in numbers. This was the sight for which they had waited four weary months.

Clemens, from his post east of Lunga had seen the landing distantly, but sufficiently well to assure him it was a success. He cached his radio and set out for Lunga, arriving there a week later. He was immediately taken before the intelligence staff to give all the information he could of the terrain to the east.

Rhoades and Schroeder, at the western end of the island, were not faring so well. The Japanese who had been driven out of Lunga fled in their direction, endangering them and the Roman Catholic missionaries near them. The naked, bayonetted bodies of two priests and two nuns found east of Lunga were a warning to the missionaries of the fate which awaited them should they fall into Japanese hands. Rhoades and Schroeder moved farther around the island, but were blocked from further retreat by a Japanese outpost. So they holed up in a cave near a river and, with their supplies now exhausted, were fed and protected by friendly natives.

Marchant on Malaita heard the gunfire and bombing at Tulagi and knew that he had won his brave gamble. He had retained control of the native population in the southeastern portion of the protectorate, and the recapture of Tulagi would now ensure loyalty even farther afield. The tide of actual war had passed him by, but he continued to play an important part in it, sending on to Vila our watchers' reports.

To Kennedy, at Segi, the occupation came as an inspiration to capitalize the advantage. It was not in his nature to stay still, and as he had not been disturbed since his boat was burned at Isabel, he now moved about New Georgia, visiting the natives in their villages and impressing them with his own determination to resist the Japanese anywhere and at all times. Now he could point to Tulagi and Guadalcanal as proof of his past assurances. His dark, heavy face and powerful frame, his determination and transparent faith in his own words convinced the natives that he was not only a leader to be followed, but a power that it would be perilous to disobey.

On Kennedy's instructions, Geoffrey Kuper, whom he had stationed on southern Isabel, now came on the air with regular reports. Previously he had signaled to Kennedy only, and at odd intervals. His first official report was of the presence of Japanese survivors from a sunken destroyer on a small island near Isabel. Natives, organized by Kuper, killed many of them.

On Guadalcanal, the Japanese were wreaking vengeance on any native who failed to assist them. One of those captured was Vouza, a retired Sergeant-Major of Police. When he refused to tell the Japanese of the position of American forces, they tied him to a tree and threatened him with bayonets.

Still holding out, he was stabbed five times, with questioning intervals between. Then, still silent, he lost consciousness and was left for dead. After the Japanese had gone and a little of his strength had returned, he chewed through his bonds and reached the American hospital at Lunga. Whenever consciousness returned, as he teetered between life and death, he whispered, 'I did not tell them.' His will to live won out, and when he recovered, he was awarded the George Medal for his bravery.

Mackenzie's information-gathering and disseminating system at Vila was functioning like clockwork. Satisfied that the local Naval Intelligence staff could handle that duty, he prepared to move to Guadalcanal to establish a station where warnings from coastwatchers could be received and collated on the spot and passed directly to the forces in battle.

With him he took his assistant, Train; Eodie, civilian radio operator at Vila; and Rayman, a New Ireland native. Rayman, a mechanic and driver, had been engineer on an evacuation boat, and in unfamiliar Vila he had attached himself to Mackenzie, who spoke the same brand of pidgin; much as a country boy in a big city attaches himself to someone from his own hometown. The four men arrived at Lunga a week after the Marines. Their first job was to select a site for their radio. To be efficient, it would have to be some distance away from other radios and from radar, generators, and other sources of electric disturbance. The best sites had already been pre-empted so, taking what was left, Mackenzie's party established itself in a Japanese dug-out on the northwest edge of the airfield, among the coconut palms that bordered the grass plains. Here the radio was housed, while a forlorn Japanese tent nearby, tattered by bomb splinters, was used as an office.

The day after they landed, their radio was on the air and in contact with the coastwatchers. Eodie, who had to return to Vila as soon as possible, trained three Marine radio operators so that a continuous watch could be kept. Reports of movements of enemy parties, signaled by Rhoades and Macfarlan, were passed from Mackenzie by telephone directly to Marine headquarters.

Two Marines were also allotted to Mackenzie as coders, but proved to be better fitted for fighting with bayonet and bomb than with the pencil, so Mackenzie set them to work digging a slit trench in which to take shelter from air raids. They provided a good illustration of how men's minds work under sudden excitement. As all sensible men do when they are likely to be bombed, they had made a mental note of the nearest shelter, a Japanese steamroller about a hundred yards away. Just as they finished digging the trench, the alarm sounded. Without a moment's hesitation, they ran to take cover under the steamroller, while Mackenzie and Train stepped into the newly completed trench.

The radio dugout was a miserable affair, simply a hole in the black soil, roofed with coconut-palm logs and decaying sandbags. When it rained, which was frequently, the water soaked through the rotten sandbags and dripped from the log roof. The radio instruments could be kept dry only by covering them with raincoats, while the owners of the coats got wet. The floor turned to a black adhesive mud, which clung to clothing, food, and instruments. The Marine operators slept in the battered office tent, Mackenzie and Train in the Base Radio Station nearby.

This was the base of D.S.I.O. Lunga: a hole in the ground and a dilapidated tent in the coconut palms in which six men worked and lived under conditions varying from discomfort to acute misery. Not an impressive sight, but it was part of the hinge on which the whole success of the Solomons campaign was to turn.

On the day of his arrival, Mackenzie had noticed a Japanese light truck standing forlornly by a muddy road. Days later, it still stood there, drab and forsaken, its engines refusing to respond to any treatment. Mackenzie, who felt an urge to expand his miserable equipment, sent Rayman and one of the Marines to delve into its innards. In a few hours, they drove it away, along the quagmire that was called a road. Envious glances were cast their way. A Seabee officer pleaded with Mackenzie, pointing out that the radio station did not need a truck but that the Seabees, with hundreds, no thousands, of tons of supplies to shift, did. Mackenzie admitted that he did not really need a truck; what he really needed was a jeep. A trade was made on the spot, and Mackenzie proudly drove off in a new jeep with 'R.A.N.' painted on it in letters as large as the sides would allow.

The brief respite from Japanese air attacks was soon over. Mackenzie passed on news of the coming raid as soon as he received a signal from Read or Mason. Ironically, because of the more-than-ample warning time this allowed, confusion and uncertainty among the men resulted. So it became the practice not to sound 'Condition Yellow'—'raid expected'—until the enemy was within half an hour of Lunga, or 'Condition Red'—'raid near'—until ten minutes before the planes were overhead. With this modification, Read's and Mason's alarms were highly effective. Kennedy's position on Segi, 160 miles northwest of Lunga, fitted in admirably with the system. His reports gave a check on the speed of the enemy planes so that the time of their arrival could be forecast within a minute or so.

A fortnight after the capture of Lunga, on 20 August 1942, the first Grumman Wildcat fighters flew into Henderson Field. Immediately, a new element of sheer precision and co-ordination entered into the coastwatching-fighting pattern. Up to this time, the Japanese Zero had been supreme in the Pacific as a fighter. It had had some hard knocks at Port Moresby, but it was still on top, as it had been in Malaya, the Philippines, the Netherlands East Indies, and Burma. The Wildcat was a robust machine, superior to the Zero in gunpower and ability to take punishment, but lacking the speed and maneuverability of the enemy plane. Only if it were above the Zero, and so able to dive on it, could it depend on shooting the Zero down.

The day after the Wildcats' arrival, word was passed by Read and Mason, via Mackenzie, that Japanese raiders were approaching. Had the Wildcat pilots had to depend on local alerts they could never have reached sufficient altitude before the Zeros arrived. But with more than two hours' warning, pilots were able to take off at their leisure and climb to 30,000 feet, ready to dive on the Zeros when they arrived. Day after day for a month, the same routing was followed. At every raid the Wildcat pilots, forewarned, intercepted the enemy raiders and shot them down in enormously disproportionate numbers, generally reported by Macfarlan, who gave a Zero to Zero description from his Gold Ridge vantage point. Read, at Buka Passage, made a count of returning enemy aircraft, information which often showed that Japanese losses were greater than Air Intelligence at Henderson Field had supposed.

This is not the place to tell the heroic story of the Henderson Field flyers, who fought on day after day, while their friends were killed around them. Compared to the enemy's, the Wildcat pilots' losses were light, but they were severe against their own unaugmented numbers. It was their unabated aggressiveness, taking to the air at every alarm, that began the decline of the Japanese Air Force. The beating which the Japanese were taking in the air had its effect on the Marines on the ground. Only those who have watched the enemy do what he willed in the air can know the relief felt by Guadalcanal groundlings when they saw the Japanese aircraft defeated with heavy losses at each visit.

About this time, W. H. Brooksbank, civil assistant to the Division of Naval Intelligence, visited Mackenzie at Lunga. Brooksbank had fought in World War I and had been decorated and commissioned in the field, so he felt quite at home in the front-line scenes of Guadalcanal. But his Palm Beach suit and Panama hat were a source of joy to the Marines, who did not spare their comments.

Early in October, Macfarlan and Andressen came into Lunga from Gold Ridge, easily passing through scattered Japanese forces in the jungle. Hay, who was too fat to run if a Japanese patrol were encountered, was left at the camp with the teleradio, to signal any Japanese movements reported to him by natives. Macfarlan developed severe malaria and was dispatched to Australia immediately, while Andressen remained on Guadalcanal.

The position of Rhoades and Schroeder, on the northwestern side of the island, was now becoming acutely dangerous. Mackenzie applied to the Marine command for a vessel in which to rescue them, but Japanese reinforcements were collecting to the westward of Lunga, and the Marines, intent on holding their perimeter, did not feel they could afford this help. Mackenzie begun to feel that Schroeder and Rhoades were regarded by General Vandegrift as 'expendables.'

Mackenzie's position at Guadalcanal was solely as a receiver and relayer of coastwatchers' reports, and he knew that the General would rightly be resentful if he, Mackenzie, took independent action outside his allotted scope. Nevertheless, he was determined not to expend Rhoades and Schroeder.

Knowing the wrath that would come, he borrowed a launch from Marchant's group at Malaita—Marchant was away at the time in Fiji—and sent Horton, one of the two FERDINAND men who had acted as landing guides for the Marines, to rescue everyone he could from among the Japanese encampments on the northwest coast. It was a dangerous mission. Both U.S. and Japanese surface craft were in the area, and both would shoot first and ask later whom they had hit.

Horton successfully ran the gauntlet during the night and crept into a creek at dawn, where Rhoades, Schroeder, thirteen missionaries, and a shot-down airman were taken aboard, together with Rhoades' teleradio. That night they made the run back, again without mishap. Schroeder, sick and elderly, was sent to Australia for recuperation. Rhoades remained at Lunga for a time; then, suffering from severe malaria, he also was sent south. Later, both were to return. As Mackenzie expected, General Vandegrift's wrath fell upon him for initiating the trip. Mackenzie had no defense, but he had the satisfaction of having rescued sixteen people with no harm done, so he could afford to take his ear bashing philosophically. It was not until sometime later, when Mackenzie's organization continued to give him valuable information while shells and bombs were falling, that the General relented.

During October, the situation on Guadalcanal had not improved. The perimeter had been held intact, and dive and torpedo bombers were now at Henderson Field.

But the Japanese had landed more forces; their aircraft, in spite of terrific losses, continued to raid Lunga; and the Henderson Field bombers, although they were causing the enemy heavy shipping losses, could not blockade the coast. The balance of sea power was so uncertain that both sides could send ships to the island; the Japanese dribbling in reinforcements, the United States dribbling in supplies. When the U.S. aircraft carriers Hornet and Wasp were lost, the enemy achieved local command of the sea, and in mid-October Japanese battleships, cruisers, and destroyers bombarded Lunga by night, while Japanese transports could be seen by day at anchor to the westward. The Allied forces on Guadalcanal became enmeshed in a vicious circle.

Few of the old destroyers that were being used for gasoline transport could get through the enemy cordon. Henderson Field began to run short of aviation fuel, making it difficult for our bombers to attack the enemy ships. Finally, only transport aircraft could get through, bringing in fuel and taking out wounded. The Japanese infantry pressed hard against the Lunga perimeter, while the Marines, holding their lines, drove back attack after attack.

During the heavy enemy bombardments of October, Mackenzie and all his staff members had narrow escapes. They had built themselves a better radio dugout; a really commodious hole floored and roofed with iron plates left behind by the Japanese. Roof and entrance were protected by sandbags, and electric lights were fitted. Nearby, they erected tents and huts as working and sleeping quarters. Just before the new camp was completed, shellfire from enemy destroyers damaged the old dugout but did not destroy the precious radio instruments. Shortly after the station had been moved, a bomb destroyed the old dugout completely, and another demolished the Base Radio Station where Mackenzie and Train had previously lived.

One night, Mackenzie, one of his Marine radio operators, and six natives took shelter in a trench roofed with palm logs and sandbags. A bomb struck close to their shelter roof, severely injuring one of the natives and causing a lung hemorrhage to the Marine, who had to be evacuated. Mackenzie carried on, although it was a month before he fully recovered from the effects.

During another of the bombardments, Train and Rayman shared a trench. The shells fell nearer and nearer and, in a short lull, Rayman whispered, 'I'm frightened.'

'So am I, Rayman,' whispered Train, which cold comfort reassured Rayman completely.

The Japanese had now begun preparations for a final thrust to reconquer Guadalcanal, preparations which took place largely in Read's and Mason's bailiwicks. Mason had already reported that the Japanese had brought tractors, trucks, guns, equipment of every description, to Buin and were preparing an airfield there.

During October, the area between Buin and the Shortlands became the anchorage for more and more ships, so many and of such divergent types that Mason had difficulty in identifying them. In Townsville, photographs were taken of pages of Jane's Fighting Ships and the prints sent to Mason in a supply drop. Thereafter his identifications were remarkable in their accuracy. Reconnaissance aircraft would fly over Buin and in their reports would list a number of 'probably this's' and 'possibly that's.' Mason would signal an exact list of each class of ship. Only once was he baffled and then, from his description, we were able to identify the ship as a seaplane tender.

Mason's natives worked for the Japanese at the Buin airfield, then returned to him, with information. How complete his information was can be gauged from a typical signal:

> Our scouts being employed Kahili aerodrome state aerodrome is expected to be completed in a week's time. Many hundreds of natives being forced to work on aerodrome. 27 lorries, 6 motorcars, 10 horses, 6 motorcycles, 4 tractors and aerodrome working equipment at Kahili. Stores and fuel under tarpaulins spread along foreshore from mouth of Ugumo River to mouth of Moliko River. Two anti-aircraft guns near mouth of Ugomo River in fuel and ammunition dump and one anti-aircraft gun on northwestern boundary of aerodrome. Wireless station on beach in front of aerodrome; also, eight new iron buildings. Priests and nuns interned in iron buildings on beach. Enemy troops in green uniforms with anchor badge on arm and on white hat. Scouts state about 440 enemy troops but coolies too numerous to count. Weather too hazy to observe ships today.

A typical signal from Read is quoted:

> A ship, which may be cruiser, and probably another, entered Kessa 1 p.m. believe from north. Heavy destroyer and light cruiser, derrick on stern, just entered Buka Passage. Unusual air activity today; nine fighters landed at drome. Believe about twenty fighters and bombers now here. First mentioned ship now leaving Kessa believe may come this way.

Their reports went on, day after day, so that little the enemy did was not known to us. As often as they could, planes from General MacArthur's command, guided by these reports, bombed the enemy bases and shipping at Buin, in the Shortlands, and at Buka Passage. At the end of October, the Japanese High Command was ready to launch its great attack on Guadalcanal. As a precaution, the Japanese decided to chase away the cheeky coastwatchers in Bougainville, to prevent them from reporting the movements. Dogs, trained in tracking, were shipped to Buin and kept in a wire cage until the hunting party should be ready. A bomb, dropped at night by a Catalina, killed the lot, for which Mason expressed grateful thanks by signal.

Minus the dogs, a patrol of more than a hundred soldiers—very flattering to the fighting prowess of Mason's party—moved out from Buin toward him. Mason took his party into rough mountain country, his scouts keeping tabs on the Japanese patrol and informing Mason of its progress. After a day and a half, the Japanese considered their duty done, probably reasoning that the Europeans must have been driven away. They turned for home and Mason, apprised by his scouts, returned to his camp and was on the air reporting the incident before the last enemy straggler was back at Kahili.

Read's scouts, too, warned him that a patrol was about to set after him from Buka Passage. Read signaled us that he was moving further inland and we immediately advised him to keep wireless silence so that his position could not be discovered by direction-finding apparatus. Read moved leisurely toward the high mountains, confident that the Japanese would not penetrate so far. The second day of his trip was hot and hazy in the forenoon, and in the afternoon heavy rain fell. Wet and miserable, Read, his soldier signaler, the police, the carriers climbed a steep, slippery track to a village perched on a mountain top.

Just as Read reached the peak, the rain stopped and the sun shone through the clear, rain-washed air, giving unlimited visibility. There, on the horizon, as clear as though within stone's throw, was a convoy of twelve large passenger ships, each more than 10,000-ton, headed southeast. Patrol or no patrol, this was more important than maintaining radio silence. The teleradio was hastily set up, and a signal sent, reporting the convoy. On board, it was the Japanese Army on its way to attempt the reconquest of Guadalcanal.

From Mason at Buin came the signal, 'At least 61 ships this area vis: 2 Nati, 1 Aoba, 1 Mogami, 1 Kiso, 1 Tatuta, 2 sloops, 33 destroyers, 17 cargo, 2 tankers, 1 passenger liner of 8,000 tons.' These were ready to meet additional battleships and the convoy reported by Read, all together forming the Armada for retaking Guadalcanal.

That night, Japanese battleships bombarded Lunga, but withdrew to be clear of our bombers at daylight. During the day, enemy bombers raided the hard-pressed base. On the following night, the battleships returned, accompanied by cruisers, but were surprised north of Savo by Rear Admiral Callaghan with four cruisers. One of the Japanese battleships was sunk and another damaged, while Japanese cruisers, also damaged, were left firing at their own battleship.

In the morning, the Japanese transports reported by Read were found by the dive bombers from Henderson Field. They crashed their bombs into the big frail hulls, returning for more bombs again and again, calling themselves buzzards. Torpedo bombers attacked the remaining battleship, which, deep in the water because of its flooded compartments, proved nearly unsinkable. That night Rear Admiral

Lee's battleships moved in and mopped up. Only four Japanese cargo ships reached Guadalcanal, and these were set on fire by dive bombers and beached by their own crews. Again, the coastwatchers had played a vital part at a critical time in the campaign.

With the tension eased by the Japanese defeat, our rear signal system was reorganized. A radio was installed at Santo, in the New Hebrides, to receive signals direct from Mackenzie at Lunga. These signals were also passed onto Vila and to Noumea for Admiral Halsey's Headquarters.

When Mackenzie stopped at Noumea, in process of reorganizing the system, Admiral Halsey arranged for him to address senior officers of the staff on the subject of coastwatching. Mackenzie is not at his most insouciant on a lecture platform before an audience of distinguished strangers. Hesitant in speech, a little red in the face, he gave credit in fumbling words to everyone but himself.

But however diffident his words, they had the right effect. On his return to Guadalcanal, the coastwatchers were confirmed in status as a separate unit under the orders of the Commanding General, with no staff officers intervening, and supplies and equipment to be had for the asking.

In October, General MacArthur had awarded the Distinguished Service Cross to Read, Macfarlan, Rhoades, and Mason. Marchant, Clemens, and Kuper were among those given British decorations in the southern Solomons. The citations were not published; the Japanese could not be told how valuable the coastwatchers were. Now, after the Japanese defeat, Read was asked for recommendations of those who had been of greatest assistance to him and to Mason. He cited Lieutenant Mackie and three of his soldiers, Sergeant Yauwika of the native police, and Usaia Sotutu, the Fijian mission teacher. Mackie and his men were awarded the Silver Star and Yauwika the Loyal Natives' Medal. As Usaia was moving within the Japanese' clutches and any such recognition of his worth might have been an added danger to him, his award was deferred. Mason at this time was also promoted from his rank of petty officer to sub-lieutenant.

After the Japanese defeat in November, there was no further need for a coastwatcher at Gold Ridge, where Macfarlan and Andressen had left Hay. However, it was not until January 1943 that Hay came in. He had been sheltering an aged nun for much of this time, the sole survivor of a Japanese massacre.

Hay walked down the mountain and, being extremely fat, by the time he reached the roadhead he was exhausted. He sent on a note by a native, saying he was 'knocked up.' In Australian slang, this means too fatigued to travel further; in American, it means pregnant.

A puzzled American officer set off in a jeep to meet Hay. When he saw him, he took one look at that ample belly and said, 'My God! It's true!'

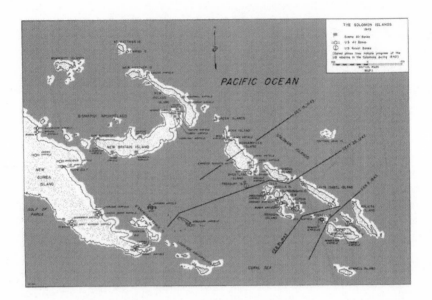

The Solomon Islands Campaign

11

ON GUADALCANAL, THE MARINES WERE RELIEVED by fresh Army troops. Before he left, General Vandegrift, in his final Order of the Day, referred to the coastwatchers as 'our small band of devoted Allies, who have contributed so vastly in proportion to their numbers.'

Having failed to retake Guadalcanal, the Japanese now prepared for an attempt to seal it off. This involved the building or expansion of bases in the central Solomons. For our coastwatchers in that area, troubles were just beginning.

Kennedy, at Segi, had determined to hold his position. The Japanese were unlikely to approach by sea, as the waters were uncharted and unknown to them. No tracks led to Kennedy's station by land, and the approach along the beach could be watched. The natives could be relied on to give the Japanese no aid. The ridge on which the house stood was in a good defensive position, and at the foot of it, on the beach, Kennedy built a stockade. Fish and plantation cattle provided plenty of food.

Segi itself was a plantation with a romantic history. Thirty years ago, when there was much money to be made in copra, a sailor, tired of the sea, settled on Ontong Java, an atoll 300 miles north of Tulagi. There, to solace his loneliness, he took a native wife, a clear-skinned Polynesian girl with black, wavy hair, and in the course of time they had a daughter.

As the years passed, his daughter's future became the dominant note of the old sailor's existence. He sent her to school in New Zealand and left Ontong Java to make a home for her nearer to Europeans and farther from her mother's people. He chose Segi, where the southernmost ridge of New Georgia runs down to the narrowest part of the strait, fifty yards wide, between that island and Vangunu. There was deep, sheltered water here; an old sailor would not choose a bad anchorage.

At Segi, the jungle was felled, coconuts planted, fruit-trees set, a house built, and cattle and poultry brought in. The old sailor settled down to comfort. When his daughter returned from school, she married a white trader nearby and the square-built, vigorous old sailor lived on at Segi alone until the Japanese invasion forced him out.

The enemy drew closer to Segi as the Guadalcanal campaign went on. Early in October 1942, Gizo, 80 miles to the northwest, was occupied. Kennedy's native scouts kept it under observation, relaying reports of Japanese activity to him by canoe at night.

Kennedy signaled the information to Lunga, and dive bombers made the position so uncomfortable that the Japanese evacuated it, leaving behind 100,000 gallons of aviation fuel. This was hidden so effectively by Kennedy's scouts that the Japanese never recovered it.

Then the enemy occupied Viru Harbour, only nine miles northwest of Segi along the New Georgia coast. Soon afterwards they occupied Munda, then Wickham Anchorage on the far side of Vangunu Island, and then the Russell Group, between Vangunu and Guadalcanal. This left Kennedy surrounded by Japanese outposts, all staging points on the shipping route by which they ran supplies to Guadalcanal. Completing his encirclement, the enemy then occupied Rekata Bay on Isabel Island to the northeast.

But Kennedy held on to his position. His natives watched Viru Harbour and Wickham Anchorage, while a half-caste, Harry Wickham, organized natives to watch Munda. As information came in, Kennedy signaled it to Mackenzie, who passed it on to the air command. The U.S. aircraft bombed and strafed the pinpointed targets so successfully that Japanese casualties were severe and damage heavy. Meantime, Kennedy built up a strong native armed force.

One day, a Japanese barge, straggling from its course, headed for Segi. Kennedy, reasoning that the secret of Segi could be kept inviolate only by wiping out the Japanese, waylaid the barge at an anchorage with his native force, and killed every Japanese in the party. From the barge, he obtained Japanese arms and ammunition, which he issued to his expanded force. Later, two more barges were reported approaching and again Kennedy ambushed them and wiped out all except two men, whom he captured.

Then his scouts at Viru reported a patrol of twenty-five enemy soldiers moving overland in the direction of Segi. Kennedy attacked them in their camp at night, but they escaped in the darkness. Their equipment and diaries were captured, the latter showing that the coastwatcher was the object of the patrol. In this last action, Kennedy was wounded by a bullet in the thigh, and two of his scouts were also wounded. But in all the affrays there were no other casualties in Kennedy's forces, while fifty-four Japanese were killed. Kennedy treated his own wound and continued on duty.

Meanwhile, also, Segi became a center for the rescue of shot-down airmen. Aircraft following the Japanese fleeing from Lunga and others on bombing missions to Japanese outposts were sometimes forced to bail out over New Georgia or its surrounding islands.

Kennedy offered a standing reward of a bag of rice and a case of tinned meat for each airman brought in, besides pay at a daily rate for each native taking part in a rescue. The same value was set on Japanese airmen, who were overpowered and brought in lashed in vines. In all, 22 U.S. airmen and 20 Japanese pilots were brought to Segi. The Japanese were kept in the stockade until picked up by aircraft.

While Kennedy held his position, Mackenzie had received approval to place more coastwatchers in the central Solomons.

Observers were required, in particular, at Vella Lavella and at Choiseul Islands, on either side of the channel between the central Solomons. This channel, known as 'The Slot,' was a regular Japanese route to Guadalcanal. Indeed, destroyers made night runs along this route so regularly that they were called the 'Tokyo Express.' Mason, at the southern tip of Bougainville, was too far away to keep a precise check on these movements.

Mackenzie arranged to place Henry Josselyn on Vella Lavella and Nick Waddell on Choiseul. Josselyn had helped with the landing at Tulagi and Waddell had been assigned to the same task but had been attacked by malaria just before the invasion. Mackenzie had met them both on Vila, where Waddell was in a jam. He, together with Dick Horton, who also assisted in the Tulagi landing, had left his post as a district officer in the Solomons shortly before Japan entered the war, and had gone to Australia to join the armed forces.

Since Waddell and Horton had taken this action without approval of the Colonial Office, the High Commissioner of the Western Pacific had peremptorily ordered them to return and at the same time had requested the Australian Government to discharge them. There had been nothing they could do but return.

However, when they reached Vila, it had become impossible to go further because of the Japanese invasion and there their paths had crossed Mackenzie's. Josselyn, meantime, had been sent to Vila in a schooner with the official records of the Solomon Islands Administration. Mackenzie rightly considered these three a good bag for FERDINAND, and signed them up.

Experience had shown us that the strain on a single coastwatcher was apt to be too great for endurance over a long period. So from headquarters at Townsville, we informed Mackenzie that the parties would be increased by sending Sub-Lieutenant J. H. Keenan with Josselyn to Vella Lavella, and Sergeant C. W. Seton with Waddell to Choiseul.

Keenan was a patrol officer from New Guinea, a tall, dark young man with a deep cleft in his chin, who had joined the Navy on his arrival in Australia from New Guinea, and had been transferred to FERDINAND. Seton, like his partner Waddell, was a large man, a planter from the Shortland Islands who had joined the Australian Imperial Forces and had been assigned to Port Moresby, where his knowledge and experience were not being used. Now that we had this assignment for him, his transfer was quickly arranged.

The four men gathered at Brisbane. There they collected three months' supplies of food and arms, and a teleradio for each party. Equipment was tested and packed in watertight covers. On 6 October 1942, the four embarked in the U.S. Submarine Grampus. En route, the sub attacked a destroyer, and was counterattacked in return. Then, a week from the day of departure, it drew near the shore of Vella Lavella, where Josselyn and Keenan were to disembark.

Disconcertingly, a Japanese destroyer was anchored a few miles north of the landing place that had been selected. The submarine commander naturally wanted to attack the destroyer, but Josselyn dissuaded him, fearing that if she were sunk, survivors would land on the island and make FERDINAND's position there untenable.

Looking long and carefully through the periscope, Josselyn watched for a break in the reef through which he and Keenan could reach the shore. Since they could see nothing but reef, they decided they would have to take a chance. That night the submarine surfaced, and Josselyn and Keenan loaded their gear into two rubber boats and a collapsible canoe. One of the rubber boats sprang a leak, keeping Keenan as busy as the little Dutch boy at the dike, so Josselyn had to paddle alone, towing the rubber boats and Keenan.

Progress was so slow that, although they had left the submarine at 1:30 a.m., it was almost dawn when they reached the breakers. With no time left to seek a passage, they paddled straight ahead and just before daybreak got through, the leaky boat swamped but still floating. At full speed, they carried everything ashore and placed boats and supplies undercover. Then exhausted, they lay down to sleep. When they woke, they found themselves on an uninhabited part of the island, a few miles from Mundi plantation. They spent the day drying out their clothes and arms. Some of their supplies, they discovered, had been lost in the breakers. Their most serious loss was one of their two pairs of binoculars.

The next day, they made a reconnaissance of Mundi and its vicinity and found it clear of the enemy, so they selected a campsite on the boundary between plantation and jungle. Days of the most exhausting and backbreaking work were then required to transport their supplies. By night they moved the stores along the shore in the rubber boat, then up the tree-sheltered Mundi River, with finally a portage to the campsite. Next they built a lean-to of corrugated iron taken from the plantation, and set up their teleradio. On 22 October, they put through their first signal to Lunga.

During the days they had been ashore, they had seen large formations of Japanese aircraft flying toward Guadalcanal, and it had been galling to watch them go over without being able to report them. Now, at last, they thought, they could begin their real work.

But on their second attempt to reach Lunga, the transmitter broke down and defied all their efforts to repair it. With the heavy flights of Japanese bombers overhead making their frustration almost more than could be borne, Josselyn decided to take the faulty transmitter to Kennedy at Segi. Keenan was to remain and hold their position against Josselyn's return.

Segi was more than a hundred miles away, and there were formidable Japanese posts in between. Native canoe was the only possible means by which the journey could be made. The two coast-watchers, therefore, made contact with the first natives they sighted; seven men in a canoe. Among them was Silas Lezstuni, chief of the Jorio district. He and his men were immediately very friendly, and utterly astonished to learn that two Europeans had been on the island for more than a week without their knowledge. Silas informed the watchers that a Japanese party had landed from the destroyer they had seen from the Grampus, and was now camped a few miles farther along the coast. He told them, also, that a clergyman and a nurse of the Methodist Mission were still on the southern part of the island.

Josselyn packed up his bedding, a few cooking utensils, a little food and the transmitter, and set off. His first stop was at a village where he arranged for natives to keep watch on all roads leading to the mission so that if Japanese approached, the two missionaries there could be warned. Then, traveling by canoe at night and resting by day, he moved toward Segi. At each village, he changed canoes. This meant putting his safety in the hands of each village in turn, but his trust was not misplaced. In the dark, he and his native paddlers stole across the strait from Vella Lavella to Ganonga, then down the coast of that island and across to Gizo, which the Japanese had recently evacuated. The silence of each night was broken only by the sound of paddles.

Before dawn, the canoe would be beached at a village, unloaded and hauled into the cover of the trees. Then Josselyn would eat a breakfast of fried bacon and sweet potato chips, washed down by tea, and would be down to sleep.

In the evening, while he ate a substantial meal of bully beef, sweet potatoes, tea, and biscuits, his new relay of paddlers would collect, each with a baked taro or sweet potato to sustain him during the night. When the sun was down, their canoe would be launched and loaded, and the journey would continue with the new crew while Josselyn's paddlers of the night before returned to their homes.

By this time the Japanese had occupied Munda, and on the opposite side of the strait there was a Japanese outpost on Rendova, but Josselyn's canoe stole safely between the two enemy forces. From here on, Kennedy's network of scouts operated, and the remainder of the journey presented no difficulties.

Kennedy, who was a good radio technician, repaired the transmitter, and Josselyn set out on his return journey. At Gizo he found the natives had captured a Japanese airman, and Josselyn arranged for him to be sent on to Kennedy. Then he continued, without incident, to Vella Lavella.

While Josselyn was away, Keenan had scouted the island for a better observation post. Choosing a ridge in the jungle that overlooked 'The Slot' to north and east, he had built a hut for himself and Josselyn, a storeroom, a hut for native assistants, and a lookout position in a tree. Installing the radio, the two men began reporting enemy movements.

Waddell and Seton in the Grampus reached the coast of Choiseul on 19 October, a week after Josselyn and Keenan were put ashore. They had selected a good landing spot, through the periscope, and 1 a.m. they left the surfaced submarine with their supply-filled canoe and rubber boats. Tidal currents slewed them around, however, and carried them past the harbor they had selected. Paddling furiously, they were unable to approach the shore until, with dawn just breaking, a herculean effort suddenly pushed them through the breakers and onto the reef. Both rubber boats grounded on the sharp coral, and were swamped by the waves.

Soft from weeks of inactivity in the submarine, both men were exhausted by the paddling. Now, buffeted by the breakers, falling over the uneven coral in the dim morning light, they hauled frantically at the boats. One by one, the packs were carried clear of the beach, but it was broad daylight before the tell-tale rubber boats, which they deflated with bayonet stabs, were carried into the scrub. Then, too tired to eat, the two men lay down in the undergrowth and slept.

In the afternoon, they awakened to find a native bending over them. He knew them both—Seton as a planter and Waddell as a district officer—and he was overjoyed to see them.

At once they sent him to bring in the leading man of each village in the vicinity.

Within three days, most of the chiefs of Choiseul visited the two coastwatchers. The support and assistance they promised was quickly forthcoming. Natives carried supplies and equipment to a site on a nearby hill from which there was a good view to the west and south. With their help, a hut was quickly built. Goratata and Levara, two ex-police who had previously served with Waddell, were permanently attached to the party and used to organize scouts in the villages for bringing in shot-down airmen and for warning of Japanese activity. Within ten days after Waddell and Seton had landed, they had a flourishing coastwatcher organization and were on the air with reports.

The two new parties—Josselyn and Keenan on Vella Lavella, and Waddell and Seton on Choiseul—now developed a keen rivalry in reporting the 'Tokyo Express.' The enemy destroyers were actually evacuating troops from the southern Solomons although this was not known at the time.

To ensure maximum cover from darkness during their operations, the Japanese vessels ordinarily left the Shortland Islands about noon, which brought them in sight of Vella Lavella and Choiseul in the early afternoon. The early reports of the coastwatchers gave the U.S. dive bombers time to attack the Japanese destroyers just before darkness fell.

Waddell and Seton soon discovered that they were not the only watchers on Choiseul. At Choiseul Bay, near the northwest tip of the island, the Japanese had established a post. A few natives there had thrown in their lot with the Japanese and had reported the arrival of our coastwatchers to the enemy, just as Waddell's and Seton's natives reported to them the presence of the Japanese.

In this game of spying upon one another, our coastwatchers had the advantage, however. Except for the few renegades at Choiseul Bay, virtually none of the natives on the island had accepted the Japanese occupation, and the reconquest of Tulagi and Guadalcanal had confirmed them in their loyalty.

Needless to say, Waddell and Seton were at pains to preserve this advantage. They instructed all coastal natives to build new villages inland and to avoid any contact with the enemy. They took turns patrolling the island, strengthening friendship and loyalty through personal contact. They salvaged arms from wrecked aircraft, both U.S. and Japanese, reconditioned them, and used them to arm their most promising scouts.

The Japanese watchers, of course, reported the presence of our men on the island, and in December an enemy patrol was sent in to capture them. It was an almost pathetic attempt. Having no guides, the Japanese patrol was unable even to leave the beach, and Waddell and Seton did not even find it necessary to disturb their usual routine. The Japanese contented themselves with capture of some natives who had not followed Waddell's advice to leave the coast, and took them to Ballalae to labor on a new airfield.

Although these captured natives were questioned at intervals and were ill-treated, badly fed, and threatened with worse, they steadfastly continued to deny any knowledge of Waddell and Seton. Eventually they were released. Japanese shipping losses had mounted so high by spring that barges were being used whenever possible, traveling at night and hiding by day in bays and creeks. Seton, with his armed natives, ambushed one of these barges, killed the crew of fifteen, and sank the barge in deep water after first taking from it a considerable amount of food and arms.

This barge, unlike those that Kennedy had ambushed, had not threatened the safety of the coastwatchers, so Seton's action was decidedly a breach of FERDINAND principles. The information our watchers were obtaining was of much more value than the destruction of a barge and the death of a few enemy troops, and he was so reminded. Soon afterwards, he and Waddell sighted another hiding barge, and this time reported its location to Lunga. U.S. fighter aircraft strafed the vessel, while its crew fled. Instead of keeping clear of the area, Waddell and a party of natives closed in, and were confronted by the fleeing crew. In the skirmish that followed, one of the Japanese was killed but the others escaped.

In response to the alarm they raised, Japanese aircraft strafed and bombed Choiseul, but fortunately without effect. Then in May, the enemy sent in 600 men to establish a coastal post midway along the island. Like the patrol that had previously come and gone, this party, strong as it was, never left the beach. Six months or more later, the diary of the post's commanding officer was captured, revealing that the force had been sent to extirpate the coastwatchers.

An entry, made on the day the post was established, disclosed that the officer was overjoyed at the 'subjugation' of the island. He was a fool. Had he been of the type who harried some of our other watchers, it is probable that Waddell and Seton would have been driven from the island as a penalty for their violation of FERDINAND rules.

But luck was with us; it had been against us often enough. Indeed, the two watchers became so confident as the Japanese continued inactive, that they divided and manned a second post.

The one adverse effect of the enemy post was its interference with the launch supply line we had established to Waddell and Seton. Even this was not too serious, as a new landing point on the eastern side of the island was selected and used with little inconvenience.

On unusual occasions, we even sent in and landed planes. Not only were American airmen shot down over Choiseul evacuated by this method, but in one case a party of fliers who had been brought down in the Cartaret Islands, 200 miles to the northwest, was taken out. These men had made a perilous canoe journey past Japanese bases, and upon reaching Choiseul had been taken to Waddell by their guides. Waddell amply rewarded the Cartaret natives who had saved and guided the airmen. You may imagine the astonishment of the fliers at finding an Allied outpost in what they had considered completely enemy territory.

Meanwhile, on Vella Lavella, Josselyn and Keenan were also keeping house next door to a party of Japanese. These Japanese, who were also supposed to be coastwatchers, were completely oblivious of the presence of our men. At times, Josselyn and Keenan would scout right up to the enemy coastwatcher post itself, to watch what the Japanese were doing and to commiserate with them silently for the boredom that must have accompanied their inactivity. Josselyn, who was still chagrined by the loss of his binoculars during the landing, was strongly tempted to steal a pair from the Japanese, and was only restrained by stern orders from Mackenzie.

On Vella Lavella, relations with the natives continued as excellent as on Choiseul. Josselyn wisely kept in the background as far as administration of civil affairs was concerned, leaving such matters to Bamboo, chief of the island. Thus he ensured that no native, resentful of an adverse decision, would be tempted to betray him in revenge.

Bamboo also served as chief of the scouts, who included all the able-bodied men of the island. They were trained to send in written reports in their own language, which would not be readily intelligible to the Japanese should a message be captured. When a message was sent by canoe, it was placed in a basket weighted with stones, so that it could be thrown overboard if danger appeared. Josselyn always had more volunteers for a scouting trip than he could use, and he was sometimes embarrassed by having to refuse services.

To make their position still more secure, he and Keenan built three additional camps in various parts of the island, and even planted a garden to supply fresh vegetables. Occasionally they would shoot a plantation bullock, providing themselves and the natives with a great feast, since there was no means of preserving the meat. Added to these supplies was a tremendous quantity of flotsam recovered by the scouts from bombed enemy ships. Whenever desired, a Catalina could be landed to bring in supplies and pick up rescued airmen.

In February, Keenan was withdrawn for service on Bougainville, and was replaced by Sub-lieutenant Robert Firth, who proved a worthy substitute, although Josselyn was at first very much downcast at losing his old team-mate.

Soon after Firth joined him, Josselyn had ample opportunity to indulge his piratical instincts. On two occasions, Japanese ships, disabled by air attacks, drifted near Vella Lavella. Josselyn with his scouts boarded the ships—one eye cocked for enemy interference— and looted to the capacity of their canoes. First, they would collect papers and documents for Allied Intelligence, then batteries, radio equipment and parts, food, cutlery, linen, arms, and ammunition— everything that could aid either the comfort or the efficiency of the post. Josselyn even dispatched cutlery to Kennedy by the canoe route. The enemy rifles were used to arm the scouts, and ample caches of food were hidden in the jungle. Even then, Josselyn still hankered, occasionally, to steal the binoculars from the oblivious Japanese coastwatchers.

Enemy barges, putting in at inlets and creeks to hide, were constantly reported by the two men, and about one a week was sunk by our aircraft. These losses were apparently connected by the Japanese with the Vella Lavella natives, for one day Japanese destroyers moved in and bombarded the coastal villages. The natives, after this event, moved inland, their opposition to the enemy turned to active hatred. They took their revenge by liquidating shot-down enemy airmen, a practice of which Josselyn approved, for he was always afraid that such wandering Japanese might stumble upon a watching post or unravel part of the scouting organization.

At Segi, Kennedy continued to sit like a spider at the center of a huge web. His 'grapevine' extended through the villages of New Georgia, to the island of Rendova on the southwest, to Kolombangara Island on the northwest, and to Vangunu and Gatura Islands on the southeast. To make the most of his organization in this area, we began sending him henchmen.

The first to arrive was Horton, who had been assigned, after his service in the Tulagi invasion, to Ontong Java, a lonely atoll nearly 300 miles north of Guadalcanal. After he had established the Ontong Java post, he was replaced by a party which included Schroeder, that 'frail' elderly man who had now recovered from the rigors of his Guadalcanal experience and had cheerfully accepted an assignment where no escape was possible should the enemy choose to occupy the atoll. His seasoned assistance to the inexperienced Australian naval officer and two U.S. soldiers who made up the rest of the party released Horton in December for service in Kennedy's bailiwick.

Horton disembarked at Segi in a Catalina, with an escort of our fighters weaving overhead. Kennedy arranged for him to travel by canoe to Roviana Lagoon, east of Munda, to join Harry Wickham, one of the half-castes who had previously been enlisted by Kennedy.

The Japanese had occupied Munda in November 1942, but some time elapsed before we realized that a sizable airbase was being developed here. Then Kennedy's scouts, directed in this area by Wickham, had reported that clearings were being made. Their reports foiled a clever Japanese device of keeping the treetops in position by wires while they secretly worked on the ground beneath.

Unable to find a good position at Roviana Lagoon for watching the field, Horton moved to Rendova Island, three miles across the straits from Munda. The dangerous trip was made at night, the silent canoes weaving among the noisy Japanese barges that filled the strait. Wickham remained at Roviana to continue directing the scouts there.

As soon as they landed at Rendova, Horton's scouts set off to the nearest native village, returning with the pleasant information that this island was clear of the enemy. Assisted by local natives, Horton selected a campsite 2,000 feet up the mountainside. Two leaf huts were built, one for himself and one for his native assistants, and two lookout posts, covered in ferns, were constructed in the trees.

Two scouts, already operating for Kennedy on Rendova, were taken under Horton's command, while more were enlisted from the local population. North of Munda, Horton tightened Kennedy's organization of scouts to report on developments in that area and on Kolombangara. With Wickham's scouts, this network now covered the entire Munda area. In addition, Kennedy's uncompromising policy for all natives of 'no unauthorized contact with the enemy' was rigidly enforced and loyally carried out.

Horton's natives kept the treetop lookouts constantly manned. Whenever they saw any movement on Munda airfield, they called Horton, who would climb the ladder and observe precisely what was going on. Every aircraft that landed or took off from the field was reported to Lunga. When a flight arrived from the northwest, Horton would signal immediately, and U.S. bombers from Lunga would promptly sweep in and attack the enemy planes while they were still refueling. When Munda-based planes took off to attack Lunga, the warning preceded them before the sound of their engines had died away on Rendova.

New gun emplacements, found by Wickham's scouts, were pinpointed for dive bombers to attack. Indiscriminate bombing of jungle positions is generally harmless, but this precise delivery of high explosives on selected targets was something else again. In spite of everything the enemy could do, the development of Munda was seriously retarded.

Horton had not long been established on Rendova, however, when the Japanese decided to put a post on the same island. They chose a site on the shore, about a mile from Horton's camp. Immediately upon landing early one morning, they captured three natives, who shivered so much from fright that the Japanese thought they had malaria, gave them quinine, and released them. They promptly scampered off, of course, to report to Horton.

Since there were about a hundred of the enemy, Horton had to shift to an alternative post in a hurry. He closed the path from the new Japanese post to his old station by planting shrubs and vines on a section of it and within a week nature had made it indistinguishable from the surrounding jungle.

Kennedy, on being informed of the new Japanese post, offered to wipe it out with his guerrillas but, true to FERDINAND principles, Horton asked that the enemy be left undisturbed. Occasionally, Japanese patrols worked around the island, keeping to the coast, their movements followed and reported by Horton's scouts. Though these patrols proved to be of little danger to Horton, they imperiled a camp of twenty-two Chinese refugees from Tulagi who had hidden on Rendova. Horton managed to ship these refugees to Kennedy by canoe at night, and thence they were flown out to safety without the enemy's ever having been aware of their presence.

Several of Horton's scouts were captured, but they were well able to take care of themselves. Two, who were taken to Munda, behaved like frightened idiots and were released. Another, being taken to Munda by barge, loosened his bonds and slipped overboard so quietly that his departure was not noticed for ten minutes. Still another, a cunning, likable old rogue called Jackie, was captured by three Japanese who forced him to guide them. He did so for a while, then suddenly pointed excitedly to the top of a tree. The Japs looked up, and when they looked around again, Jackie had faded into the jungle. To keep morale up, Horton encouraged his scouts to steal back canoes taken by the Japanese and to loot stranded barges.

On Isabel Island, Geoffrey Kuper still kept watch at Tunnibulli. The Japanese seaplane base at Rekata Bay was too far from his post to allow him to gain much information about it, and it was not desirable for him to leave the strait between Isabel and Malaita unwatched. Therefore, we decided to send Flight-Lieutenant J. A. Corrigan to keep watch on Rekata Bay.

Corrigan, who was new to the Solomons but had been a miner for ten years in New Guinea, was landed in February 1943 on the west coast of Isabel. With a few scouts, he made his way across the island and selected a post overlooking the Japanese base.

The natives in the area, following Kennedy's orders, had avoided the enemy, and Corrigan had no trouble getting their assistance. He selected a number as scouts and sent them into the enemy base with fish and vegetables for sale.

One scout in particular was a gem, a shrewd native who looked stupid and could act like a most convincing moron when occasion called for it. He struck up an acquaintance with the Japanese commander, to whom he always brought the choicest food, and was soon allowed to roam about the base at will. On his return from these trips, he would tell Corrigan just where the seaplanes were hidden, how many guns there were and where, and where the troops were housed. All this was passed on to the Air Force at Lunga, which made full use of it. After one raid, the scout commiserated with the Japanese commander so sympathetically that the officer told him the exact number of casualties.

In April, Corrigan was relieved by Andressen, who, after finishing his watch at Guadalcanal, had manned a post in the Russell Group until those islands were occupied by a U.S. Army division in February. After his return to Lunga from Isabel, Corrigan flew in the leading bomber on our next strike against Rekata Bay. He directed a successful bombing of camouflaged positions, which were so well hidden from ordinary observation that the Japanese must have considered them inviolable.

The next spot we needed to cover was Kolombangara Island, northwest of New Georgia, a jungle-covered cone with one small area of flatland on which the Japanese were building an airstrip as a support for Munda. Native scouts had already reported the presence of Japanese on the island, and air observation confirmed the activity. So we dispatched Sub-Lieutenant A. R. Evans to this post.

He landed at Segi, where he remained for two weeks while Kennedy made a visit to Guadalcanal. Then Evans left for Kolombangara by canoe, following the old routine of traveling by night and hiding by day. He passed so close to Munda that he could hear the sound of motor trucks as the busy Japanese worked through the night. On the western shore of Kolombangara, he was welcomed by Horton's scouts, who had already built him a house. The natives of Kolombangara were beach dwellers, and they themselves did not know their own island. No tracks led inland, and only one old chief had any knowledge at all of the interior. This added to Evans' difficulties in scouting, but it also added to the security of his position.

From his post, Evans was able to report all vessels approaching his island and Arundel Island to the west, and to supply the U.S. bombers with information about the airfield. Solitary as his post seemed, he felt far from isolated. His teleradio kept him in contact with Mackenzie at Lunga, while his scouts were in contact with Horton's to the south, Kennedy's to the east, and Josselyn's to the northwest. Thus, by March 1943, we had a chain of coastwatchers through the Solomons from end to end. Most enemy movements against Guadalcanal were initiated at Buin, and the coastwatchers were placed to check on the entire sequence of movements. When aircraft left the Buin area, they were reported from Choiseul or Vella Lavella or both.

Evans then heard them from Kolombangara, or Horton from Rendova, then Kennedy at Segi, and finally a signaler in the Russells heard and reported them just before radar picked them up off Guadalcanal. Sometimes every coastwatcher in the chain reported them.

Similarly, ships and barges were reported as they made their way down, easy marks for interception by torpedo or dive bombers or warships. Even planes taking off at night from Rekata Bay were reported. It was 'streamlined coastwatching,' so rapid and sure that enemy attempts to prevent our forces from being built up were quite ineffective, while Japanese bases, in spite of the most persistent attempts, could not be built up sufficiently to withstand attack.

Australian tank bulldozing through Buna

12

WHILE OUR OPERATIONS IN THE CENTRAL SOLOMONS were developing with a smoothness that almost made us rub our eyes in wonder, Read and Mason on Bougainville were running into troubles that were to tax all FERDINAND's ingenuity and resources.

In spite of mounting odds against them, the two men had hung on to their posts—Read overlooking Buka Passage at the north of the island and Mason in the Buin area to the south—until after the Japanese defeat in November 1942, a defeat in which these two played a major part.

The strength of the Japanese on Bougainville had continually grown as the island became the site of important bases. And the determination of the enemy to rout out the coastwatchers mounted with this increased local strength and under the spur of the defeats to the south.

Gradually, also, the work of Tashira, the Japanese who had been a resident of Bougainville and who had taken on the job of propagandizing the natives, was bearing fruit. News of Allied successes at Guadalcanal and Tulagi had only a temporary effect on the Bougainville natives, who saw no change in the local situation except for an even greater influx of Japanese.

Under Tashira's ministrations, the natives around Kieta finally threw in their lot wholeheartedly with the Japanese. Calling themselves the 'Black Dogs,' they formed bands that raided inland native villages, pillaging, raping, and murdering. Then they combined with the Japanese to wipe out the last remaining Europeans and Chinese, a project they did not dare attempt on their own. The first of the combined expeditions was aimed at Mason's group, in December 1942.

Mason's party was camped between Buin and Kieta, in the valley of the Lulaia River, with low hills between it and the east coast. Loyal natives, who deduced the plans of the Japanese from their requirements for carriers, kept Mason abreast of the preparations being made. Three enemy parties moved in from the coast, one blocking off the southern end of the valley, one moving to the pass at its northern end, and the third striking at Mason's camp. They were three days too late. Mason had slipped from the trap by leading his party westward across the main range, an arduous, breathtaking climb.

But the enemy parties did capture Tom Ebery, the elderly planter from Toimonapu whose sense of duty as a coastwatcher had impelled him to remain on Bougainville even though he had been deprived of his teleradio by panic-stricken, fleeing Europeans in the first days of the war.

Though infirm and inactive, he was forced to accompany the Japanese patrol. Driven and beaten, utterly exhausted, he fell while crossing a river and, either too weak to save himself or else welcoming the release of death, he was drowned. Sympathetic natives buried his body after the Japanese had gone.

Mason's new position was in rugged country. There was no clear place into which supplies could be dropped at night by plane. A daylight supply-dropping trip was impossible, both because of the enemy fighter strength at Kahili and because it would have disclosed Mason's position. His food was running short, and the depredations of the 'Black Dogs' were giving friendly natives nearly all they could do to protect and feed themselves.

Moreover, it seemed only a question of time before hostile natives would find the new camp. Therefore Mackenzie ordered Mason to abandon his teleradio and to join Read in North Bougainville, where conditions were more favorable. The abandonment of South Bougainville at this juncture was not the misfortune it would have been three or four months earlier. Coastwatchers further southeast now covered all movements toward our positions. Mason had done his share when he was desperately and uniquely needed, and now the time had come to save his party.

In response to Mackenzie's order, Mason and his men set off on a trek of more than a hundred miles, through country infested with Japanese patrols. Dispatching his soldiers and his natives ahead, with the exception of one police-boy, Mason himself turned aside to visit a Chinese encampment on the first day of the trip, intending to join the rest of his party next day. An alarm was given by natives that Japanese patrols were nearby, however, and the soldiers hastened on, leaving Mason and Kiabi, the police-boy, to catch up.

The alarm was false, so Mason hurried with all his strength to overtake the others. A sore had developed on his foot and had become septic, slowing him down, but for thirty-six hours he pushed grimly on without stopping. Finally, limping badly, he reached the camp of Frank Roche, a miner who had hidden since the enemy invasion. When Mason removed his boot, skin and flesh came away with the sock. He rested two days with Roche, then, still limping painfully, the faithful Kiabi carrying his pack, moved on.

A few weeks later, Roche was captured by the Japanese and killed after brutal handling. Four weeks after starting his ghastly journey, Mason reached Lieutenant Mackie's camp, where he found the remainder of his party, together with soldiers sent by Read to meet him. Next day, 28 January 1943, he joined Read. The good news was flashed to us that his party was safe, after six weeks of silence. In spite of all they had had in common during the past year, Read and Mason barely knew each other. Now, while Mason rested and his foot healed, they compared notes and a firm friendship grew between them. Just before he was joined by Mason, Read had managed a difficult evacuation operation. As time went on, he had been increasingly troubled by the Europeans still remaining on the island. They consisted, in the main, of two groups: Catholic mission priests and nuns who had remained in the hope of continuing mission work among the natives; and planters who had been scornful of Read's previous advice to leave.

The work of the missionaries had been completely blocked, with all teaching prohibited by the enemy and many of the priests and nuns imprisoned. Bishop Wade, in charge of the missions, had done his duty as far as he could, but at length he felt that the nuns, at least, should be evacuated. The planters, for their part, had taken to the hills and were constantly bombarding Read with peremptory demands that signals be sent on their behalf demanding evacuation. Late in the year, Read signaled us, explaining the situation and recommending evacuation, particularly of the women.

The signal was passed on to the authorities in the Southwest Pacific Area, but since the Buna campaign was in full swing at the time, no aircraft or submarines could be spared. The signal received favorable consideration from Admiral Halsey in the South Pacific Area, however, and he lent us a submarine for taking off women and children. The arrangements required considerable care. Safety of the submarine was of paramount importance. Thus a harbor free of the enemy had to be selected and the evacuees collected without the enemy's becoming aware that anything was afoot. We used the most guarded language in our signals, since our codes could easily be deciphered by experts. The evacuation was set for the last night of 1942 at Teop Harbour on the northeast tip of Bougainville. Read was determined to send out all the non-combatant men as well as the women, if it could be managed, so they also were notified to be ready. The gathering of the woman was managed by

Father Lebel, a dynamic little priest, who sent runners to all prospective evacuees and even provided litters for the weaker ones.

He did his part well, timing the movement so that all except a few too far away reached the point in time, but not so early that attention was drawn by the concentration of women.

From the west coast, just south of Buka Passage, came nuns and a half-caste family on whose eldest daughter the Japanese commandant had cast longing eyes. Under the noses of the Japanese, they walked across the island, unobserved. Two planters, widows, were already near Teop. From distant mission stations came other nuns, the elderly carried by natives on improvised stretchers. Among the planters who arrived was the Austrian whose loyalty had been in doubt. He was not under guard, but the others were keeping an eye on him.

The day before the evacuation, Read, after a hasty breakfast in the very early morning, prepared for the trip to Teop. He was taking the radio so that warning could be given the submarine should any Japanese appear. Carriers lined up, equipped with poles on which to carry the packs, and vines from the jungle with which to lash them on. The radio was dismantled and packed and, together with other gear, handed to the carriers by policeboys.

After a checkup to see that all was ready, the party set off, four policeboys leading, a police-boy here and there along the line, and the watchful Sergeant Yauwika bringing up the rear to see there was no straggling. Read himself walked near the teleradio, with a final warning to the carriers that it must on no account be dropped or bumped. Their care was all he could have asked for. Whenever a carrier slipped, he let his body fall but held his rigid arm aloft so that the radio would not touch the ground. His brothers, at this same time, were carrying wounded down the Kokoda Trail in New Guinea with the same care and were earning the name 'Fuzzy Wuzzy Angels' for it.

It was a long day from Porapora to Teop. Heavy rain fell in the afternoon, but the line plodded on, bedraggled carriers squelching through the mud with banana leaves placed over their poles to offer some protection to the canvas-covered packs beneath. Small streams, normally ankle deep, ran in turbid, dirty torrents up to a man's knees, tugging at his feet. The last stream, reached as dusk was falling, was a waist-deep flood. As the carriers struggled to keep their footing on the slippery stones beneath the rushing current, a floating log, unseen in the gloom, struck the two who were carrying the transmitter.

With superhuman effort, they managed to keep the instrument aloft. Had it been dropped, that might have been the end to communication, and with it to coastwatching on Bougainville.

On the beach, Read set up the teleradio and received a message confirming the plans for the evacuation that night. Quickly he sent messengers to guide the hiding evacuees to the beach. With the way faintly lighted by a dim lantern, the silent file made its way over logs, through mud and pools of water. At the last moment, one of the two widows refused to go. Read politely told her she would be put on board by force, if necessary. Two of the evacuees, a planter and his wife, had not yet arrived and when this was discovered it created a flurry of apprehension.

At last they appeared, in the nick of time, and it was seen that the cause of the delay was the quantity of luggage; enough to sustain an ocean tour on a luxury liner. At the other extreme of behavior was the American Sister Superior, who drew Read aside and, telling him that she and the other nuns had thought his action high handed when he ordered them out of Buka previously, gently expressed regret for their thoughts and for the trouble they were causing him. Swallowing the lump in his throat, Read prepared the signal fires.

At midnight, as the fires were lighted, a faint hail answered from the harbor. Read shoved off in a canoe and moved toward the sound, coming up against the powerboat of the U.S. Submarine Nautilus hard and fast on a reef. More canoes with natives were called for and the boat was shoved off the reef, after which all wished each other a Happy New Year.

The motorboat, with a rubber boat in tow, could carry only the seventeen women originally arranged for. It was hastily planned that, subject to the approval of the submarine captain, the launch would return for the men. One male planter managed to squeeze aboard with the women; no one knew quite how. It was appropriate that he had been most contemptuous of the evacuation originally.

To expedite matters—for the Nautilus had to be clear by dawn—the men were taken a couple of miles offshore in canoes where they waited until 4 a.m. Just as hope was fading, the motorboat returned and took them aboard. Read and his assistants pulled back to the beach to signal that the evacuation had been a success. With them they had firearms and new batteries sent out from Lunga and, as a present from the Nautilus crew, a package of comforts, tinned food, cigarettes, and tobacco, a gift which warmed Read's heart.

After a rest the party returned to Porapora, exhilarated by success. They were free of the encumbrance of twenty-nine civilians, glad some of them were getting to safety, glad to be rid of others.

The natives who had helped in the evacuation had their own thoughts. They discussed the event among themselves, whispering together in groups. If it were true, as the kiap said, that American forces were near and would soon retake the island, why were the missionaries and planters going? Was it true, as the Japanese said, that the war was over and Bougainville a part of the Empire of Nippon? The kiap and the soldiers were still here ... it was a time to reserve judgment ... but ...

To add to the doubts in the minds of the natives, Japanese patrols around Buka Passage now began to penetrate inland, just as they previously had near Buin. On one occasion, they reached a spot where we had dropped supplies only a few days before. With them was a Chinese who had been forced to act as an interpreter.

All the natives fled from the nearest village, except for one old man who hoped by his presence to save the houses from being burned, the usual penalty for a village that avoided contact. Trembling with fear, the old man met the patrol. The Japanese officer spoke to the interpreter, who bellowed in pidgin, 'Where are the Australian soldiers? You must tell the truth! You must not lie!' Then, in a whisper, he added, 'Say you don't know.'

The aged native dutifully 'No savvied' to all questions, and the patrol withdrew, but not before the Chinese had whispered, 'Tell the Australians to keep a good lookout.'

About this time, our aircraft made a damaging raid on Buka Passage and the Japanese sent in reinforcements. The augmented numbers indicated that they would spread further, and Soraken, with its commodious plantation buildings, appeared the next logical point for occupation. To make things a little more difficult for the enemy, Usaia and Corporal Sali slipped secretly into Soraken at night and burned all the buildings.

Time, and the Japanese strength, were unsettling even the foreign natives, the 'Redskins' who had clung most loyally to Read. To reassure them, Read bought land from the local natives and presented it to them for settlements and gardens. In return, they agreed to continue carrying for Read whenever they were required.

Near Buka Passage, a pro-Jap village had handed over friendly natives to the enemy, and Read now asked that the village be bombed at night. To ensure that the correct village was hit, Sergeant Yauwika, with three of Read's native police and his native clerk, lighted fires on its outskirts when they heard the noise of the bombers, an assignment requiring considerable courage. The bombing was a successful deterrent to such openly hostile acts by other villages, and fortunately the only casualty was one native wounded.

Late in January, we succeeded in making a supply drop, which included a complete teleradio. A party of Mackie's soldiers was given the new instrument and sent to keep watch over Kieta. Before long, this party found itself surrounded by Japanese posts and patrols, and retired only with difficulty. One of the soldiers who had become separated from the others did not make his way back for several days, and fell ill from the privations he had suffered. Meantime, news came that more Chinese had been betrayed by natives and captured. Some were brutally tortured, then killed. The fate of others was unknown.

At FERDINAND headquarters, we mulled over the whole question of coastwatching on Bougainville. With the Japanese circumscribing our watchers' activities, results in terms of information were declining. All the Europeans had been there a year and needed relief. In particular, the soldiers, not salted to the climate as were Read and Mason, were weary and splenetic, a little 'troppo' in fact.

For reinforcement or relief, we had available three FERDINAND officers: Keenan, who had just been relieved on Vella Lavella, Captain Eric Robinson, and Lieutenant G. Stevenson. All three had had previous experience on Bougainville. Also available was a party of soldiers who had gone through Jungle Training School.

It was our plan to give Read and Mason a holiday, but both refused, mainly from loyalty to the natives who had stuck to them. Therefore we decided to send in the three additional FERDINAND officers to aid them, and to replace Mackie and his soldiers with the new troops.

We planned to make the landings in two submarine trips. As soon as Read was told of this proposal, he requested that three nuns who still remained on the island and the Asiatic women and children be evacuated at the same time. The question then arose whether, in the event of there not being enough space, the evacuating soldiers or the women and children should go. Humane considerations overrode military requirements, and priority was given the women and children. In all, there were 12 soldiers, 27 children, and 12 women, including the 3 nuns who were each over 60 years old and who had walked more than a hundred miles across the roughest part of the island. Usaia's wife and children were also among those to be evacuated.

The operation was fixed for 28 March 1943, again from Teop Harbour. With the coast approaches guarded, the evacuees gathered nearby, canoes awaiting the embarkation—everything in readiness—

a small Japanese vessel turned into the harbor and anchored precisely on the spot where the rendezvous was to take place. Read hastily sent a signal, and the evacuation was postponed until the next night.

Next morning the Japanese ship left and at nightfall that evening, the signal fires were lighted. Almost immediately the U.S. Submarine Gato broke surface in the harbor. She had been there all the previous day and had actually surfaced the night before, a few hundred yards from the enemy ship. Only the coming evacuation had saved those Japanese from a sudden end.

Read boarded the submarine and explained that he had fifty-one persons to go out. There was a short consultation between captain and navigator, and then the welcome decision to take the lot. Apparently the Gato's captain, Lieutenant-Commander Foley, worked on the principle that his submarine was not full if he could close the conning tower hatch. It was a typical action for the U.S. submarine service, in which nothing was too onerous or dangerous, the worst job a part of the day's work. In a few hours, the Gato stood out to sea, with all the evacuees on board and even the government records Read had kept since he left Buka Passage.

Included in the incoming party were Keenan and some of the new troops with their officer, Lieutenant D. N. Bedkober, two Buka natives, and a Bougainville native. The Buka natives had been taken to Buna by the Japanese and had escaped to us. Back to Buka they brought tales of Japanese defeats at Guadalcanal, Milne Bay, and Buna.

Told by their own kith and kin, these stories were more convincing to the Bougainville and Buka natives than anything our men, or the Japanese either for that matter, could say. The Bougainville native had been especially trained by us in propaganda.

Before the second submarine trip could be made, a Japanese camp was established near Teop, so the next rendezvous was arranged for a few miles to the southeast. In this evacuation, Read hoped to send out all the remaining non-combatants. Of those remaining, Bishop Wade in particular was in a quandary. Sick and discouraged by the trend of events, he realized he could be of no use to the natives, but his whole nature rebelled against leaving. Read sensed his predicament and ordered him and all other missionaries to leave, thus taking the matter out of the realm of conscience. Nine missionaries, Mackie, the twelve soldiers still remaining, and the last remaining planter, a man who had helped the coastwatchers in every way he could, were to go. Seven Chinese men, the only known

Chinese survivors free of the Japanese, were also slated to go, but were unable to reach the rendezvous in time.

Evacuation by submarine was now becoming a routine performance for Read. The exchange of personnel was quickly affected, the submarine stood out to sea, and the coastwatchers faded into the jungle. Next morning, a Japanese patrol aircraft flew over the innocent scene where nothing showed of the night's activity.

With the landing of Robinson and Stevenson and the remainder of the new troops, there were now five experienced officers and an entire fresh contingent of soldiers to revitalize coastwatching on Bougainville. Added to these FERDINAND forces were the native police, Usaia, another Fijian named Eroni, and three half-castes, Anton and Billy Pitt and William McNicol. These had all become active coastwatchers under Read.

Two nights before the second submarine had arrived, a supply-dropping Catalina crashed into a hillside, killing three of the crew and injuring the other six. As soon as the complete FERDINAND forces were assembled, the coastwatchers and soldiers retreated inland to reorganize and make provision for these wounded men. Read hoped to evacuate them by submarine as soon as they were fit, but before they recovered sufficiently the Japanese occupied the whole east coast, and the west coast was much too exposed to make the attempt with wounded men.

Robinson and Read were old friends, who had served together in New Guinea years before. Fate, with a perverse sense of humor, had ordained that Eric Robinson should never pronounce the letter 'R,' so he was known far and wide as Wobbie. He had blue, innocent eyes and the expression of a child who has not yet seen any evil in the world. A veteran of the last war, he had been an assistant district officer in New Guinea and then had left the government service to keep a pub in Sydney.

Some months before his arrival at Bougainville, I had written Read in a supply-drop letter that Wobbie had been in the Battle of Milne Bay, adding, 'I don't know how the old bastard got into a combat unit at his age.' The letter was still in Read's camp and Wobbie duly read it with shocked horror, insisting that a signal of protest be sent me at once.

True to FERDINAND principles, Read had not been molesting the Japanese patrols working inland. One day about this time, however, the temptation was too much for Constable Sanei, one of his native police.

Six Japanese approached him as he hid at the bend of a path. He shot three, of whom two died later, and drove the remainder away carrying their wounded with them. Then, returning to camp, he realized the enormity of his offense. He had disobeyed the kiap. Sadly he reported to Read, every second sentence an apology, 'sorry too much,' until Read's sense of humor overcame him and the worthy Sanei went unrebuked for defeating six of his enemies single-handed.

In May, Read and the others worked out a plan to cover the whole island with a network of watchers. Keenan was to cover the north from Porapora; Read, with Wobbie, the central east coast, where the Japanese were building up their strength; a party of the fresh troops under Sergeant G. McPhee was to cover the west coast, where there was no enemy activity except for passing aircraft; and, for the south, where conditions were worst, Mason, Stevenson, eight soldiers, Usaia, McNicol, and ten native police were to make up a party. Bedkober, with a few troops, was to remain at an inland camp guarding the injured fliers until opportunity offered to move to the west coast.

Mason's party set off early in May, and the northern parties dispersed to take their positions.

Keenan, at Porapora, placed an outpost of two native police sergeants some distance toward the coast to guard against surprise. For three weeks, he and they were undisturbed, while he reported ships moving in and out of Buka Passage. Then the Japanese moved.

First, they raided the outpost, from which the two sergeants barely escaped to warn Keenan. Keenan immediately hid his teleradio and supplies and withdrew deep in the jungle. The Japanese duly arrived at the Porapora camp, burned it, and then withdrew. Keenan set up his radio in a new position and continued to report ships and aircraft.

On the east coast, Read placed his camp on a ridge and for a while the patrols passed him by. In early June, however, natives reported a strong patrol moving up the valley below his position. The enemy patrol followed the track leading in the direction of Read's camp, but instead of turning off to the camp itself, moved on. Read at once sent messengers to warn his supporting soldiers, who had made a camp five miles to the westward. Then, following normal procedure, he dismantled the teleradio, hid it in the dense jungle nearby, and posted inner and outer guards. As a further precaution, he had his natives spread thin, dry bamboo over the path between his outer and inner guard posts.

About 9 p.m. the night silence was suddenly broken by a shot, followed by heavy firing from the inner-guard post. At the camp, Read, Wobbie, and the natives dived for the jungle on the steep slope of the ridge. In a few minutes, the Japanese burst into the camp, firing machine guns and throwing grenades before them. Their fire was aimed in every direction except that which the coastwatchers had taken, which led Read to fear that another patrol was approaching from that side. Wild yelling indicated to the hiding men that natives were with the Japanese. Knowing that they might ferret out the watchers even if the Japanese could not, Read and Wobbie cautiously slid down the slope until it became too steep to proceed further. There they clung through the night.

With the first light of dawn, they began to negotiate their way farther down the cliff. Suddenly a shower of pebbles from above apprised them that they were being followed. They froze. Wobbie saw a black leg feeling its way down from above, and he opened fire with his tommy gun. The shot was followed by reassuring cries from above; some of their own natives were following Read and Wobbie. Wobbie had given the first one in line a flesh wound in the leg, but it did not disable him.

Descending further, the two coastwatchers and the natives were again stopped by a sheer drop. Here they were pinned, while hostile natives paraded the top of the ridge calling out the names of Read's boys in the hope that one would betray himself by answering. Silently, hardly moving, the men waited through the day, and then, shrouded by the gathering dusk, worked their way up the cliff again and to the side. Again, complete darkness held them immobile.

In the morning, they found a way along the slope and down into the valley, where they met more of the party's natives and together raided a garden for taro to break their two-day fast. The natives brought news that one of the soldiers who had been in Read's group and the other natives still missing had moved off to the west to join Read's other soldiers, who had fled in ample time.

Revisiting their camp, Read and Wobbie found it a heap of ashes. But to their delight, the hidden teleradio was still intact, although the charging engines and batteries had been found and smashed by the Japanese.

At the camp they also found the body of the native who had guided the Japanese. He was an old man who had visited them on the afternoon of the attack and had been given some cloth in exchange for taro. Possibly the new cloth had be trayed his association to the Japanese and they had forced him to lead them, but whether he had done it willingly or unwillingly the penalty was the same. It had been a maxim of the coastwatchers' propaganda that any native who guided the Japanese would be killed and so one of the guards' first shots had been for him. In addition, two Japanese had been killed and two wounded.

Taking the teleradio with them, Read and Wobbie made their way to the abandoned camp of the soldiers. They destroyed it, and moved off to the hills, where their scouts found the remainder of the party. A search of the caches in the vicinity produced a charging engine and batteries but no benzine, so Read was unable to send any signals.

Keenan had also been attacked again, the day after the raid on Read. Warned in time, he had hidden his teleradio. Then, since the Japanese stayed in the neighborhood, he moved south, leaving his radio in the jungle. Accompanied by some police and carriers, he joined Read and Wobbie on the sixth day after the attack.

The only area of the island still relatively free of Japanese, as far as Read knew, was the inland portion near the west coast. So he dispatched Keenan and his men in that direction to try to affect a concentration of all parties there. Then he sent natives to Keenan's old camp for benzine, so that he could go on the air again and attempt to ascertain the state of the other parties. In particular, he was worried about Mason's group, from whom he had heard nothing for some time.

Mere subsistence had also become a really grave problem. Little food remained, and as the moon was near the full, he knew it would probably be impossible to arrange for a supply-drop.

But he had not yet heard the worst.

Bedkober, at his camp near the west coast, had also run low on food. Unable to get Read on the air after the attack, Bedkober had signaled FERDINAND for a supply-drop. In his camp he had five soldiers and the six injured Catalina fliers, four of whom had not yet recovered. He decided to send the two recovered airmen and two soldiers to prepare the drop site, and arranged for Sergeant McPhee and his party to move in next day from their post on the west coast to join him.

On the morning of 16 June, three-quarters of an hour after his four men had left for the drop site, a force of eighty Japanese, accompanied by about forty natives, charged in and opened fire on the camp. Bedkober and his men, although completely taken by surprise, returned the fire. Dunn, one of the badly wounded airmen, just able to hobble on two sticks, slowly and painfully attempted to walk away. Fenwick, another who was still unable to walk, remained in a hut.

As the Japanese made a final rush, Bedkober fired the rest of his magazine, then stood with the empty gun in his hands. Dunn and Fenwick could not escape, and he would not leave them. So he threw down his gun and walked toward the enemy. At that moment, Dunn was shot dead. Bedkober and Fenwick were taken prisoner, while the others, keeping up their fire, escaped to the jungle. Without food they wandered eastward in search of the other parties and were reported later to have reached Numa, where natives betrayed them to the Japanese.

McPhee, on his way to join Bedkober, had been only ten minutes away when the firing broke out. His party had kept to the jungle and maintained radio contact with Lunga. His was the only radio on the island still on the air.

Bedkober's four men who had left for the drop site just before the attack joined up with Keenan, and together these two groups moved westward.

Read at last obtained a few pints of benzine and managed to charge his batteries. From Lunga he learned the state of affairs: Mason off the air, Bedkober's party wiped out, McPhee in hiding, no news of Keenan. In a fortnight, coastwatching on Bougainville had been completely shattered. On 26 June, he signaled:

My duty now to report that position here vitally serious. After fifteen months' occupation almost whole island now pro-Japanese. Initial enemy patrols plus hordes of pro-Japanese natives have completely disorganized us. Position will not ease. Believe no hope reorganize. Our intelligence value nil. In last fortnight all parties have been either attacked or forced to quit. Reluctantly urge immediate evacuation.

At Lunga and at FERDINAND headquarters the same conclusion had been reached. Read was informed that arrangements were being made for an evacuation submarine and was told to concentrate the parties in the west, a move he had already initiated. Read then asked that all police and loyal natives be brought off rather than left to the vengeance of the Japanese. Admiral Halsey readily assented to two trips by the submarine.

But Mason was still missing.

When Mason, Stevenson, Usaia, McNicol, their eight soldiers, and ten native police had set off for the south in May, they planned to head first for the west coast so that canoe transport could be used for part of the journey. Usaia went ahead as advance agent, arranging for canoes, and the first part of the journey was managed successfully. But when they reached Torokina, somewhat more than halfway down the coast, they found that a Japanese patrol was there before them, blocking the way. They struck inland and everywhere found evidence of the enemy. The few carriers available were insufficient for moving all the gear at once, so a few days inland a dump of rations was left in a camp with a police-boy and several carriers as guards. Before Mason could send back for these men and supplies, they were discovered by the Japanese, who killed a carrier and captured the police-boy.

The troops allotted to Mason's party made all the newcomers' mistakes. They lost small items of equipment, frittered away supplies, and failed to make the best use of native foods. It was almost inevitable that this should be so, but in this party, there was no margin for error and even small mistakes could be ill afforded.

At the foot of the main range in the southern part of the island the party successfully received a supply-drop from the air. From here Mason went ahead with four soldiers and some of the police and carriers, leaving Stevenson with the remainder of the party to wait for the carriers to return. Mason crossed to the head of the Luluai River, where he had camped the previous year before being driven out of the south, and then sent the carriers back to Stevenson's group. But disaster had overtaken the rear section. Stevenson had camped at a hamlet on a rocky ridge to which three tracks led. Two of these were guarded but the third, apparently used only by native women, was considered safe and left unwatched.

In the afternoon, natives led the Japanese up this path, reaching the outskirts of the hamlet unseen. Stevenson, who was resting under a small roof of palm-leaf, was the member of the party nearest the approaching enemy. He jumped to his feet, alert, as he heard twigs snapping but the first shot from the Japanese struck his heart and he fell. Usaia rushed to his assistance but, finding him already dead, retreated while the soldiers and police returned the fire, killing five Japanese. Then, with only their arms, they retired. A short way off they found one of the natives who had betrayed them, and executed him on the spot.

Next day, the bedraggled group joined Mason. Now the party had little food, and the Japanese were definitely on its trail. The rough mountain country precluded another supply-drop at night, while a daylight drop would advertise their position.

In spite of these almost unsurmountable difficulties, Mason was still willing to remain, trusting to resource to pull them through. But men who are continually hunted are not able to obtain information.

At FERDINAND headquarters, word had already been received of some of the reverses suffered by the parties to the north, and so when Mason paused to signal his willingness to remain, he was ordered to join McPhee on the northwest coast instead.

So Mason and his men who were left began the long trek back. They could not follow the route toward the east coast which Mason had used on his retreat the previous winter, as that was now all enemy country. The harder route, near the west coast, would have to be followed, and even this was overrun by Japanese patrols, while local natives, now thoroughly demoralized, could be depended upon to betray the party's movements. Nevertheless, all went well for a day as the men crossed the higher mountains. On the second day, while they were following a rough path, they were fired on by a Japanese patrol. They killed one Japanese in return, then retreated, while the carriers bolted, dropping all the gear. When the party rallied, McNicol, a police-boy, and several carriers were missing. The others had only their arms and what was in their pockets.

Mason led the remnants of his group along the bed of a stream so that the water might cover their tracks. The stream, it turned out, led into a gorge. But the men had no course open now except to follow it. They spent a miserable night, hungry, damp and frightened, feeling that the gorge was a trap rather than a haven. But slowly the wretched night passed for the sleepless men and they pushed on with the first light of day.

Following the stream that morning, they suddenly saw, ahead of them, three natives. Obviously, these were lookouts, awaiting their arrival. Unobserved, Mason and the police crept up and captured two but the third escaped. Topping a ridge to the right was the village from which the sentries undoubtedly had come. Mason held one of the two captives and sent the other, a mere boy, to the village to report that his brother was held as hostage for the safe passage of the party. With the hostage leading, the men made their way safely past the village, from which they could hear the beating of drums and the wailing of women.

So far so good, but where the gorge widened into a valley a little way beyond, a Japanese patrol was waiting, doubtless informed of the party's course by natives from the village above. The Japanese opened fire and, although none of Mason's men was hit, the hostage escaped in the melee. Mason and his men ducked into the jungle and struck on rapidly until they reached a track which the Japanese were patrolling. There, by the side of the path, they lay silently in the thick jungle, watching the Japanese run back and forth until after dark. Occasionally the enemy soldiers would fire their rifles, apparently in the hope that answering fire would disclose the coastwatchers' position.

When night had fallen and the Japanese seemed to have given up temporarily, the men darted across the track. Heavy rain was falling, which helped obscure their movements but added to their misery. When they were well clear of the track, they huddled together for warmth and spent another forlorn and hungry night.

Next morning Mason led the men barefooted, so that their tracks would not betray them. By afternoon they seemed clear of immediate danger and, having eaten nothing at all for thirty-six hours and not much for the previous twenty-four, they divided the last tin of emergency rations. While they were resting, some of the carriers who had been missing since the first ambush rejoined them, but McNicol, a police-boy, and four carriers were still missing.

Next day they found a garden from which they took taro. They cooked and ate it, considering the risk of making a fire preferable to the weakness of starvation. Refreshed, they put on their boots and struck off again. They were now near the main east-west track across the island, nearer than they realized, for suddenly a Japanese on a bicycle passed them not thirty yards off. They froze, then as soon as he was out of sight crossed the track and struck off into the jungle again.

Assuming that the bicycling Japanese might have seen them, they kept going all during the night, Mason leading with his compass and each man with a piece of luminous fungus attached to his back so that the next might follow. With most of the night gone, they reached a jungled ridge, where they slept within sight of the campfires of a Japanese post in the valley below. In the morning they again found a deserted garden and took food, then moved on northward, tired and weak but buoyed by the feeling that they were reaching safer ground. On 6 July, a week after their journey northward had started, they had a red-letter day. They shot a pig and for the first time really had enough to eat. While they were feasting, one of the missing carriers arrived bearing one of the packs, of which he was justly proud. He also had a letter, given him by another native. It read:

My dear Ansacs,
We all admire your bravery. You have done your best for Great Britain. You are advised to give yourselves up. The Japanese are not cruel people as the propaganda of the United States would tell you. You will die of hungry in the jungle. You will never reach your friends in Buka as

*all the jungle trails are watched by the Japanese soldiers and the
sharper eyes of the natives.*
    Commander of the Japanese Army.

With their bellies full of pig, the most dangerous part of the
journey past, and the intimation of the note that the northern parties were still free, the missive was treated as a pretty piece of
whimsey. 'Come and get us!' one of the young soldiers shouted to the
unresponsive jungle.

The carrier had also heard native rumors, one being that the
Japanese had captured Usaia. As Usaia was with the party, it was
assumed that the enemy had probably, in reality, taken McNicol.
But this was not the case either, for McNicol was to turn up a year
later, having hidden all that time.

Next day, the party met friendly natives who fed and hid them.
Their track now tended westward and two days later they reached
flatland where, every day, they found signs of Japanese patrols but
no immediate danger.

Although the worst part of the trip, as far as danger from the
Japanese was concerned, lay behind, the hardest walking still lay
ahead. A limestone ridge, rising to 5,000 feet, cut them off from the
north. They had avoided this on their way south by using canoes,
but the coast had become too unsafe to repeat this venture.

So, for a week they climbed and descended trackless ridges and
gorges by day, and by night slept blanketless beside fires, generally
in dry watercourses; the only land even approximating level. At the
high altitudes, the cold was intense. They passed through villages
whose inhabitants had never before seen a European and in these
places they were treated as honored guests. Up to this time Mason,
who was the oldest in the party, had been weakest. Now he grew
stronger while the others weakened.

As they left the high ranges and passed into the foothills, they
were told by natives that there was a coastwatcher party ahead. At
first, this news was only in the form of a vague rumor, but as soon
as he heard whispers of it, Mason sent two police ahead to investigate.

On 18 July 1943, more than three weeks after the party had begun its nightmare struggle north, the scouts met two of Keenan's
police. Swiftly they returned to Mason and the entire party was
guided to what had now become the main coastwatcher camp.

Read had already reduced his party to himself, Wobbie, and a
few police and had sent the others, together with McPhee and his

party and the four men left from Bedkober's original group, to Keenan. He had started the seven last Chinese remaining on the island across to the west by a different route, and then he and Wobbie had set out for the west themselves.

He was still several days' journey from Keenan when the radio told him that Mason had rejoined. From FERDINAND headquarters, where there was unrestrained rejoicing that Mason for the third time had wiggled through a complete Japanese net spread to catch him, Read was immediately signaled that the evacuation submarine was available at four days' notice. He signaled to go ahead at once with the evacuation of those already on the coast.

Four nights later, Mason, Keenan, the soldiers, the two surviving Catalina fliers, police, Chinese, and loyal natives collected on the sand at the water's edge.

It was a calm night. The waves broke with a hollow thud, followed by a swishing; the only sounds in the still darkness. The jungle behind the beach raised its blacker, jagged edge against the dark sky. Eyes peered into the empty darkness to seaward, ears strained against the silence. Restlessly, the Europeans moved from place to place, groups forming, whispering a few uneasy words, and disintegrating. The natives sat silent and passive.

At the appointed hour, Mason lighted the signal fires. For a few almost unbearably tense moments nothing happened; then those watching the dark sea saw black shapes which resolved themselves into rubber boats shooting through the low breakers to the sand.

Offshore, too far to be seen from the beach, the U.S. Submarine Guardfish lay on the surface. Trip after trip was made with the rubber boats until, somehow, sixty persons were crowded into the hull of the Guardfish. Only the redoubtable Usaia with a few of the fittest police remained ashore to join Read and Wobbie thirty miles up the coast.

The Guardfish transferred its passengers to a sub-chaser bound for Guadalcanal and then returned the next night to pick up Read and his companions at the second rendezvous.

For the last time, Read lighted the signal fires and watched the rubber boats creep in among the uncharted reefs. For the first time, he himself was an evacuation passenger. On board the submarine he found that the captain was one of the shadowy figures he had met in the darkness of Teop Harbour when the Gato had called there.

Wobbie, Usaia, and twenty natives were taken off with Read. Billy Pitt, one of his half-caste assistants, failed to make the rendezvous but months later, when FERDINAND returned to Bougainville, he was found to have survived as a refugee in the jungle.

A few of the loyal foreign natives, 'Redskins,' married to local women, preferred to remain. Read arranged for supply-drops to these men. The first was successful, but a month later no fires showed when the aircraft flew over the appointed site.

So ended the first phase of coastwatching on Bougainville. For seventeen months our parties had operated in enemy-controlled territory, sending out information of priceless value. There had been severe losses—Stevenson, Bedkober, the fliers, the soldiers, natives—but the greater part of our force had been saved to fight another day.

The Europeans were sent to Australia for leave and recuperation, while the natives were rested on Guadalcanal, by this time a back area.

To Read and Mason, in particular, many appreciative words were spoken by senior officers of the South Pacific Command, words said with that sincerity and courtesy of the Americans which enable them to praise a man to his face without embarrassment. Most treasured were those of Admiral Halsey, who said that the intelligence signaled from Bougainville had saved Guadalcanal, and Guadalcanal had saved the South Pacific.

Japanese tank Type 97 Chi-Ha

13

THE FIRST SIX MONTHS OF 1943 HAVE SOMETIMES been called the 'lull' in the Southwest Pacific. During this period the Japanese were building up the defensive capacity of their bases in the central and northern Solomons, while the American and New Zealand forces were concentrating for attack. In the attrition that accompanied these preparations, the Japanese fared much the worse.

During the lull, FERDINAND was engaged not only in supplying much of the information which made it possible to wear down the Japanese, but it was also intimately involved in the preparations for the coming South Pacific offensive.

A malignant turn of fate permitted me to have no part in this offensive, except for the initial planning stages.

In March 1943, I made a trip to the Solomons to familiarize myself with details of our organization there and to ensure uniformity of procedure when operations of FERDINAND overlapped with coastwatcher operations in the unoccupied areas. After finding that the work at Guadalcanal under Mackenzie was running on ball-bearings, and conferring with Army and Marine staffs on FERDINAND's part in the advance, I prepared to leave for Malaita to visit Marchant.

As I took my place in a small plane, a severe pain attacked me. I was promptly put in the hospital at Tulagi, where a doctor took my name and particulars and then wrote 'coronary thrombosis' beneath. Those words spelled the end of my activities in FERDINAND.

Mackenzie was my logical successor but, until a replacement for him had been familiarized with the work at Guadalcanal, he could not leave for Australia. The week before I arrived at Guadalcanal his assistant, Train, had gone out one night in a bomber to help guide an attack on an island owned by his wife's family, and his aircraft had failed to return. Nothing was ever learned of its fate.

In the interim, Long, Director of Naval Intelligence, appointed as acting head of FERDINAND his most experienced officer and assistant, Lieutenant-Commander J. C. McManus. In May, Mackenzie and McCarthy conferred with him on plans for the immediate future and then, as Mackenzie was preparing to take over, he was stricken with blackwater fever and had to fight with all his tenacity to keep alive. It was long before he regained a measure of his strength.

So it was McManus who took over permanent direction of FERDINAND. As time went on, he showed a grasp of the problems and an ability to solve them. Before long, too, his tact, patience, and consideration won the loyalty and respect of those difficult, critical people, the islanders. At first, they wondered how they would fare under the direction of a stranger who was not an islander, and their tendency was not to give him the benefit of any doubt. But amazed that their new director managed to put up with their tantrums so forgivingly, they were won over.

In preparing for the offensive, the commanders of the fighting forces naturally wanted all the information possible about the terrain and approaches of the bases they planned to attack. As the area was badly charted and the islands themselves were unmapped, photographs from the air were relied on for the basic outlines. These were interpreted by experts with the aid of our coastwatchers. In connection with Munda, Kennedy's henchman, Wickham was particularly valuable, because he had lived nearby all his life.

Of course this left many details wanting. Specific information on depth of water, slope of beaches, space for deployment after landing, sites for airfields, artillery, hospitals, and roads was necessary. Details like these were beyond the technical abilities of any one man to obtain and the solution was to organize parties of technicians to be led into the areas by coastwatchers.

Corrigan was relieved from his post at Rekata Bay by Andressen and was brought back to Guadalcanal to instruct the American technicians in jungle life. He took the men camping, taught them how to build shelters, how to split a dead, rain-sodden branch to start a fire, how to recognize changes of terrain in the jungle by changes in vegetation, how to pack and carry jungle equipment. His students lived in the jungle until the feeling of strangeness had worn off.

Indeed, this rather intangible part of the training was more important than the specific techniques he taught.

As his first class of students was completing its course, a further difficulty arose to hamper the planners. Some of the features of the islands—bays, capes, and mountains—had both European and native names. Others had only native names, which differed with different groups of natives. It became apparent that the nomenclature must be standardized if signals and maps were not to become hopelessly confusing. So Rhoades, newly returned from Australia, relieved Corrigan as jungle teacher and Corrigan was sent to visit the coastwatchers in the field and establish a uniform nomenclature, as well as to bring in topographical information that demanded diagrams as well as words.

He flew first to Segi, where Kennedy's maps were brought into line with the standard, and new names added from Kennedy's local knowledge; then to Rendova and Kolombangara, where he worked with Horton and Evans on the Munda area.

One of the immediate results of his trip was that coastwatchers in the central Solomons could now signal the position of a barge as off a certain point or creek and feel assured that the staff at Lunga would find the place immediately.

On the heels of Corrigan, and practically under the noses of the Japanese, the technicians moved in to examine Segi, where an airfield was to be built to support the Munda attack. Other parties slipped into Rendova Harbour, where the first landing was to be made, and to the northwestern side of New Georgia, above Munda, to select additional landing points and cut tracks toward the rear of the Japanese positions at Bairoko. Some of the American officers remained at these places to await the landings. Corrigan too halted at New Georgia, where he collected and held ready a large force of natives to act as carriers when the landing took place.

During this period, Kennedy's wisdom in wiping out stragglers approaching Segi, instead of retiring, bore its full fruit. Segi became an important base, the point of insertion for all parties preparing for the Munda attack. This traffic, of course, made a great deal of extra work for Kennedy. He had to receive and house the many transients, provide them with canoes and handle their signals. To help him, FERDINAND sent a thoroughly Allied party, a U.S. Army sergeant, an Australian Navy coder, a New Zealand Navy telegrapher, and a captain of the British Solomon Islands Protectorate Defense Force.

Our air activity around Segi became so extensive that it was feared the Japanese might send a strong patrol against the post and disrupt our plans. To ensure its safety, 400 U.S. Marines were landed on 21 June.

Gone completely was the solitude of Kennedy's plantation stronghold. The Marines were so itchy-fingered that it became dangerous for scouts to enter the area, so Kennedy himself moved across the strait where he could recapture some of the old-time quiet and where his scouts could come and go without danger from sentries. A few days before the Munda attack, FERDINAND sent an Australian, a New Zealander, and an American, under command of Flight Lieutenant R. A. (Robbie) Robinson, to relieve Horton at Rendova, so that he could guide the forces landing there. To make sure of communication with these coastwatchers up to the last minute, the flagship of the invasion convoy carried another FERDINAND man with a teleradio.

The convoy proceeded unobserved through the night, and just before dawn of 1 July 1943, our forces landed simultaneously at Rendova, Wickham Anchorage, on Vangunu Island, and Viru Harbour on New Georgia.

At Rendova, Rhoades landed with the first wave, showed that his knowledge of jungle fighting was not merely academic or his reputation for ruthlessness undeserved, and for his courage he was later awarded the Silver Star. Horton was in constant demand because of his local knowledge, and he was kept busy locating sites for various units and pointing out tracks, water supplies, and other desiderata while the enemy aircraft bombed the beachhead.

On the mountain above the harbor, Robbie's replacement party kept watch in Horton's old lookout. It was not long left in sylvan solitude. Retreating remnants of the Japanese forces stumbled on the camp, and for some hours a strange duel was fought, both sides firing at shadowy forms in the ill-lit jungle. Throughout the affray, the signaler stood by the teleradio, sending and receiving messages as coolly as if he were in the dugout at Lunga. Finally, when the Japanese brought up a machine gun and rushed the post, Robbie and his men retired with their codes, making their way next day to the forces on the beach.

FERDINAND at once sent in new equipment to replace what they had lost, and Robbie set up a post at Rendova Harbour to receive and disseminate air-raid warnings; much the same role as that played by Mackenzie during the fighting at Lunga. Although the enemy sent flight after flight of raiding aircraft, warnings from Vella Lavella or Choiseul enabled the landing forces to weather the attacks with few casualties.

Five days after the landing at Rendova, another landing was made north of Munda. Corrigan was waiting for this force, his guides and carriers in readiness to move the Marines inland for an attack on the Japanese rear. For the next month, Corrigan and his natives carried food up to the firing line and took the wounded out, while Corrigan himself also handled the radio traffic. Corrigan was not at all the wild Irishman his name suggests. He was, in fact, quiet, soft-voiced, and super-sensitive. When his feelings were hurt, he hid the fact until they suddenly boiled over. Although he exploded at the Marines occasionally, they showed their appreciation of him in a practical way; they tried to have him permanently attached to their outfit. He was awarded the American Legion of Merit with the citation, '...his performance reflects great credit, not only upon F/O Corrigan, but also on the Service of which he is a part.'

From Rendova, the attack on Munda itself was launched. Soon after the battle began, Robbie moved his party across the straits from Rendova. During the landing, he fell and bared his shinbone for three inches, but he smothered the wound in sulfanilamide powder, bandaged it, and carried on. One or another of his men remained at the teleradio constantly, taking and passing on air-raid warnings throughout the battle. The Japanese held out in well-concealed foxholes and returned artillery fire from hidden guns, and it was not until August that Munda was finally subdued. To the north, Japanese communications were becoming precarious, and finally the remnants of the enemy's Munda forces slipped away.

On Kolombangara, Evans, who had been reinforced by Corporal B. F. Nash of U.S. Army Air Communications, had the backwash of the campaign. The Japanese made frantic barge movements, first to reinforce Munda, then to withdraw troops from it. The two men were kept busy reporting barges, many of which were sunk by U.S. aircraft and PT boats. Nash had adapted himself quickly to the life of a coastwatcher, one of the very few outsiders to do so. Possibly he was fitted for it by his early life in the wide-open spaces, for he came from Arizona.

With the fall of Munda, the Japanese escape route along the channel west of Kolombangara became the principal scene of activity. Evans and Nash then moved from Kolombangara to a small island along this route. The difficulty of finding hidden barges, the inadequacy of charts in spite of the best that could be done, and the inexperience of new pilots resulted in the strafing of many friendly villages. This had always been a problem throughout the Southwest Pacific, but probably the natives of Kolombangara suffered worst.

New pilots arrived, convinced that the country on our side of the lines was friendly and that on the other side hostile. Yet, in fact, the occupied country was friendly, too, except for spots controlled by the enemy. To many, natives were just 'expendables,' and not even 'human expendables.'

In spite of warnings and pleas, the friendly natives were so shot up that Evans' scouting organization was seriously dislocated. Only the coastwatchers knew how essential was native good will, how much success was due to native assistance, and what risks the natives had run. And only those who had worked with natives, apparently, would go to real trouble to protect them. When, in spite of every precaution, an area in which Evans' scouts were hidden was bombed by our own aircraft, Evans felt he could no longer ask the natives for their co-operation and he asked to be recalled. He was relieved, and in a short time the station was closed.

While our forces were attacking Munda, Josselyn and Firth on Vella Lavella were not only kept busy signaling warnings of air attacks, but they were also going into the hotel business on a large scale. To prevent any large reinforcements of Munda by the Japanese, the U.S. Navy was ranging far forwards toward Buin. On one of these sweeps, a Japanese naval force was encountered at night. It was defeated, but in the action the U.S. cruiser Helena was sunk. When 161 survivors drifted ashore on Vella Lavella in rubber boats and rafts, Josselyn's and Firth's native scouts, patrolling the beach, helped them ashore and led them to safety in the jungle. The Japanese outposts, probably deterred by the numbers, did not interfere except to send out a patrol of twenty men, who did not leave the beach.

The two coastwatchers, assisted by the Methodist clergy man who had been on the island when they arrived, organized food supplies from the natives and contributed their own stores, issued arms to the sailors for self-defense, and posted native guards around the survivors' camps. One party of four Japanese came too near a camp and was wiped out.

Immediately the survivors began to land, Josselyn had sent a signal and on 13 July an evacuation destroyer arrived. A screen of native scouts was posted around the embarkation point to ensure that there was no interruption while the Helena survivors bade farewell to Vella Lavella. In the six days the sailors were sheltered on the island, they almost exhausted the coastwatchers' food and medicine.

As another measure for smothering counterattacks against our forces at Munda, we were at this time making constant air attacks on Buin, and as a result a good many airmen were shot down over Vella Lavella. Hardly a day went by that there was not an airman at the coastwatchers' post. At one time, there were eleven. The total number rescued was 31, with only one casualty, a gunner who was lost in a skirmish with a Japanese patrol while he was being led to the post.

Of the Japanese airmen shot down over the island, twenty-two were killed and one taken prisoner. There was seldom any alternative to killing the enemy airmen, since most of them were armed and would not surrender. Further, the natives had hardened their hearts after bombardment of their villages by Japanese destroyers.

The Japanese on the island had done quite a rescue job themselves. The garrison of 600 enemy troops had been augmented by an additional 500 men from Japanese barges sunk by our forces. As the number of Japanese on the island increased, it became difficult to bring in a Catalina unseen, and finally it became impossible. So, the evacuation of our airmen and the landing of supplies was carried out by PT boats at night.

Even before Munda had fallen, it had been decided that our forces would occupy Vella Lavella, bypassing Kolombangara and Rekata Bay, and so forcing the enemy to abandon them.

In spite of the numbers of Japanese on the island, six U.S. officers were landed to select sites for airfields. Josselyn guided them past the Japanese positions while they made their surveys. In operations such as this, the coastwatcher invariably took charge, regardless of rank. Unfortunately, as the date of invasion drew near, friendly villages were bombed and strafed by our planes. It was heartbreaking to the natives who had stood loyally by us and time and again risked their lives in our cause.

On 12 August, the first troops landed unopposed at a spot selected by Josselyn. Four days later, the main force landed, and on the southeast point of the island formed a perimeter inside which the Seabees started the construction of an airfield. Outside the perimeter, Vella Lavella was left to the Japanese and the coastwatchers.

At the northeast tip of the island, the Japanese posts continued to act as control and lying-up bases for barge traffic; so, although enemy aircraft were growing scarcer, the coastwatchers still had numerous barges to report. Before long, large parties of Japanese began to move across the island, some coming uncomfortably near the coastwatchers' post. This was a partial evacuation, though we did not realize the fact at the time. When the movement was finally over, it was found that the Japanese were holding only the north coast of the island. In early September, New Zealanders were sent in to wipe out the remaining Japanese. For this operation, Josselyn collected scouts from the north coast to pilot the landing craft through the reefs. The operations were highly successful, and a month later the last Japanese was gone from Vella Lavella.

Josselyn, who had been on the island a year, had grown a luxuriant brown beard which gave him a specious air of age and authority. He was sent on leave, and in Brisbane feminine influence did what Admirals and Generals had failed to achieve. The beard came off, to reveal the boy underneath. The only coastwatchers still in enemy-occupied territory in the Solomons were Waddell and Seton on Choiseul. Seton, always bloodthirsty, applied for permission to arm more guerrillas and wipe out Japanese posts on the southwest coast, but he was refused. Killing a hundred or so Japanese would not have affected our campaign, while the loss of information might have been serious.

During September three reconnoitering parties were sent to the island and were met and guided by Seton. In connection with one of these expeditions, native runners traveled 35 miles through rough jungle in 9 hours, mainly in the dark; a remarkable feat.

However, the plan to land large forces on Choiseul, of which the scouting parties were forerunners, was discarded. Instead, it was decided to occupy Torokina on Bougainville for the purpose of bypassing Buin and putting a fighter strip within reach of the main enemy base of Rabaul. To cover this operation, Marine paratroopers, landed in barges, were to stage a merely diversionary raid on Choiseul.

Late in October, Waddell was left in charge on the island and Seton was taken off, together with a selected group of scouts, to accompany and guide the Marine raiders. On the night of 27 October, the first landing craft was piloted ashore, and soon the whole battalion with supplies and equipment was hidden in the jungle. For the next two days, camps and positions were secretly prepared. Colonel Krulak, commander of the battalion, decided to wipe out the enemy's Sangigai post first. One party approached the post along the coast while another, guided by Seton and commanded by the Colonel himself, moved to the rear of the position. The coastal party arrived at the enemy post first, and the fleeing Japanese ran head-on into the second party. Seton, two natives, and five Marines were in the lead, and they succeeded in driving back the leading Japs.

The whole Japanese garrison then rallied and charged with bayonets and automatic weapons. The main body of the Marine party, hurriedly forming, mowed down the advancing Japanese with heavy, accurate fire, then charged and scattered the remainder. The Marines had 4 killed and 13 wounded, while the enemy's casualties were more than a hundred.

Accompanied only by native scouts, a Marine detachment was then sent to raid Choiseul Bay at the northwest end of the island. None of the Marines could speak pidgin, however, and consequently could not understand the information of the scouts. Under this handicap, the expedition was only moderately successful.

Shortly afterwards, the Marines withdrew from the island. This had a devastating effect on native morale. The natives did not understand broad strategy; they knew only what they saw. They had seen a large body of U.S. troops land and had assumed that Japan's day was over. Now the troops had gone, and the Japanese remained.

The next time Seton, with three armed natives and some carriers, ran into a patrol of Japanese, the carriers ran. Fortunately, the Japanese were equally scared and retreated after firing a ragged volley. Possibly they mistook Seton's 200-pound bulk for a tank, and a bearded tank at that.

A month later, Waddell and his scouts ambushed and annihilated a patrol of seventeen Japanese who had ventured into the interior. It was a justified attack, because the patrol endangered the existence of the coastwatchers. To some extent, the Japanese were now playing our own game on Choiseul. Cunningly concealed on a ridge, one of their posts was watching and reporting our shipping movements. Seton and one of his scouts were flown out to guide our aircraft in attacks on this position, and after three raids, the Japanese coastwatchers were no more. After guiding a number of other air raids on the Choiseul area, Waddell and Seton were both sent on a well-earned leave. For fifteen months they had sent out information that enabled our aircraft and ships to damage seriously the enemy's supply lines at a time when they could ill afford such damage. We were really moving up the road from Guadalcanal. The central Solomons were now in our hands. The next strike was to be at Bougainville, an island with which FERDINAND had an account to settle.

Australia's sloop HMAS Yarra

14

WITH POETIC JUSTICE, FERDINAND'S RETURN to Bougainville was made in the U.S. Submarine Guardfish, the ship that had spirited away the harried coastwatchers, soldiers, and natives three months before. FERDINAND's return was no quixotic gesture, however. It was a well-laid plan for covering the landing of U.S. Marines at Torokina on the west coast of the island.

Three FERDINAND parties were prepared; one to land with the troops, one to be placed at the north end of the island, and one for the south, the two latter to land before the invasion.

Leading the northern party was Wobbie, whose sojourn in the lush pastures of Sydney had made him, he said, fit as a fiddle. Actually, he more nearly resembled a cello. Because of his age, he had at first been passed over in the plans for the return to Bougainville, but this had made him so indignant that he was hastily designated a party leader.

Assisting him was Sub-Lieutenant K. W. T. Bridge, who had served as an administrative officer at Buka Passage in peacetime and had already served FERDINAND in New Guinea. Poor Bridge had a one-day honeymoon before the party left.

Keenan, Mackie, and Sergeant McPhee made up the southern party. Both groups included natives who had been evacuated with Read in July. Sergeant Yauwika and his trusty men, having had a rest at Guadalcanal, were more than ready for another tangle with Japanese patrols.

On 26 October 1943, Keenan's party was disembarked on the southwestern coast and then the Guardfish continued northward to the point from which it had evacuated Read and Wobbie.

As it arrived at the selected spot, two fires could be seen on the beach. Obviously, these were enemy fires, for no natives lived on this part of the coast. Nevertheless, Wobbie's party landed, sneaked quietly between the two fires, and penetrated immediately about 60 yards into the dense mangrove swamp. There, with the Japanese almost in earshot, they huddled in their rubber boats until daylight, bitten by millions of mosquitoes.

At dawn they hid the boats and cut their way through the mangroves, reaching dry land several hours later, when they were all on the point of complete exhaustion.

Wobbie sent out scouts, who returned with the news that a large Japanese party was passing through the nearest village, immediately between the coastwatchers and the mountains. This village lay on the only route the men could take to the high country, so they pushed on in spite of the news and crossed the path of the Japanese patrol two hours after it had passed.

Within a few days, they reached the settlement of Redskin's who had not been taken by the Japanese or killed by hostile natives as we had feared.

Next morning, they heard the bombardment at Torokina and, setting up their radio, made contact with Robbie Robinson, who had landed with the American troops.

Robbie had handed over Munda, by then a rear base, a fortnight before. With him he had R. Stuart, the last planter off Bougainville, a man who had been of great assistance to Read in his evacuation of civilians and who was now a sub lieutenant in the Navy. He also had Nash, the U.S. soldier from Arizona who had made such a good coastwatcher, two other Americans, two Australian sailors, a New Zealand telegraphist, and seventeen natives. FERDINAND had certainly acquired an international character.

The firing was still hot when Robbie and his watchers put ashore on the low-lying, swampy beachhead. Robbie immediately spied a breadfruit tree, which his jungle lore informed him meant firm ground, and he appropriated the hut nearest it, outside of which Japanese washing was still hanging on the line. Experience had led him to the highest land in the area and as an additional blessing there was a well of passable drinking water nearby. While he received and disseminated signals for the fighting men, Stuart guided landing parties to the south of the beachhead perimeter.

FERDINAND's southern party, led by Keenan, had meantime had slow going. Loaded to full capacity, he and his men had to cut their way inland through swamp from their disembarkation point. Deluged by a heavy tropical rain, but pushing as hard as they could from dawn to dark, they made only two miles their first day. Next day, they reached the bank of the Laruma River, where two Marine officers who had accompanied the party were detached, together with five scouts, to head for Torokina. Keenan and the others pushed on and by dusk were about five miles from the beach; five miles in two days of sweating, exhausting effort.

Two days later, with the rain still pouring, they reached the first foothills. The teleradio was set up but the constant rain had soaked through its covers and in spite of all they could do it would not function. Early next morning, gunfire and bombing told them the landing was taking place, and climbing to a hilltop they watched our cruisers and destroyers shelling the beach, dive bombers striking at Japanese positions, transports unloading, and landing craft scurrying back and forth. For men who had long watched the Japanese lord it over these beaches, it was a sight to lift the heart.

During the landing, the only enemy interruption from air or sea was a strafing run by six zeros. This was particularly fortunate for us because there was only open ocean between Rabaul and Torokina and no coastwatchers could be placed to give warning of attacks from the great enemy base.

As Keenan's radio remained obdurate, Mackie took it and set off for Torokina to repair or replace it. During his trip, Japanese troops moved into the intervening country and although he eluded them it was three weeks before he returned with Robbie's spare instrument. During this time, Keenan collected a number of natives who had lived at Torokina and sent them to the beachhead for use as scouts.

With his new teleradio, Keenan moved inland to a position from which he could observe the trail leading to the west coast from Numa. But there was no enemy movement from the west coast, and he had little to do beyond wiping out a few Japanese stragglers and transmitting information obtained by his scouts to the east.

Some of the natives from the area in which he camped were sent to Torokina as sightseers, to impress them with the fact of our advance. When they returned and told their villages what they had seen, Keenan had the whole local population assisting him. Not only militarily, but psychologically, the tide was turning on Bougainville.

To the north, Wobbie's party established itself on a mountain giving a good view of the west coast from Torokina to Soraken. Natives in the vicinity now eagerly helped him, also, with food and information. Before long, Billy Pitt, the half-caste who had missed the evacuation and hidden in the jungle, turned up and joined the group. On the information he and the scouts provided, our forces carried out numerous bombing strikes in which the enemy suffered heavy casualties.

On 12 November, Wobbie was told by his scouts that the Japanese knew all about his party and were planning to search for it next day. Wobbie moved the group to rough country to the northeast, while local natives guided the Japanese everywhere but to the new camp. Then he moved still again to a position overlooking the east coast, while his natives continued to report the positions of enemy forces. Japanese shipping was being so heavily hit that the enemy's mobility was seriously reduced; troops and supplies could hardly be moved about the island.

A supply-drop had been made at Wobbie's old camp shortly after he left it, and although four parachutes were subsequently recovered, his group was running out of food. One day during this time of scarcity, a police-boy returned from a scouting expedition with a bag on his shoulder and a large grin on his face. Asked what was in the bag, he replied with an even wider grin, 'Beer belong Japan.' Magic words! An enemy ship had gone ashore on a reef not far from Wobbie's camp and the natives who had been forced by the Japanese to unload it had hidden some of the beer for a present to Wobbie. He reported it, 'a good brew.'

Three days before Christmas came another report that a Japanese patrol was about to move after the group. Retreating inland, the men happened to witness a strange and moving Christmas ceremony. At a lonely spot in the jungle, hundreds of natives from miles around collected on Christmas morning, brought together by Catholic and Methodist native mission teachers. In the morning, both denominations held church services, attended by Wobbie's natives but not by the Europeans in the party. Then in the afternoon, about 200 natives from the congregations assembled near the camp and invited the three Europeans, Wobbie, Bridge, and the telegrapher, to attend a meeting.

To the watchers, the effects of war were easily discernible among these natives. Bodies were not so well nourished as formerly, clothing was scantier and more bedraggled, skins smelled for lack of soap, and sores stank for want of medicines and treatment. It was a still, silent crowd, lacking the noise and movement of happier times.

The three Europeans were set in a place of honor before the gathering, while Mika, a Methodist teacher, made a speech. These three, he said, were representatives of the good people. He exhorted the natives to assist them in every way, even in the killing of Japanese. Wobbie replied with a speech of gratitude and of assurances that one day the Japanese would be driven out and the good times would come again. Then Mika led the assembly in a prayer for the coastwatchers' safety and the entire group, natives and Europeans, sang the National Anthem. When the three men returned to their camp, they found that in their absence natives had left generous gifts of food, gifts which could be ill spared by these people, hungry themselves.

Continuing to follow a policy of frequent shifts to keep the enemy puzzled, Wobbie and his men moved on north. They had had about five weeks of peace when again they received news that a

Japanese patrol knew of their whereabouts and was moving to round them up. In continuous, torrential rain, they made their way back to the Christmas camp. Bridge had fever during the trip but kept on manfully, even drawing on some reserve of energy when at last they stopped, to put up a notice, 'Hudson Bay Fur Trading Company.' It had been his practice to give equally incongruous names to their other camps and the party frequently wondered what the Japanese thought when they found these signs.

A supply-drop would have endangered disclosure of their position during these wanderings, so the men obtained their supplies and mail from the southern group; Wobbie's carriers and police avoiding the enemy patrols coming and going.

By this time many natives in Wobbie's vicinity were enthusiastically killing Japanese. One, Tomaira, had five notches cut in the handle of his pako, a club made of swamp ebony. His method was simple. While walking with an unsuspecting Japanese he would simply point upwards. The Jap, fearing aircraft, would look up and would never look down again. Other natives, to prove they had made a kill, brought in Japanese equipment and identity badges, and were rewarded.

In his checkered career, Wobbie had once been a medical assistant and now he was kept busy giving injections of N.A.B., the specific for yaws, one of the few medicines in which the natives really have faith. Having been without any treatment for two years, virtually all the natives were suffering badly, and they were extremely grateful for his help. When a native would arrive late in the day asking for an injection, and Wobbie was tired, he would remember the Christmas ceremony and set to work to boil a needle, ever cheerful.

With the New Year, a Fijian patrol, 200 strong, serving under our forces, moved into Keenan's area to the south. Keenan joined them at their camp at Ibu, about seven miles from the east coast. Their teleradio had broken down, so Keenan passed their signals to Torokina, a service they could not have done without.

At Ibu, the Fijians constructed a small airstrip, sufficient to take a Piper Cub, while small detachments from the patrol circulated in the surrounding area, frequently clashing with the Japanese. Piper Cubs flew in daily bringing reinforcements and supplies.

All went well until February, when the Japanese attacked the patrol's outpost to the eastward and, with a strong force, moved in to cut it off from the west. A retreat was ordered. Mackie, with a vanguard of Fijians, took out all the friendly natives, while Keenan remained with the main body. The vanguard was attacked by a superior force, blocking the retreat, but Keenan's scouts led the main body to safety by a little-known track.

Then the vanguard managed to disengage itself and follow. Keenan made contact with a small American force which had established a beachhead on the west coast nearby, and on 19 February 1944 the whole Fijian force was evacuated by landing barge. The vanguard—now the rear guard—had inflicted a hundred casualties on the enemy without loss to themselves.

Wobbie, knowing that the retreat of the Fijians to the south would release large numbers of enemy troops to chase him, also decided on retreat. While he waited for information from his scouts, he managed to rescue a Fijian lieutenant who had crashed with a U.S. Army flier in a Piper Cub a month before. He took time, too, to bury the remains of the airmen who had been killed in the Catalina crash a year before.

Informed that the way to the coast was clear, Wobbie and his men, accompanied by 200 loyal natives who could not be left behind, moved off. A last addition to the party was 'Yamamoto,' a Japanese prisoner brought in by natives. His real name was not known. He appeared to be quite tractable but could not understand a word of English. In the long marches ahead, his detention was a problem which Wobbie solved by drawing a sack up to his waist and tying it securely whenever the party stopped. Sergeant Yauwika was dubious of this device so, to convince him, Wobbie fired his revolver behind the prisoner's back. 'Yamamoto,' alarmed, jumped up and immediately fell over. 'He would never win a sack wace,' Wobbie explained.

The first night on the march, 'Yamamoto' asked in pantomime to have the sack pulled over his head; indignity notwithstanding, he preferred to be warm.

On 28 February 1944, the party reached an appointed spot on the coast, where Keenan was waiting for it. FERDINAND was no longer needed on Bougainville. The beachhead at Torokina was secured, the entire Solomons campaign was virtually over. Japanese forces still on Buka, Bougainville, and Choiseul, cut off by sea and air, could do nothing but make a holocaust of themselves in futile attacks on Torokina. So, again the coastwatchers left the island. No surreptitious flight by night this, but an evacuation by barge in broad daylight under air cover; so much had the face of the war changed in Bougainville.

15

In the New Guinea area, which includes New Guinea and Papua on the New Guinea mainland, New Britain, New Ireland, and the smaller specks of land off the coasts of these larger islands, FERDINAND had to begin operations nearly from scratch. All our men in New Ireland had been driven out immediately after the Japanese occupation. In New Britain only Bell, Douglas, and Olander had been left behind after McCarthy's and Mackenzie's evacuations, and these three, unable to do much except be low, were finally brought out by 'Blue' Harris; still the commodore of the 'Harris Navy,' in June 1942. On the New Guinea mainland we had a rather random sprinkling of watchers, including Harris and his group on the shore of Vitiaz Straits. In the summer of 1942 the Allied forces were planning, over-optimistically, it turned out; to recapture Rabaul, which the enemy had turned into a tremendously strong naval and airbase.

FERDINAND's part in these plans began early in July, when Sub-Lieutenant Malcolm Wright, a dark, soft-voiced young man who had been a patrol officer in New Guinea, was landed secretly by submarine on the New Britain coast near Rabaul. Although it was impossible, at this time, for us to maintain watchers in New Britain, we knew there might be a chance for an experienced officer to land, stay a few days, and be taken off. The whole success of such an operation would depend on whether the natives assisted or betrayed the officer, but this fact in itself was something worth finding out.

Wright was eager for just such a venture. Unable to obtain his release from the civil service just before Japan entered the war, he had resigned and joined the Navy and then had deliberately flunked his examination in anti-submarine school so that he might serve in FERDINAND. On the night of 12 July 1942, the U.S. Submarine S-42, with Wright aboard, surfaced off the New Britain shore for the secret landing. It was the season of the southeast monsoon, and the wind and rain were sweeping the angry sea under low-lying clouds. Slipping, sliding, and falling, the submarine crew launched a rubber boat from a wallowing vessel, and a few moments later, Wright and his meager equipment were afloat.

As soon as he cast off, the submarine disappeared into the dark void. His boat tossed wildly in the seas and for a time he thought he would not make land. For hours, it seemed, he fought the heaving waters, until at last a breaking wave picked up his boat and tossed it ashore. With every muscle aching, his gear and himself drenched by sea and rain, he pulled the rubber boat to the beach, hid it and his equipment, and then, in utter weariness, lay down and slept, little caring for the moment what became of him.

Waking with daylight, he found his landing place could not have been better chosen. He was on a windswept beach on which the surf broke and creamed into a mat of vines. No human habitation was in sight, and the scattered bushes and pandanus palms made a sufficient screen between him and the road a hundred yards inland.

Wise in the ways of natives, he made no move to disclose himself until mid-forenoon, when the young men and women would be at the gardens. The first person to see him as he moved cautiously down the road was a small native girl who ran back to her village and called the Luluai, the chief. Wright watched the old man advance, hesitant, while curious faces peeped here and there from the village huts. Then, his heart pounding, he called the chief a greeting.

There was nothing inimical in this visitor's friendly smile or voice; the Luluai hesitated an instant longer, then advanced confidently. Immediately other natives tumbled out of the huts to follow, and Wright was engulfed with questions. Was this a kiap? There were kiaps left then? The Japanese had said they were all finished and would never come again. Where had he been? Where was he going? Out of the clamor of questions came also the information that they were glad to see him, that they did not like the Japanese. Then one, furtively, not wishing to show disrespect but wanting reassurance, touched Wright's arm to make sure he was not a ghost.

Turning to practical matters as soon as their curiosity was satisfied, the natives led Wright to a hut a short distance from the village, well hidden in the jungle. More natives arrived and one young man appointed himself cook and personal servant while others posted themselves to be sure no Japanese or Jap-employed native police might come on the scene unexpectedly.

Next day, Wright visited a camp of seventeen Chinese a few miles away. They met him with suspicion. One, who had been a law student in Melbourne, called him a Quisling. Only one of the Chinese had been in Rabaul since the Japanese occupation, and he offered to give Wright his information only on condition that the seventeen Chinese be taken off when Wright himself left. Wright was, of course, unable to make any such promise. Having some doubts himself about the Chinese, he told them nothing of his means of arrival or of the time and place of his departure.

For the seven days he was ashore, Wright's presence was kept secret, although native police in the service of the enemy passed through the village several times. After a few days, the Chinese who had been in Rabaul thought better of his previous decision, visited Wright, and told him all he knew of the Japanese defenses. Information was also collected from reliable natives, but it was disappointingly scanty, because most of the people had been staying in their own villages to keep out of harm's way.

On the seventh day, Wright told the Luluai that he would be leaving that night and asked for a few men to accompany him on the road. The Luluai had been expecting this and was ready. He had two gifts. One was a piece of bark cloth, a present for the 'Number One of Australia' and a token of loyalty to the King. The other gift was for Wright himself, a pair of pig's tusks, nearly circular in shape, very precious; indeed so priceless that to be allowed to hold them was to have been shown the highest mark of esteem. This is the type of gift which is meant to be returned. Only the experienced can recognize the subtle distinction between that which is given and that which is lent.

That night at midnight, Wright flashed a signal to seaward with his torch, and the submarine broke surface a few hundred yards offshore to the utter astonishment of the natives. Ten days later Wright landed in Brisbane, where his information was passed on to the staffs. That done, he saw to it that the Luluai's bark cloth was sent to higher authorities for transmission to the Governor General, then took the tusks to a jeweler, who joined them on a silver mount and hung them on a neck chain for return to the Luluai when opportunity should offer.

Wright's venture had been successful, but the information he had gained was less than had been hoped for. However, it did establish, roughly, the enemy defense perimeter south of Rabaul and, most valuable to FERDINAND, it revealed the under lying native goodwill. We had something to go on now, for future planning.

Quickly we began preparations to land five parties for covering both coasts of New Britain toward Rabaul, and to augment these with a chain of posts reaching back to our own main bases. But before our plans could be put in effect, the Japanese upset our calculations. While we had been thinking of recapturing Rabaul, the enemy had been considering the capture of Port Moresby so that he could push on to the New Hebrides and Noumea without a threat to his flank. His first attempt on Port Moresby had been frustrated at the Battle of the Coral Sea. This second attempt was to be made by a series of jumps.

The first jump was to Buna on the Papua coast, where we had no forces. Though our aircraft struck at the enemy convoys and damaged them heavily, the Japanese were soon in possession of a beachhead, from which they pushed through the swampy jungle over the foothills to Kokoda, then across the Owen Stanley Range and down the trail toward Port Moresby. A month after the Buna landing, more enemy forces landed at Milne Bay, but we got there first with the most men and they were defeated. In spite of the Milne Bay victory, our plans for attacking Rabaul had to be deferred. The Buna campaign would have to take precedence.

Almost at once there was an assignment for our ship Paluma, in which we had planned to transport our watchers to New Britain. The Paluma had been an examination vessel at Thursday Island, and although the Navy was desperately short of small craft, she had been lent to us while the New Britain plans were being made. Her speed was only ten knots, while we would have preferred one of fifteen, but in every other way she was satisfactory. Sixty-six feet long, she was large enough to carry several FERDINAND parties and their gear, but small enough to hide in creeks and inlets. We refitted her, built extra accommodations, mounted two fifty-caliber machine guns aft, and camouflaged her outside in green and gray.

Although the Japanese were pushing over the Owen Stanley Range toward Port Moresby, Allied headquarters knew that they would shortly be driven back. That done, ships would be needed, to carry supplies to Buna. But the sea between Milne Bay and Buna was unsurveyed and it would be months before a Navy chart could be completed. We were asked whether the Paluma could lay buoys and place lights along the route and at two anchorages in time for ships to get through by early November.

Our preparations, which had been hectic enough for the proposed New Britain landings, now reached fever heat. Lieutenant Ivan Champion, who had helped in the New Britain evacuations, had the greatest knowledge of the area and he was placed in command of the ship and its survey work. For the shore parties at the anchorage sites, McCarthy was selected as overall commander.

Sub-Lieutenant P. J. Mollison, a young patrol officer from New Guinea, was placed in charge of the party that was to land at the Sewa Bay anchorage. Lieutenant H. E. Hamilton, another patrol officer, who had been interrogating native deserters from the Japanese, was chosen for the Cape Nelson area. Lieutenant B. Fairfax-Ross, a fair, noisy man who had been an assistant district officer and had just recently returned from the fighting in the Middle East, was put in charge of forward reconnaissance. The rest of the party included an engineer, first officer, eleven soldiers of the Independent Companies as crew, and three natives. Being islanders, the coast-watchers were not going to do their own cooking and washing if they could possibly have natives to do it for them.

Peter Figgis, Mackenzie's companion on the evacuation from Rabaul, was sent to Milne Bay with a teleradio to act as control station for the other radios of the expedition.

At Townsville the Paluma lay alongside a wharf, while supplies were handed aboard and stowed away by the soldiers. Fairfax-Ross, with more soldiers, stored arms and ammunitions. McCarthy tripped people with aerials and Mollison muttered imprecations while he untangled the wires. Clashing, getting in each other's way, all of them were cursed impartially by the engineer whenever he bobbed up, covered in grease and carbon, from the engine room. Everyone was swearing and snarling at everyone else, so it was clear that at least each had his heart in his own work.

Townsville itself was a fitting setting for the confusion aboard the Paluma. By this time, it was so crowded by Australian and American troops that hotels, restaurants, and cinemas were filled to capacity and shops of all kinds were bare. Even the bordellos had such an oversupply of patronage that it was not unknown for an impecunious Aussie to line up before one early in the evening and later sell his place in the queue to an affluent, late-coming Yank.

General Headquarters kept making inquiries about our progress, which became less polite as time went on. Soon after the Paluma finally set off on 26 September, her water tanks burst and the Army patently lost faith in us. Luckily, she ran like a clock after that, and we redeemed ourselves. Mollison was safely landed at Sewa with a teleradio, lights, and motor dinghy. Then the Paluma carried on to Cape Nelson, where the reefs were thick and uncharted. The key point here was a reef situated 12 miles southeast of the Cape, and the first to sight it was Corporal L. P. V. Veale, one of the soldier crew. 'Veale Reef' is now its official name on the charts.

Marking it with a buoy on which a light could later be hung, the Paluma then passed on to Porlock Harbor, 40 miles from Buna, where Fairfax-Ross was landed with an assistant and three soldiers to push ahead to Oro Bay. The Paluma then moved back to the Cape Nelson area, where Hamilton was put ashore with a teleradio and lights. The bays in the area were then examined and a clear channel chosen. In this operation, the usual surveying procedure was reversed. Normally obstructions to navigation are charted. The Paluma crew searched out clear water and, except in a few instances, did not fix the position of anything else.

The Japanese at Buna took no notice of the insignificant vessel that seemed to be plodding aimlessly about to the southeast. They did not realize that here was the key which was opening the door to their back gate. After a time, the Paluma was joined by several other small vessels and a survey ship, and the prosaic search for channels went on until 4 November 1942, when Champion reported that the route was ready.

During this time, Australian troops had pushed the Japanese back along the grim Kokoda Trail and had hemmed them into an area of swamp fronting Buna and Sanananda. Then, harried by Japanese planes operating from Rabaul and Gasmata, the Australians hastily constructed airstrips inland of Buna. The Japanese held tenaciously to their earthworks and could not be routed out by light, airborne arms however, or by the strafing and bombing of our planes. Only sea transport, bringing up tanks and heavy guns, could destroy the enemy bastion.

Early in December, the Paluma led the Allied ships through to Oro Bay, the first sizable indentation southeast of Buna. Their movements were controlled from Port Moresby over FERDINAND teleradios. A good new cypher, called 'Bull' since it was prepared especially for FERDINAND, was supplied by the Navy. Heavy tanks, guns and troops were landed to spell, eventually, the end of the Japanese at Buna. At the end of the operation, the Paluma collected her shore parties and returned to Port Moresby. She had not had a dramatic mission. Probably the facets of the voyage most memorable to her crew were the heat, the overcrowding, the lack of ventilation. The work itself had been tedious, painstaking, and, it seemed at times, endless. And always, on everyone's mind, had been the nerve-racking realization that a slip-up might cause the loss of a transport or of the campaign.

16

WHILE PREPARATIONS WERE BEING MADE FOR the sea-borne assault on Buna, the Army was optimistic about the early fall of that bastion. The Japanese had lost a great part of their Air Force at Guadalcanal and during the earlier phase of the Buna battle. Their ships could not reach Buna in the face of Allied air superiority, and so their supplies came in only in driblets by submarine and barge.

Three divisions, two Australian and one American, were scheduled to attack Buna. These, it was believed, would also be adequate to retake Salamaua and Lae, north on the New Guinea coast, as soon as Buna fell. In this projected advance, warnings of enemy air attacks from Rabaul would be invaluable, just as Read's and Mason's warnings had been so vital to the success of Guadalcanal. So we were asked in November 1942 to place parties on the western half of New Britain and at Finschafen, across from New Britain on the New Guinea mainland.

At Vitiaz Straits, north of Finschafen, we had sixteen watchers, most of whom had been waiting for about eight months on the New Guinea coast and were demanding action. Among them were Bell, Douglas, and Olander, who had been brought off New Britain in June; 'Blue' Harris, who had made this area headquarters for his motley 'Navy'; J. B. McNicol, a half-caste; Captain L. Pursehouse, patrol officer at Finschafen; the Reverend A. P. H. Freund; three mission lay brothers, A. Obst, V. Neumann, and G. Kustis; Andrew Kirkwall-Smith, a man who had followed nearly every occupation the islands afforded; W. A. H. Butteris, B. G. Hall, and C. K. Johnson, planters; and Tupling and McColl, who had escaped from the Admiralty Islands early in the war. Among them they had six teleradios, five launches, and ample supplies.

It would be nice to record that these men had lived in courteous, considerate amicability during the time they waited on the coast, but it would not be true. A few, whose skill marked them for work on boats and radio sets, were reason ably busy and contented. The others, sturdy individualists all, with not enough to do, bickered, clashed, or brooded in petulant silence. They were continually sending us signals asking that the authority of this one or that one be defined, or that active work be given.

The only thing that really disturbed us about this situation was that their signals—some of which were particularly verbose—might well attract the attention of the Japanese. By the time we were ready to give them an assignment, they were using Palgrave's Golden Treasury as a source of keywords for their abundant signals.

Physically, they had not been badly off. Dr. Braun, at the American Lutheran Mission hospital near Madang, ministered to them when they were sick. On one occasion, for instance, Douglas capped an illness of malaria and asthma by breaking his denture, and was unable to eat as a convalescent should. We obtained materials for repairing it, dropped them by parachute, and Dr. Braun fixed the plate.

We decided to spread this party into six groups, stationed at Talasea on the northwestern New Britain coast, on Witu Island to the north, at Cape Gloucester at the western tip of New Britain, on Rooke Island between New Britain and the New Guinea mainland, at Arawe on the southwestern New Britain coast, and at Finschafen on the New Guinea mainland. From these posts, any movement from Rabaul to the neighborhood of Lae and Salamaua was certain to be observed.

Bell, who had already been requesting that we move him to Rooke Island, was assigned with Hall to that position on 16 November, and a few days later the other parties embarked. The launches traveled together to Rooke and then parted for the five destinations. Three days after the move commenced, all but the Arawe party were in position. First blood came from Bell, who reported five destroyers steaming southward through Vitiaz Straits, bound for Lae or Buna. Our aircraft sank at least two of the destroyers and drove the others back. In the meantime, however, Buna would not fall. The Japanese fought with a suicidal stubbornness, defending their foxholes to the last, wearing gas masks against the stench of their own rotting dead. Reduced to a few thousand, but buoyed by hope of relief, they held out. Meantime, our attacking troops were suffering far heavier battle casualties than the Army had expected, and malaria and dysentery were taking an even greater toll.

It was largely due to FERDINAND that the fanatic Japanese defenders were not getting the relief they expected. Earlier in the campaign we had fallen heir to four Allied Intelligence Bureau parties with mixed information and sabotage duties who had been made coastwatchers when it became evident they had little or no scope for sabotage. One of these parties, led by Lieutenant L. C. Noakes, former assistant geologist for the New Guinea Government, was situated near the mouth of the Mambare River, 40 miles northwest of Buna.

The Mambare debouches into the sea between low, muddy banks along which pipa palms stand knee-deep in water. Behind the palms, a creek here and there makes a tunnel in the dark mangrove jungles, the tunnel's treetrunk sides supported on a maze of gnarled, twisted, obscene roots in oozy mud. The sun never penetrates to these crocodile-haunted black waters.

Here the Japanese decided to make a landing and establish a bridgehead for the relief of Buna. This was a serious threat to us. The enemy might push up the Mambare, which could carry barges for 30 miles, and then swing southeast to take our troops in flank and rear. Noakes, who was camped on a small ridge about two miles from the mouth of the Mambare, heard aircraft one morning and suspected that a landing was being made. Slim, boyish, and enthusiastic, he was the perfect terrier. Sneaking through the swamp, he arrived at the edge of the Japanese encampment, noted the tents and supply dumps, and placed them in relation to a sandy beach easily seen from the air. Back at his camp, he hastily coded a signal giving the exact position of everything the Japanese had landed.

Next morning at daylight, our Bostons and Beaufighters swept the area with their machine guns. Useless was the careful camouflage of the Japanese. Telltale smoke rising through the jungle foliage apprised the pilots that they were hitting their mark. Run after run was made until the Japanese supplies were mostly wreckage and ashes, their barges sunk, and their men killed.

After the aircraft left, the remnant of the enemy troops shifted what few supplies were left, but again Noakes was watching and again he reported the new position. Again next morning, the aircraft came in at treetop height with spitting guns and more supplies went up in smoke. A few days later, the Japanese landed still more supplies and men at another position; Noakes found them and again our aircraft destroyed the dump. The Japanese then shifted their last remaining launch up a tree-covered creek where it was so well concealed that, in spite of Noakes' minute directions, it was three days before it was finally destroyed.

Refusing to give up, the enemy sent in still more barges with supplies. Noakes again crept through the noisome, crocodile-ridden swamp to within a few yards of the dump, and again signaled a report. For a month, the Japanese kept up the struggle to establish the beachhead, but finally they gave up and instead attempted to land at the mouth of the Waria River, somewhat farther north.

At the Waria, Bridge, whose adventures in Bougainville have already been related and who was another FERDINAND heritage from the discontinued A.I.B. operation, was upon them immediately. Although enemy patrols kept him at a distance from the camp, he was close enough to direct air attacks. The Japanese held their position for a few weeks, huddling in their trenches by day, and then withdrew. The threat to our Buna communications was completely frustrated. During the two series of attacks, there were a number of casualties among friendly natives, casualties for which the pilots could hardly be blamed in this instance.

For the speed of the aircraft was so great and the Japanese were so spread out, that a pilot had little time to distinguish whether figures were native or Japanese. Bridge's party itself was strafed by our own aircraft and one of his natives was killed and one wounded.

The Japanese High Command met the situation at Buna as best it could. Buna could not be saved for them, so their men were left to die. Meantime, while their troops at Buna still held, they arranged to create a fresh front of bases from Lae to Rabaul, supported by airfields in the rear, to meet our next advance.

Enemy convoys from the Carolines moved down to the New Guinea coast. Japanese troops occupied Wewak, Madang, and Finschafen in force. Some of the ships were sunk by our aircraft, but the move was successful. On the same day, 19 December 1942, other enemy convoys from Rabaul landed troops at Cape Gloucester and Arawe. On the day before the Japanese move, Bell reported that Hall was sick and that he was taking him across the straits to Dr. Braun's hospital. During the night he must have passed close to the convoy then approaching Finschafen. At Sio, on the New Guinea mainland, he found two Allied airmen and Douglas, who had remained behind because of illness when the six parties were sent out.

Bell took the three up the coast in his launch, to find that Japanese patrols were already in Bogadjim, closing the easy route inland to our airfield at Bena Bena. There was now only one way out for them; over the top of the 10,000-foot Finisterre Mountains. We instructed Bell to send Douglas and the airmen along this route, but to remain himself on the coast to assist the other parties. After two months of walking, Douglas and the fliers reached Bena Bena and were flown from there to Port Moresby.

The Cape Gloucester party, consisting of Kirkwall-Smith, Obst, and Butteris, had established itself in the rest house at a native village a little east of the Cape. The natives were friendly, and life went on about the watchers undisturbed. In the mornings the young men and women went out to the gardens, leaving the old men and women pottering about in the village. In the afternoon the men returned, followed by the women carrying taro in string bags suspended from their heads, a bundle of firewood above the taro, and, topping the load, a child perched with its legs dangling.

Kirkwall-Smith and his men saw no sign of the convoy that landed troops at Cape Gloucester. It approached from the north, at night. Next day the natives informed him that the Japanese had arrived, and he signaled the report, then set off by canoe to investigate, leaving Obst and Butteris in the village.

In the meantime, the Japanese had been told of the coastwatchers and at once a force was sent to wipe them out. Creeping close to the village in the dusk, a Japanese patrol opened fire on the houses. Obst, Butteris, and their natives escaped uninjured but without their arms, and took refuge in a small hut in the jungle.

Kirkwall-Smith, meantime, was returning by canoe, keeping close to the shore to escape observation. Suddenly, around a point, a barge appeared and opened fire. Kirkwall-Smith and his natives dived overboard and swam ashore. Next morning, unarmed and barefooted, he set out for camp. Obst and Butteris also made their way back to the village in the morning. The villagers reported the enemy had gone. Actually, the Japanese had left a small patrol in the jungle nearby. Whether any of the villagers were aware of this is not known. Still cautious, Butteris decided to remain in the jungle close to the village. But Obst returned to the rest house and lay down on the floor. It was raining, and possibly he had a fever. Also, being a missionary, he was apt to have more confidence in the natives than his fellow watchers.

Suddenly, from the side of the village opposite the rest house, a dozen Japanese rushed the hut. One fired through a crack in the split palm floor, wounding Obst in the head. With ferocious cries, they dragged him into the open and began to torture him.

Butteris saw it all from the jungle and his gorge rose as bestiality was piled on bestiality, until all else seemed worthless if this were allowed to go on. Chivalrously, foolishly, he rushed out unarmed and felled the nearest Japanese with his fist. The others fell upon him and soon subdued and bound him. Mercifully, Obst had been killed in the struggle.

Butteris and two of his natives were immediately taken by barge to Cape Gloucester. One of the natives, though bound, slid overboard in the dark and swam ashore. Butteris and the other were beheaded. Kirkwall-Smith, informed by natives of the fate of his companions, was also told the surprising fact that Neumann and his launch were not far away. Neumann, assigned to Witu Island, had been having trouble with the natives there and, not having had much experience with natives, had overestimated the probability of their damaging his boat. So he had moved to the New Britain coast, unfortunately commit ting the cardinal sin of not telling anyone of his move.

Kirkwall-Smith's own launch had been found by the Japanese, so he trudged on to Neumann, exhausted, his bare feet badly cut by the coral. Late next day, he found Neumann and the two set out in the launch for New Guinea.

Neumann's move had put Harris, McNicol, and Johnson, stationed near Talasea, in a serious predicament. Conditions had become too threatening for them to remain at their station, and their launch was in such poor condition that they were depending for escape on Neumann, whom they still believed to be at Witu. Ordered to retire, they reached that island where the engine of their launch broke down completely.

From FERDINAND headquarters we signaled Neumann to pick up Harris' party. But before he received the signal, he and Kirkwall-Smith had already reached the New Guinea coast and had joined Bell. We then ordered Bell to take the launch and rescue Harris. At this point, the native crew refused to make the dangerous trip again, and, to add to Bell's troubles, Neumann developed cellulitis in the arm. Bell was forced to suspend his efforts to make the rescue trip while he treated Neumann under teleradio directions from the naval doctor at Port Moresby.

As though luck were not already sufficiently against us, one of our aircraft now bombed and strafed Bell's position, wounding a half-caste member of the party. This put the final seal on the distrust of the natives and quashed any hopes Bell might have had of regaining their co-operation. To ensure that they would not be shanghaied aboard the launch, they slipped her mooring lines, and, in the morning, it was a complete wreck on the reef.

At Witu, Harris had found an abandoned launch in very bad condition. While he was desperately trying to put it in order, a Japanese patrol plane flew over and spotted him. Next day for three hours his position was bombed and strafed by ten aircraft, but without injury either to the men or the teleradio. He signaled his predicament and we turned to our old friends, the Catalinas.

On the night of 18 January 1943, the rescue plane with McCarthy aboard as guide landed in the bright moonlight in the large submerged crater of Johann Albrech Harbour at Witu and taxied to the eastern shore of the basin. A canoe glided toward the aircraft in the shadow. 'Is that you, Blue?' called McCarthy. 'Yes,' came the answer. 'Will you have room for my dog as well as everything else?'

The dog, the teleradio, Harris, his two assistants, and two police were all taken on board and then the Catalina waited, silent under the shadow of the steep side of the crater, so that the landing might be made in daylight at Port Moresby. At 2 a.m. the engines roared into life and the Catalina sped across the flat, moonlit basin. As she cleared the island, signal flares were seen rising from the northern shore. A Japanese ship had been sunk about 50 miles to the north that afternoon and apparently these signals were from survivors who were expecting a plane of their own to land on the tiny island. 'Blue' Harris had been lucky. He had gotten away at the last possible moment.

Olander and Tupling, who had been dispatched to Arawe on the southwestern coast of New Britain, had not been able to reach their station before the Japanese occupation. The sea around Arawe was littered with reefs and was uncharted, so that Olander had found it impossible to take the launch through in darkness, while to move by day was to invite attack from enemy aircraft. A week before the Japanese landing at Arawe and Cape Gloucester, he signaled us that he intended to go forward to Arawe by canoe, leaving Tupling to follow in the launch at full moon. This was the last word we received from either man. Realizing that Olander's arrival at Arawe would have coincided, roughly, with the Japanese occupation, we concluded that he encountered the most disastrous situation in the catalog of coastwatcher dangers; arrival at a place at the same time as an enemy force.

Our supposition was confirmed a year later when we learned from natives that Olander, unsuspectingly on the heels of the Japanese, had paddled into Arawe and had been shot as he landed. Pro-Japanese natives had then led a patrol to Tupling, who was hunted down and killed.

When the Japanese landed at Finschafen, Freund was at nearby Sattelberg, while the other two members of his party, Pursehouse and McColl, were further southwest, overlooking the Japanese post of Hopoi. The natives around Sattelberg became restless immediately the Japanese landed. They were all adherents of the German Lutheran Mission, some of whose workers were Nazis and had been interned. Even the non-Nazi missionaries at this station had taught the natives that this was not their war and that they should remain neutral in the event of invasion. One missionary, Wagner, was still at the mission when the Japanese landed.

The natives requested Freund to leave so that they could make their own terms with the Japanese. They provided him with carriers and he sensibly withdrew inland, taking his teleradio with him.

When, a few days later, a patrol of Japanese visited Sattelberg, Wagner and the leading natives met the troops and expressed their desire for neutrality. The Japanese reply was unequivocal. Sattelberg was now part of the Empire of Nippon; religious and other teachings were to cease; the natives were to supply labor and food when called upon; there would be no neutrality.

As soon as the patrol returned to Finschafen, Wagner advised the natives to assist our coastwatchers by every means in their power, and then he set out for the high mountains of the interior, where he hid until our forces later recaptured the area.

Pursehouse and McColl joined Freund a few days after he left Sattelberg, and made a rear base at which Freund was left with a teleradio while Pursehouse and McColl went forward to reconnoiter Finschafen. By night they stole in close to the enemy camp, counted the guns, located defense works and huts, and estimated the numbers of the enemy and the areas occupied.

Then, examining an abandoned airfield to the north, they saw that its twelve-month growth of tropical vegetation was not being cleared and concluded that the enemy's Finschafen position was a staging point for barges supplying Lae and Salamaua. They signaled us the results of their scouting expedition and then, establishing an observation post in the jungle near Sattelberg, settled down to watching and reporting the enemy's comings and goings.

At last, at the end of January 1943, Buna fell. But our hopes of an early advance on Salamaua and Lae, for which the coastwatcher parties had been prepared, had already evaporated. Battle casualties, malaria, dysentery, hookworm, and tropical ulcers had taken such a toll of the three Allied divisions at Buna that the troops were in no condition to undertake a further campaign.

FERDINAND's venture to cover the advance which did not take place, though the best organized and executed operation we had carried out up to this time, had ended in complete failure except at Finschafen. We had lost a quarter of the personnel dispatched to New Britain, and those left had been either driven out or were in danger.

The enemy now held the whole north coast of New Guinea from the Dutch border to Lae, the whole of New Britain and of New Ireland. FERDINAND's plans, which had anticipated an early attack on Rabaul and a quick end to operations in the New Guinea area, had to be recast for a long, slow campaign with victory in the distant future.

Australian assault units approach Balikpapan

17

IN NEW GUINEA, AS IN THE SOLOMONS, the first half of 1943 was a period of preparation, a lull in battle, while the Allied forces prepared to attack, and the enemy entrenched himself in newly invaded territory. For FERDINAND, however, the New Guinea 'lull' represented one of our most harrowing periods.

Although we knew that occupation by the Japanese could only cause progressive deterioration in the native attitude, we also felt that, in spite of the risk, we must keep men in New Guinea to observe the enemy's activities. So with a calculated imprudence, paradoxical as that may sound, we sent more men into the enemy-riddled New Guinea mainland to weave hunted trails westward to the Dutch border.

One of Allied Headquarters' most urgent intelligence needs involved the Japanese forces at Wewak, on the New Guinea coast northwest of the great Sepik River. We had already anticipated this need as soon as the Japanese moved into that area and had organized a party under Captain A. H. J. Fryer, an oil surveyor who had previously been employed north of the Sepik.

He and his party had sat in Port Moresby for weeks, cooling their heels, while we tried vainly to get them air transport to the Sepik. Finally, together with a Dutch party, they had been flown to Bena Bena and from there had set out on an arduous 300-mile tramp to their destination.

When, early in 1943, Allied Headquarters pressed us for information from Wewak, Fryer's party and the Dutch group, which was bound for the Dutch side of the border, were trudging across the center of New Guinea.

Fortunately, we had another party available, commanded by Captain L. E. Ashton, who had been an assistant resident magistrate in Papua but, caught by the lure of gold, had resigned fifteen years before to mine in New Guinea. He was now in his forties and graying, but his springy, energetic step still belied the lazy drawl of his voice. As assistants he had Hamilton and Veale from the Paluma, and Lieutenant G. R. Archer, a quiet dour young miner who had fought the Japanese at Salamaua, two native police, and two natives trained in propaganda.

The Sepik River, to which this group was flown by Catalina, is one of the evil places of the earth. Lying between the coastal

Torricelli Mountains and the central massif, a hundred miles to the south, it drains the enormous amount of water precipitated in this great valley. And that describes the Sepik; a big, dirty drain winding sinuously through a swamp 200 miles long and 20 miles wide. Here and there, horseshoe-shaped cut-offs lie stagnant and weed-covered. A hundred miles from the mouth, at the point where Ashton's party was landed, a low range of hills stands in the swamp.

In March and April at the end of the northwest monsoon, the river is in constant flood, reaching beneath the high stilts of the native houses built on its marshes. In the center of the vast stream, the dirty, brown water rushes madly, bearing a procession of flotsam. Sometimes an island of matted floating grass, an acre in area, is swirled along. When the waters fall, they reveal oozing mud banks on which crocodiles bask in the sun.

The natives, dark brown Papuans with Semitic features, were ardent headhunters until fifteen years before the war. Each village was in constant strife with its neighbors, and the possessor of many heads was loud in the village council. The practice was untarnished by any code of chivalry; one head was as good as another, however obtained. A man wishing to launch a favored son in life would sometimes purchase a child captive and allow his son to kill her and so qualify as a man.

Everything in this people's environment offers a dismal prospect. For example, the millions of mosquitoes, rising from the unlimited breeding grounds of the swamps, are a curse and a menace, deterred by nothing. In voracious hordes, they settle on any exposed skin, sucking blood painfully from the victim so that only by retreat under some sort of net can any relief be obtained. The natives sleep in baskets of closely woven rushes, in which less air is admitted than in burlap sacking. Into these foul, airless containers, sometimes 20 feet long and about 3 feet high, a whole family crawls, rolling a piece of wood over the end to close it. By day each man carries a whisk broom made from the backbone of a sago leaf, with which he constantly switches.

The native food consists largely of sago, garnished sometimes with fish, pig, or dried mayflies. A more repulsive food than sago can hardly be imagined. It is made from the brown pith of the sago palm, which is beaten to friability and then washed in a trough. The washed fiber is thrown away while the sago, which is almost entirely starch, settles in a grayish deposit on the bottom. It is scraped up and stored in earthenware jars, kept wet so that the starch ferments and stinks with its own peculiar acrid smell. However cooked, it is glutinous and tasteless and, to those not inured to it by years of consumption, it leaves the belly distended with the feeling of hunger unappeased.

Bound by their swamps, with no horizon beyond the bend of the river, the distant blue mountains as unattainable as the stars, tortured by mosquitoes, the Sepik natives had evolved a life in which no man in any circumstances forgave his enemy. Their only relaxation from the grim duty of killing their neighbors occurred during the low-water season, when they indulged in orgiastic dances in which the sex unbalance resulting from polygamy was redressed. At these times, the adolescent boys were cut about the arms, breasts, and back; the cuts treated to leave up-raised scars. Yet, in spite of their sinister practices, most Europeans who had come in contact with Sepiks rather liked them; there was no hypocrisy in them, at least.

When the Government had at last come to the Sepik it had shot some natives and hanged others until a forced peace settled over the swamps. Most of the young men then went away to work and to see the outside world, while Catholic missionaries moved in and established stations, gaining converts under the new conditions. After war with Japan broke out, the Government had left, and the old enmities again came to the surface. A few missionaries remained, maintaining some semblance of uneasy peace.

This was the area in which Ashton and his men were landed, and, as might be expected, they met with difficulties at once. To make the overland trip to Wewak, they required more than a hundred carriers for their extensive supplies and equipment, and it was almost impossible to obtain this number. The natives were afraid to travel toward Wewak, as they had heard rumors that the Japanese had moved inland. On the river itself, the nearest Japanese were at Marienburg, 60 miles, airline, downstream.

Making up their expedition each morning was a nerve-racking task for the party. Sometimes sufficient carriers for all but the last 20 packs would present themselves, and the whole line would have to wait while numerous other carrier recruits hung about out of sight, watching to see whether it was possible to steal anything without making the trip.

The first day's journey toward Wewak was through swamp. Next day, with the mosquitoes undiminished, the swamps lay between hardly discernible ridges of coarse kunai grass. As the party progressed, the kunai ridges became broader and higher, the swamps narrower and the mosquitoes less ubiquitous. Ahead, the top of Mount Turu, the last and highest peak on the Torricelli Mountains before that range falls away to foothills, turned from blue to green as the distance lessened.

All this while, the party was moving through the country of the garamuts. The garamut is a wooden slit-gong, a section of the trunk of a tree hollowed out through a narrow opening which, when beaten by a length of sapling in piledriver fashion, produces a sound that carries miles. Some garamuts are ten feet long, hollowed from a trunk four feet in diameter. These produce a dull, reverberating boom, while smaller garamuts give a higher note. A code, common to the various language groups, carries garamut messages from village to village.

Every time Ashton's group left one village, the garamuts would strike up, telling the next village that the party was on its way. Ashton bribed and threatened, but could not silence them. As a countermeasure, he conscripted two natives from each village so that their relatives would warn them of any Japanese approach.

About twenty miles from Wewak, the party left supplies at a deserted mining camp. Two missionaries nearby, who had not been disturbed by the war, could tell Ashton nothing of the Japanese forces. A day's further journey, however, brought the watchers into an area where the natives were obeying the Japanese' orders to send laborers to Wewak.

They had accepted the Japanese as the new Government, having seen the precipitate retirement of the Europeans and having reasoned that men who would not stay to fight would not return.

Ashton reconnoitered Mount Turu as a lookout, but found it too far from Wewak and too often obscured in cloudbanks. Moving toward Wewak, he found a site on a ridge from which the Wewak peninsula, with the airfield across its base and the anchorage alongside, could be seen.

Resolving to stay at this post if possible, the party made camp on the evening of 31 March. But shortly after midnight a friendly native warned them that a Japanese patrol was hunting them and was only two hours away, while another patrol was moving to cut them off. The garamuts had done their work.

Ashton immediately broke camp and moved westward. The natives through whose villages they passed that day resented their presence, fearing it would bring Japanese reprisals. At some places obstructions were put across the track, and at others the party had to move through jungle to avoid meeting open hostility in the villages.

At sundown, tired out, they camped but again they were away at daylight next morning. The only hope of evading the pursuing patrols was to travel fast until distance from Wewak deterred the Japanese from following further.

By late afternoon, they felt that they had outdistanced their pursuers for the day and that they could stop long enough to send a signal to McCarthy at Port Moresby. They stopped at a village rest house, set up the aerial of their portable radio, and prepared a signal. Meantime, they had taken off their sweat-drenched clothes and replaced them with dry shorts, while all but Veale had taken off their boots to allow their feet, softened by constant sweating and wetting, to dry and harden.

While Hamilton was adjusting the transmitter and the others were coding, a shot rang out from the front of the hut, followed by a yell and a fusilade of shots into the house. A hurried glance showed half a dozen Japanese firing from the front of the house and another half dozen firing from the left. The coastwatchers threw themselves out of the back door and a few seconds later a grenade exploded in the house.

The four dashed toward a belt of trees, while the natives disappeared. Somehow, Hamilton became separated from the other three. Consulting together, Ashton, Archer, and Veale decided to set out for the Sepik, traveling by night and hiding by day. Alone, Hamilton made the same decision.

All were clad only in short trousers, and Veale alone had boots. The first part of the journey lay across kunai plains intersected by patches of swamp and bush. The butts of the kunai bruised their bare feet while in the swamps sago thorns tore at their flesh.

But with no food or equipment, constantly stung by vicious hordes of mosquitoes, and with the Southern Cross for guide, the three pushed on through the night. By day they slept uneasily in a patch of jungle, then with nightfall pushed on again. Veale unselfishly handed over his boots to Ashton, whose feet were the first to give out.

On the third night, they entered a swamp and were ten hours crossing it in the dark, floundering from one mudhole to another and, as always, plagued by mosquitoes. Leaving their hideout early the next evening, they were seen by natives, who became threatening. Ashton, holding a large nut in his pocket, which he told them was a grenade, demanded food and was grudgingly given a pawpaw.

At the end of the fifth night, a night of torture from myriads of mosquitoes and burning thorns in their hands and feet, the three reached the river village of Marui, close to the point at which they had been flown in. There a missionary, Father Hansen, fed and clothed them and told them the good news that Hamilton had arrived the day before and that the natives of the party had also escaped.

Hamilton, on getting clear of the house after the attack, had been sure that the others were also safe and had reasoned that an attempt to find them in the dark would be a waste of time and a risk. He had set off at once and upon arriving at a creek had decided to follow it to the Sepik, since all streams on this side of the range lead to the one great river.

By night, he had followed the stream, wading in mud most of the way, and each dawn he had rolled in mud until he was completely covered as a protection against the mosquitoes while he slept. On his last night he had to swim several times. His guardian angel must have been constantly alert to protect him from the crocodiles.

The recuperating watchers learned from friendly natives that their reserve supplies had been pillaged. Better news was that an Angau party, under Captain J. L. Taylor, was in the area.

Ashton and his men, rejoined by the native police who had escaped to the Sepik in the same manner as the Europeans, moved some miles upstream to meet Taylor. They not only found him, but on the same night were joined by Fryer's group and the Dutch party, who had spent three months in walking a distance which could have been flown in three hours.

On 31 April, a fortnight after the three groups had come together, a Catalina was flown in with supplies, and Ashton's party was brought out.

We had planned to assign Fryer's party to keep watch on Japanese developments at Vanimo and Aitape, close to the Dutch border, while the Dutch group was to strike off for the hinterland of Hollandia. It was plain, however, that any group attempting close observation of the enemy would not last long, so Fryer was ordered instead to remain on the southern side of the Torricelli range and to try to build a 'grapevine' through the villages to the coast.

With him he had three men, Lieutenant H. A. Aikon, who had worked with him on oil surveying jobs north of the Sepik before the war; Lieutenant G. B. Black, who had been a clerk with the New Guinea administration; and Navy Supply Assistant W. B. Baillie, the signaler, who had had no previous experience in New Guinea. Several natives had gone in with the party and Fryer had recruited more on the journey from Bena.

The Dutch party, commanded by Sergeant Stavermann, included an Australian signaler, Sergeant Siffleet, and two Indonesians, Pattiwal and Reharing. None of its personnel had been south of the Sepik, so Fryer had served as its mentor and guide on the trip to the river.

After Ashton's party was flown out, these two groups crossed the Sepik together and reached the firm ground beyond. Then they separated, the Dutch making their way northwestward toward Hollandia while Fryer established a base in the area into which Japanese influence had not penetrated.

From his base, Fryer sent natives to collect information from the villages to the north. But the natives there were hostile, and in any case, they knew little. So the party largely marked time, traveling among the natives nearby to establish confidence in case the Japanese pushed in. Our forces were not contemplating operations in that part of the country, so the lack of information was not too serious.

Meantime, news filtered back to Fryer that disaster had overtaken the Dutch party. Stavermann and Pattiwal were killed near the border, and later Siffleet and Reharing were captured while attempting to return.

In early September 1943, on one of their confidence-building rounds, Fryer and Aikon with some of their natives visited Seinum village, about 40 miles south of Aitape. A large number of people gathered from other nearby villages, and Fryer was addressing them from the verandah of a hut. Since the natives were unarmed, Fryer was not suspicious, but ordinary caution had prompted him to place an armed native on guard behind the door of the house.

Suddenly, one native gave a shout and threw himself on Fryer. It was a general signal for all natives to attack the party. The guard's rifle misfired, and the natives swarmed over the two coastwatchers. Aikon, struggling with several natives, managed to fire a rifle. The sound of the shot momentarily demoralized the attackers, and Aikon, with his second shot, killed the leader. The natives ran and he threw a few grenades, which completed the rout. From the surrounding jungle, however, the natives continued to fire arrows at the coastwatchers as they retreated. The attack, Fryer discovered, had been made at the instigation of the Japanese.

It was plain that our men were going to find it almost impossible to obtain information while the natives were not on our side. It was also plain that the natives would not be on our side until they were convinced, we were winning. In this predicament, it was suggested that a larger force be sent to the Sepik, upon which smaller parties could retire if pressed. The idea was attractive. Angau was keen to try it and the Army agreed, since it seemed to be the only alternative to withdrawal. Angau organized the party, about 75 in number, and control of all operations on the Sepik passed to Angau, McCarthy being given an appointment on its staff to ensure liaison.

The Angau party was flown in and a camp established on a Sepik tributary nearly 200 miles from the mouth of the river. It was not a well-selected site, for it could be reached by barge. The Japanese soon heard of its presence and sent a small force to attack it. When this attack was beaten back, Japanese aircraft bombed the camp. The party was too large for mobility, and it was only a question of time before a large force would be sent to wipe it out.

So it was withdrawn, and with it Fryer and his men and an Allied Intelligence Bureau propagandist, who had been working to the west of Fryer. Fryer and the propagandist could have remained where they were indefinitely, although they probably would not have been able to obtain information of any immediate value. God was still on the side of the big battalions, but He will sometimes close an indulgent eye on a small, unobtrusive force.

At about the same time as Fryer's group had set out from Bena, early in the year, another of our parties under command of Lieutenant G. Greathead, a former patrol officer, was dispatched from Bena toward Madang. Before he crossed the Ramu River, less than halfway to his destination, rumors reached him that the Japanese were patrolling the other side of it. Since his scouts brought him word, however, that the area was clear, he crossed to the east bank of the river. He had not gone far when he was warned that a patrol of a hundred Japanese was close by, guided by a captured American Lutheran missionary.

He recrossed the Ramu and withdrew into the highlands, where he learned that the American missionary had been forced into his role of guide much against his will, and that he had attempted to escape and had been recaptured and executed. Another captured missionary, he learned, was the good Dr. Braun, who had treated our sick coastwatchers before the ill-fated New Britain expeditions. Braun survived, however, to be released more than a year later.

Greathead and his party swung northwestward, across the open highlands to the west of the river, where carriers were plentiful and Japanese influence had not penetrated. From Mount Hagen, the group then walked eastward, its course leading through an area not previously traversed by Europeans. The track grew rougher, deep valleys intervening, the crossing of which exhausted the party and slowed it to a snail's pace. The Stone Age inhabitants, regarding all strangers as enemies, resented the intrusion but, experienced in dealing with natives, Greathead and his men were generally able to pass peacefully through the villages and to buy native foods with trade goods.

About the middle of March, the men again cut to the Ramu River, where they found a group of Europeans who had evacuated from the coast. One of Greathead's men was ill and the party's supplies were running low, so it made camp and signaled for a supply-drop. After many delays, a Liberator was detailed for the duty, with Leigh Vial, the 'golden voiced' watcher who had warned Port Moresby of raids in the early days of the war, as guide. In the mountains over Central New Guinea the Liberator crashed, killing Vial and the entire crew.

It was not until May that supplies were finally dropped to Greathead. By this time he had decided to move to the high land country again and, since the Japanese were patrolling actively west of Madang and there was danger that they might penetrate to Bena, he was ordered to Mount Hagen to keep the airfield there available to us if Bena Bena were lost. Here his party settled down to a negative role, until it was eventually withdrawn.

At Finschafen, where Freund, Pursehouse, and McColl were stationed, the high mountains inland had deterred the Japanese from penetrating further than Sattelberg. Three days' journey inland, Freund was camped with his radio. He was the rear base for Pursehouse and McColl, who were keeping watch on Finschafen from a forward position.

These two lived in a hut well hidden in a jungle-covered gully at some distance from the tracks normally used by natives. The jungle screened them from view and only a few local natives, who had not fraternized with the Japanese, knew where it was. A path led through a belt of bamboos to a point on a ridge from which Finschafen, Vitiaz Straits, and the sea to the southeast could be seen. Turn by turn, Pursehouse and McColl watched from this observation post. On some days, they saw barges or aircraft, on most days nothing.

On a day in March, they saw a Japanese convoy of 22 ships making for Lae. The convoy had already been spotted from the air and the two men watched our aircraft attack from masthead height, through a storm of anti-aircraft fire, to sink the enemy vessels. It was the Battle of the Bismarck Sea, a battle which so asserted our air supremacy that there after the Japanese could no longer send ships, other than barges and submarines, to Lae. From the beach the watchers' scouts learned the number of Japanese who had survived and made the shore.

The morning of 3 April was McColl's turn to watch. He walked down the path toward the observation post, his Owen gun in his hands, leaving Pursehouse in the hut. As he reached a turn in the path, he was suddenly fired at from the bamboos. He could see nothing in the shadows, but blazed a magazine in reply, then turned and ran. He had gone only a few yards when he slipped and fell. Several Japanese rushed him and fired from a range of a few yards as he scrambled to his feet, his empty gun still in his hands. Again he ran, miraculously still unhit, and gained the cover of the jungle. His spare magazine had been jolted from his pack when he fell, and he made for the hut where there was more ammunition. But the Japanese were there before him. He watched them surround it, fire into it, then rush and capture it, empty.

Pursehouse and McColl had long before made their plans for just such an emergency. They had reasoned that if one were fired at and hit, the other could do nothing to help him, while if he were unhit he could make his own escape without aid. So at the first sound of firing, Pursehouse retired to the jungle.

Both made their ways separately to the rear and at the end of the day met in a village. Together they moved to Freund's camp and signaled their news.

Natives had betrayed the position of the post and they could be expected to do it again. Freund, McColl, and Pursehouse were therefore ordered to withdraw to Bena Bena and from there were flown to Port Moresby. Just before the attack we had formed another party to operate in the Finschafen area but, realizing that the expedition would be suicidal, we abandoned this plan.

Yet one more tale of failure during the 'lull' remains to be told.

At Saidor, on the New Guinea side of Vitiaz Straits, Bell and Hall had remained hidden after the Japanese advance. They were in a place that appeared as safe from enemy attention as any in New Guinea. Their part of the coast, which runs parallel to the Finisterre range, is known as the Rai Coast, because at Madang to the north it seems to be from here that the 'Rai,' the southeast monsoon wind, comes. On the Rai Coast, the mountains rise abruptly from the sea, spurs leading directly from the water to the blue, cloud-covered peaks which rise 10 to 14 thousand feet. Here are no kindly, gentle slopes, but soaring cliffs, razor-backed ridges, and deep valleys overhung by jagged rocks. Jungle covers all but the bare stone of the cliff faces; steaming, tropical jungle on the lower slopes; moss-covered trees growing out of moss-covered ground at the higher altitudes, where the clouds settle in a gray, dank mist.

Halfway along the Rai Coast, nature had left a level ridge, which, after many years of over-cultivation by the natives, had become covered with kunai grass. In peacetime, this had been cleared to make a landing strip, and its name, Saidor, had thus become known to the outside world.

The mountainous shores, the lack of roads, the scarcity of anything useful, and the distance from a settlement made the Rai Coast an unlikely spot for enemy occupation. The scattered native population had had no contact whatever with the Japanese. Ordinarily, in these circumstances, we should not have been fearful for our men.

But Bell and Hall had been in these rugged, steaming jungles for a year. Their health could not be expected to hold out much longer, and with a deterioration in health would inevitably come a slackening of initiative and vigilance.

To relieve them, we formed a party from Paluma personnel. Led by Fairfax-Ross, it included Lieutenant D. A. Laws and four soldiers. Laws was the radio technician who had succeeded in escaping from New Britain by launch in the early days of the war. He was to put Bell's teleradio in order and then return with Bell and Hall.

On 9 February 1943, the party landed at Bena Bena. Eight days later, on foot, the men crossed the Ramu River and slipped quietly by night across the flat Japanese-patrolled valley to the foothills of the Finisterres.

From here, the men followed rudimentary tracks up steep slopes, where hands and feet had to scramble to gain a hold, down precipitous banks to boulder-strewn streambeds, through icy water and up again over slippery rocks and greasy red clay. They sweated until the green shirts clung to their shoulders, while at every stop their wet feet chilled. Leeches in thousands infested the track, clinging to feet and legs and sucking the men's blood until, at a halt, they would be burned off with the lighted end of a cigarette.

At last, after fourteen days, they reached the summit, where the rarity of the atmosphere made breathing a labor and every step an effort. Slowly they descended, the moss-covered heights giving way to tropic jungle. In early March, down near the coast, they met Bell and Hall at a village inland of Saidor.

Fairfax-Ross at once established a base, hid supplies in subsidiary bases, and appointed trustworthy natives to guard against looting. FERDINAND dropped more supplies at Saidor, the only open space for miles. All seemed well.

But the Rai Coast was not to remain such a convenient backwater. The Battle of the Bismarck Sea, won by our forces, made it impossible for the Japanese to get ships through to Lae and Salamaua. So they instituted a barge service to these points from Rabaul and Madang. The barges from Madang naturally followed the Rai Coast, and one of the staging points selected was Saidor. Three weeks after Fairfax-Ross and his men arrived, the Japanese landed at Saidor, while other enemy patrols moved along the coast from Madang.

Fairfax-Ross immediately reported the landing and the positions of the patrols. Our aircraft strafed and bombed the Japanese positions but, because of the concealment of the thick jungle, with little effect.

The natives were impressed by the enemies' numbers and terrified by the savage punishment meted out to those of them who disobeyed. Most tried to be neutral, some openly assisted the Japanese, and a few remained loyal to the coastwatchers, helping them with food and information at great danger to themselves.

In the early days of the war, most enemy landings had been made by Japanese Special Naval-Landing Parties.

As Navy's interest had been to hold only the bases, the Japanese, except for short, perfunctory patrol expeditions, had not usually moved into the hinterland. But the landing at Saidor, like the other landings on the New Guinea mainland, was made by the Japanese Army. Although the mission of these troops was primarily to defend bases for the use of the Navy, they were true to the Army policy of conquering the country, and did not hesitate to send strong forces out to comb the hinterland.

Late in March, one of these patrols was led by natives to Maibang, a village where Fairfax-Ross and some of his party were camped. At the same time, other natives led a second Japanese patrol to cut off the men's retreat. Fortunately, this body was seen by the second portion of Fairfax-Ross's party, camped nearby.

The enemy platoon was led past the coastwatchers' sentries and, unnoticed, gained Maibang and rushed the camp. In the melee which followed, Fairfax-Ross was wounded in the hand and knee by a bayonet, but he and the others successfully shot their way out. At the sound of firing, the second group of coastwatchers attacked the other Japanese patrol and kept open the retreat.

The attack impressed the natives with the power of the Japanese, and further native defections promptly followed. The Japanese were led to two of the supply hideouts, which seriously reduced the provisions of the watchers. They're treated to the higher mountains, where Fairfax-Ross developed pneumonia but was nursed back to health.

On 2 May, Bell, Laws, and a half-caste who had hidden at Saidor left for Bena, Hall remaining with Fairfax-Ross. Bell and Laws had come through much more dangerous situations, and merely to walk out to safety appeared the easiest assignment they had yet been given.

For a year, however, nothing more was heard of the two men or their companion. Then, after reconquest of that part of the country, we learned that natives who had met them in apparent friendship and were carrying their equipment, treacherously turned on them and killed them. Whether or not the attack was Japanese-inspired was never established. The loss was a severe blow. Bell was a courageous, self-reliant man, of whom there can never be too many. Laws, as a radio technician who understood our needs and difficulties, was never fully replaced.

Back in the mountains near Saidor, Fairfax-Ross set himself to discover a site at which supplies could be dropped. But the jungle-covered ranges were all alike from the air, and there were no accurate maps of the area.

Food was running short. Japanese patrols, a hundred to two hundred strong, were searching for the watchers, and another affray would cause the loss of the few supplies that remained. Even if there were no casualties, the party would be liquidated by starvation.

Withdrawal was the only course open, and Fairfax-Ross was ordered to return to Bena. Just before he and his men began their journey, they reported two small steamers bound for Madang and then watched our aircraft sweep in and sink them. To the men in the mountains, leaving their post, it was one last satisfaction.

The return journey over the Finisterres was even grimmer than the trip out. Food was short, boots were wearing out, and the natives were frightened and unhelpful, in one place even attacking the watchers with an arrow fusillade. One of our aircraft, sent to drop supplies, mistook the location of the track and deposited its load in enemy territory. The mountain trip, which had taken two weeks when the men were fresh, took the now weary and haggard party half again as long.

When they reached the dangerous valley of the Ramu, however, they at last had a piece of luck. A friendly native chief helped them cross at night among the Japanese patrols. Then, in safety, they toiled wearily on to Bena, where they augmented the small force which was holding that area against an expected Japanese attack; which fortunately did not eventuate.

Finally, they were flown out to Port Moresby and sent to Australia to recuperate. Sergeant Hall was awarded the Distinguished Conduct Medal for his long Rai Coast watch and was commissioned.

Bridge, who had helped prevent the Japanese from reinforcing Buna, remained in the Morobe area. While Australian troops were defeating the attack on Wau, inland from Salamaua, and driving the enemy back in what was probably the hardest fighting of the Pacific war, Bridge led an American intelligence party toward Salamaua. This group discovered that the farthest Japanese outposts, lightly held, were at Nassau Bay. The Americans returned to their division, which was to attack the area they and Bridge had reconnoitered.

In spite of this and a few other small successes, it was evident that only an advance in strength, an advance that would hit the Japanese so hard that its effect could not be concealed from the natives, would make it possible for FERDINAND really to operate in New Guinea.

18

ON 30 JUNE 1943, THE SAME DAY THE Allies attacked Munda in the Solomons, the offensive in New Guinea was launched. The first landing was made at Nassau Bay, where Bridge had continued to supply information of the enemy's strength. From this beachhead American troops attacked Salamaua, while Australians who had fought down from Wau attacked outposts on the inland side of the enemy base.

For the New Guinea offensive, FERDINAND personnel was absorbed into the landing Amphibious Force. A group, including Harris, Pursehouse, Noakes, and Kirkwall-Smith, was sent to a special training school, where they practiced landing from rubber boats under all conditions, and in turn lectured Army and Navy officers on jungle traveling, pidgin English, and the handling of natives.

Bridge's continuous reports of the enemy's weakness at Nassau Bay were confirmed by the landing forces which soon made a junction with the Australian troops behind Salamaua. As soon as the beachhead had been established, Bridge was sent on leave.

With the enemy troops at Salamaua pinned down, Lae was now ripe for the taking. American paratroopers were dropped 25 miles to the west of Lae, where they prepared an airstrip on which an Australian division was landed. On 6 September, while the airborne division was pushing down the valley toward Lae, another Australian division was landed on the coast, twelve miles to the east of the Japanese stronghold. Two FERDINAND men landed with this force but, as the whole operation moved with clock-like precision, their services were not required. Lae was soon taken, and Salamaua fell immediately afterwards, leaving Finschafen next on the list.

For the Finschafen attack, a landing beach a few miles to the north was chosen. To determine depth of water offshore, declivity of the beach, area and nature of the flatland nearby, and tracks leading off the beach, an Amphibious Force party, of which Harris was a member, made a reconnaissance.

Unobserved, the party landed in rubber boats launched from PT boats and hid in the strip of jungle fringing the shore. All day the men crouched in the undergrowth, while Japanese passed back and forth along the road only a few yards away. That night the men stealthily took soundings and made measurements, then took to the jungle again before daybreak.

To keep the Japanese occupied, it had been arranged for our aircraft to bomb Finschafen while the reconnaissance party was ashore. Some enthusiast decided that a greater measure of safety would be achieved if the bombing were extended nearly to the party's refuge. As the crash of bombs came close to the road, a band of Japanese scattered to the jungle where Harris and the others were hidden.

Crouched under some ferns, Harris suddenly heard a rattle in the undergrowth nearby. He turned his head and found himself staring into the eyes of a Japanese. Harris was in a quandary. He did not know whether to shoot the Japanese and so risk calling attention to himself, or to let him live and risk having the party reported. While these alternatives flashed through his head, the Japanese solved the problem by dashing away. No hue and cry followed, so Harris could only assume that the Japanese either mistook him for one of his own side or decided that he was bomb-happy and seeing things.

A week after the party was safely withdrawn, the Australians landed and quickly took Finschafen, though Sattelberg was not captured until two months later.

Late in September, the Amphibious Force sent Kirkwall-Smith with four American soldiers and four natives to Grass Point, south of Cape Gloucester, the tip of New Britain. Kirkwall-Smith protested before leaving that the party was too large for mobility, but he was overruled. Once ashore, he fixed things to suit himself. He placed three of the Americans in a hideout in the thickest part of the jungle. With the others and the natives he spent the next ten days traveling over a large area and speaking to many villagers.

The natives could tell him little about the enemy, for they had all been excluded from the Cape Gloucester base for the past two months. He did learn, however, that there had been a decided change in native attitude since the earlier acceptance of and obedience to Japanese domination. Rapes, robberies, and murders had convinced the Cape Gloucester natives that there was no good in the Japanese.

One instance in particular had caused universal resentment. An old man who lived alone in the jungle had been visited by Japanese troops, who began pulling up the young, still in edible taro in his garden. The old man protested. He could concede hungry men taking food from his garden, but this was pure vandalism. The Japanese cut off his protests by shooting him. Violence for a purpose, even for the most selfish purpose, the natives could understand, but they never forgave this wanton, purposeless murder.

After twelve days ashore, Kirkwall-Smith and his men were taken off. In addition to his information on native attitudes, he brought reports on beaches and terrain, and on guns, roads, trenches, and barbed wire; everything he had been able to piece together about the enemy's defenses.

Noakes was next given the task of reconnoitering Gasmata for the Amphibious Force. Gasmata, on the southern coast of New Britain, had been occupied for eighteen months and we had no indication that the natives there could be trusted. So Noakes, the three American soldiers, and the five natives accompanying him would have to be entirely dependent on their own resources. The plan was for them to land twenty miles west of Gasmata, then to strike inland and pass behind the base to a point ten miles east of it.

Noakes did not like the plan but he did his best to carry it out. Early in October, he and his men were landed from PT boats. Carrying their own food and equipment, they struck into the jungle; completely trackless in this area. The lay of the land was against them. For a week they pressed on, breaking through jungle up a steep slope to the top of a razorback ridge; then through jungle down a milder declivity to the inevitable creek at the bottom; then again, a climb and again a descent, always in oppressively dank, sticky heat and most of the time in rain. Always their clothes were wringing wet with rain and sweat. At night they camped under hastily built leaf shelters, with the camp of the night before a scant four or five miles behind.

Seven days of this and the men were completely exhausted. Examining the map, they decided that if they kept on as originally planned there was little likelihood, they would survive to reach their objective. So they turned back. By following the ridges, the going was easier and at length they reached a point near their landing place. During their wanderings they had met no natives and had not even seen Gasmata.

Making camp, Noakes sent the natives of his party to infiltrate the local villages. This was risky, but so far Noakes had nothing to show for his efforts and he was determined to bring something back. The results proved well worthwhile, for the village natives had worked for the Japanese at Gasmata and were able to give a fairly comprehensive account of the installations there. With considerable accuracy they recounted numbers of troops and positions of guns, bunkers, and pillboxes.

Having done all he could, Noakes signaled to be taken off. To his alarm, however, he could get no reply from the Amphibious Force. Some staff officer had changed the radio frequency without signaling Noakes about it, and the watcher's messages were crying in a vacuum. Finally, he was able to adjust his radio to the FERDINAND frequency and had got a response. His signal was passed on to the Amphibious Force and at last the men, by this time starving, were picked up.

So severe had been their privations during the three weeks ashore that they all had to be sent to the hospital. Noakes, on whom the additional strain of leadership had fallen, was in the worst state. Coupled with his earlier exertions at the Mambare River mouth, the hardships of the Gasmata trip affected his physical condition very seriously and he took no further part in FERDINAND activities. Noakes was a man who always gave all he had, and he was now worn out.

Early in December, after Sattelberg in the Finschafen area was taken, Pursehouse and five natives landed near Arawe on southern New Britain. The landing was made in bright moonlight and was seen by the Japanese. Nevertheless, the six men got ashore safely in a rubber boat, obtained information from local natives, and after an hour ashore made a safe getaway.

This was the last FERDINAND operation conducted under the control of the Amphibious Force. The organizational experiment was not an unqualified success. Landings had been made and some information obtained without any casualties, but owing to lack of knowledge of local conditions on the part of the planners they had been happenstance adventures, not really calculated operations.

In addition, the coastwatcher could produce the best results only if he had complete trust in his base staff. Lacking this, he naturally kept looking back over his shoulder. Like other fighting men, he was willing to die if necessary, but suicide was a Japanese privilege and he wanted no part of being an 'expendable.'

As a result of this lack of confidence and of faulty planning, the coastwatchers did not produce the results expected of them and the Amphibious Force, in turn, lost faith in the watchers. FERDINAND personnel was therefore withdrawn, to the relief of both units.

19

WITH SALAMAUA, LAE, AND FINSCHAFEN IN ALLIED HANDS, the next task was to clear Vitiaz Straits, through which lay the route to the Philippines. From the east the straits were still threatened by the Japanese bases at Cape Gloucester and Arawe on New Britain.

The way from Finschafen to Cape Gloucester lay past Rooke Island. To the northwest was Long Island. Either of these, if occupied strongly by the enemy, would be a serious obstacle to the attack on Cape Gloucester. Not only was information about the forces on these islands needed, but in addition a coastwatching station on Long Island was required to report enemy air attacks from Madang.

Lieutenant Hall, who had been Bell's assistant on the Rai Coast and at Rooke Island and who had made the grim return trip to Bena Bena with Fairfax-Ross's party, was assigned to Long Island soon after the Allied attack on Finschafen. It was his first independent command. With him went Sergeant Veale, now recovered from his trip to the Sepik River, Corporal F. A. Young of the Paluma crew, and four natives. On 6 October 1943, they landed on the unpopulated northwest shore of the island. Establishing camp in the jungle, the men set off to examine the west coast, moving warily and keeping to the jungle. On the second day they saw a Japanese camp on the beach, but on closer examination found it was only the crew of a wrecked barge. Hall reasoned that they would not remain long and did not constitute a danger to his nearby camp.

Next the men sneaked down the east coast of the island, where they discovered a Japanese encampment with preparations for departure in full swing. For a day, they watched the Japanese pack their gear and load it on a barge while their sentry sat on the beach and gazed idly out to sea. Hall's natives reported the island's two villages and their environs free of the enemy, so Hall moved the camp to the outskirts of the settlement. The inhabitants built the watchers' huts and made them welcome. Hall, Veale, and Young each took turns standing watch for aircraft at this station, while the other two and the party's natives patrolled the island. By late November, Hall had established that the island was completely clear of the enemy. His signal to this effect was received by McCarthy, who was temporarily attached to 6th U.S. Army Headquarters, on the birthday of the Commanding General. McCarthy rewrote the signal to read that FERDINAND was presenting Long Island as a birthday gift, an offering which General Krueger accepted with satisfaction. A week after Hall's party had been dispatched to Long Island, we sent Captain Bill Money, with two soldiers and five natives, to Rooke. Money, who was by no means young but very vigorous, had had a colorful career in New Guinea. He had been one of the syndicate which discovered Edie Creek Goldfield, and after his mining days he had settled down on Rooke Island, felled the jungle and made a plantation. Just before the war he had sold his place to the Australian Lutheran Mission. The island, about thirty miles long and half as wide, is rugged and mountainous, with no extensive flatland and with many reefs offshore. The native population is fairly heavy so, although the irregular hills are jungle-covered, a pattern of tracks covers the island.

Money and his men had just landed on Rooke and were still on the beach when a canoe came around the nearest point, just visible in the darkness. As it approached, the watchers could see that in it were three Japanese and three natives. Silently, they waited in the darkness, machine guns at the ready. Just as the canoe came opposite them, it grounded on a reef about twenty feet from the beach.

Money whispered instructions to a native, who nonchalantly waded out and shoved the canoe off into deeper water, casually asking one of the natives where the Japanese had come from. No one in the canoe regarded the native's presence as exceptional. He was told where the Japanese had come from and where they were bound, and the canoe moved on. The party promptly moved some of its supplies inland into very rough country, leaving the remainder to be carried later from the jungle near the beach. Two of the local natives with the party, Kalo and Baital, were sent to the nearest village to obtain any news they could of Japanese in the vicinity. The two did not return, and next day the Japanese came within a few hundred yards of the watchers' hideout. Again, the following day, Japanese patrols approached; Money and his men watching them from a swamp in which they stood waist deep.

It was evident that the enemy suspected their presence, and the days and nights were passed in anxious watching and listening. At night, one of the party's natives, who had previously been taken to Buna by the Japanese and was apparently shell-shocked, would scream hair-raisingly in his sleep. When awakened, he would recount his blood-curdling dreams, which added nothing to the peace of mind of the others.

Tied to his patch of jungle, with two of his scouts gone and their fate unknown, Money could obtain no information, and he and his party, except for the disappeared Kalo and Baital, were taken off.

Three months later, we learned the story of the missing scouts. After leaving Money, they had walked toward the nearest village, meeting two natives on the way. To these they told their prearranged story; they had been at Lae and had run away from the battle there, had stolen a canoe and crossed Vitiaz Straits.

They were taken to the village and fed, but detained to meet the Japanese-appointed headman. This official was highly suspicious. First, he sent other natives to question the two. Then the next morning he cross-examined them himself. They stuck to their story, adding some convincing embellishments. They had been frightened of the battle. At a small island to the southeast they had been bombed by an American airplane. They had paddled away from there as fast as possible and when they reached Rooke Island had been too exhausted to drag the canoe beyond high watermark. Doubtless it had drifted away. That was why they could not produce it to verify their story. They did not know anything about Europeans landing.

The headman was still unsatisfied. He took them before a Japanese officer, who first threatened but then dismissed them. By the time they returned to the village the supplies, Money had been unable to remove from the beach had been found, and again the hue and cry arose. Kalo and Baital again disclaimed all knowledge of Europeans and suggested that the supplies had been washed ashore. They were taken before a second Japanese officer, who was sufficiently impressed with their protestations to say that if they remained quietly in their village, he would believe them.

Realizing that their own and Money's only hope of safety lay in living out the deception, Kalo and Baital returned to their own village. The headman continued his accusations but, with the Japanese unable to find Money's party, the two were able to hold their ground. Knowing they were watched, they made no attempt to communicate with Money and did not even tell their wives and mothers the true story. Stoically, they followed the daily village round and let the time pass.

On Christmas night, a U.S. Army detachment occupied Long Island, releasing Hall, Veale, and Young from their post. Hall, Veale, and two of their natives were thereupon landed on Rooke, but heavy surf soaked their radio, so they returned. On the night of 5 January 1944, equipped with a new radio and accompanied by two additional natives, they made a second landing, this time successfully. A few days earlier, the U.S. Marines had landed at Cape Gloucester and

FERDINAND was particularly anxious to know what the Japanese on Rooke Island were contemplating.

Finding no enemy in the vicinity of their landing place, Hall and Veale moved slowly down the east coast, then struck across the island toward Gizarum on the opposite coast. Meantime, natives informed the Japanese of the party's presence. The Japanese jumped to the conclusion that we had made a landing in force. Hall took no steps to disabuse them of their error, and the enemy island garrison began a withdrawal. At least 500 Japanese were being chased off the island by two Europeans and four natives, with the pursuers taking every care not to catch the pursued.

Near Gizarum, Young joined Veale and Hall, bringing with him a U.S. Army officer and three enlisted men. The combined parties moved along the southwest coast through recently abandoned enemy positions, then over to the east coast. Here they saw fresh Japanese tracks and shortly afterward a body of unarmed enemy troops overtook the rear of the coastwatcher party. The Japanese retreated precipitously to the beach, from which they made their escape that night. Hall reported them to FERDINAND, but a heavy overcast prevented our planes from attacking. This group of Japanese proved to be the last of the garrison. Hall, Young, and Veale had 'captured' their second island.

They remained on the island for another month, reporting air movements and sending out patrols. It was on one of these scouting expeditions that Kalo and Baital were found and their story was learned.

On the New Guinea side of the straits, Australian troops were pushing up from Finschafen to Sio. Pursehouse, who of course had an excellent knowledge of this area, was lent to the Army to accompany the forward troops. When the force reached Sio Mission, Pursehouse turned back to obtain labor from Sio village, which is on a small island separated from the mainland by a narrow, shallow strait.

Accompanied by a soldier, he was crossing the strait in a canoe when suddenly a solitary Japanese, who had been left behind and was hiding in the jungle, shot at the two men. The soldier was wounded. Pursehouse, who had so bravely and capably come through his dangerous assignment at Finschafen, was killed.

To cut off the retreat of the Japanese fleeing up the coast from Finschafen, a U.S. division was landed at Saidor in January 1944. It encountered little enemy opposition and soon established a perimeter surrounded by observation posts. This left the Japanese only ill-defined foot tracks through the mountains to Madang, tracks on which starvation, exhaustion, malaria, dysentery, and tropical ulcers reduced the retreating Japanese to a sorry remnant of a fighting force. Kirkwall-Smith, who had accompanied the forces to Saidor, moved inland toward the high mountains to discover what trails the retreating enemy troops were using. With him he took an Australian corporal named Binks, three native soldiers, and fifty carriers, some of whom were armed.

They had gone less than a day's travel when they reached a native garden and heard the sound of Japanese voices. Two of the native soldiers were sent to investigate to the left, while Kirkwall-Smith himself reconnoitered the right. For nearly half an hour, they watched the garden, looking over its reed and bamboo fence, but they could see nothing. Finally, Binks and the native soldiers moved into the garden. Immediately they were inside, one of the natives spied a Japanese fumbling with a grenade, under a groundsheet just the other side of the fence from Kirkwall-Smith. He fired, killing the Japanese. Immediately the armed carriers opened fire, which was returned by Japanese on the right. Binks was hit by the first enemy shot, the bullet piercing his thigh and lodging in his body. The native soldiers held their ground like veterans and the Japanese fled.

Binks was badly wounded and would have to be taken back to Saidor at once. The country in which the skirmish had taken place was the roughest imaginable, high mountains cut by deep, steep gorges through which turbulent streams rushed among slippery boulders. The party's salvation lay in the fact that none of the carriers, in spite of the firing, had fled. There could not be a higher tribute than this to Kirkwall-Smith's leadership.

Up and down the cruel slopes, across streams and around rock faces, the carriers struggled with Binks on a stretcher improvised of saplings and vines. It had taken four hours to walk up to the scene of action. It took five days to carry Binks back. He survived and recovered completely, but he still has a Japanese bullet snuggled away near his pelvis.

One of the last of FERDINAND's jobs on this part of the coast was to search for enemy coastwatching parties. It was known that the Japanese occasionally attempted to play the same game as FERDINAND, leaving watchers in the areas from which they were driven. The search turned up nothing, however, proving that if there were Japanese coastwatchers, their activity was so slight as to be innocuous.

20

IN PLANNING THE ATTACKS AGAINST ARAWE and Cape Gloucester, Allied Headquarters anticipated air opposition from Rabaul at the other end of New Britain. To provide warnings, FERDINAND planned to insert three parties across the eastern neck of New Britain not far from Rabaul, a fourth on the north coast east of Talasea, and a fifth near Gasmata.

FERDINAND's card of entry to the far end of New Britain was a party placed on the southeastern coast during the 'lull' before the New Guinea offensive. It was the first that had successfully managed to remain on New Britain and give us a continuous supply of information.

At the time this party was landed, in March 1943, cold reasoning indicated it was still impossible to maintain a station so close to Rabaul. But, like a hunch in poker, some instinct born of experience whispered that the situation was not as bad as it appeared. And no FERDINAND operation was planned more carefully than this one.

The party was made up of Wright, Figgis, and Lieutenant H. L. Williams. Wright had already landed once near Rabaul in the optimistic days when we expected an early attack on that base. Figgis, on the retreat from Rabaul, had passed through the area and learned its features. Moreover, as a trained military-intelligence officer, he was exceptionally well equipped to interpret and evaluate any reports brought by natives. Williams was a patrol officer, experienced in handling natives, with a good amateur knowledge of radio and some accomplishments in first aid. The three were good friends and teamed well.

Three of the four natives accompanying them were carefully selected by Wright from among the several hundred who had been brought to Buna by the Japanese and had deserted to us. Having experienced enemy treatment, they could be relied on to be anti-Japanese in their sympathies and to influence others on New Britain to the same point of view. The fourth was Sergeant Simogun of the native police, who had served with Wright in Talasea. Simogun, a native of Wewak, was big and cheerful, with a commanding personality, able to handle other natives; ordering one here, jollying along another there, all without friction.

The point selected for the station was Cape Orford, thirty miles south of Wide Bay. From Wide Bay north to Rabaul, the Japanese held the coast in strength, and of course they had other posts spotted here and there to the south. The terrain around Cape Orford is mountainous, with large unpopulated areas and, so far as we know, nothing had happened there to arouse enemy interest. The Air Force took special photographs of the area at our request, which we carefully examined for signs of enemy occupation. Baien, a village lying in a bay in the cliffs, was selected as the landing point.

To guard against the radio of the watchers being picked up by enemy direction-finding apparatus, Ken Frank of Amalgamated Wireless designed an aerial that gave a beam effect to the transmission of signals. The special aerial required a suitable area in which to erect it, and this would entail considerable time spent in searching as well as extra work for installation, but the results would be worth it.

While they awaited embarkation, Wright, Figgis, and Williams practiced landing in the surf at Southport, an Australian seaside resort. This fitted in very well with the resort scene, and the sight of three young men disporting themselves in a collapsible canoe caused no comment and aroused no curiosity.

Before leaving, Wright was given complete freedom of decision. He was told that if he did not like the look of things at the landing place, he was at liberty to call a halt to the expedition and no reason would be required of him other than that 'the place smelled bad.'

After some difficulty in locating Baien Bay through the submarine periscope, the first installment of the party—Wright, Figgis, and two natives—was launched. Steering, in their collapsible canoes, for a patch of lesser blackness in the dark walls of the cliffs, the men passed between towering rock walls into the bay. The light offshore breeze brought to their nostrils the smell of a native village, a blend of wood smoke and cooked food, pigs, decaying vegetation, beach at low tide, and the sickly-sweet scent of the flower of the betel nut palm, an unmistakable compound to anyone who has lived in New Guinea.

The village was in darkness without fires or movement, and the men drew up their canoes unnoticed. One of the natives of the party was from this very village, a home he had never expected to see again when he lay on the bomb-drenched beach at Buna. Now he was unsure of his welcome. He slid into the shadows of the trees that lined the shore and moved toward the houses, Simogun following him, machine gun at the ready in case there were Japanese in the village. Wright and Figgis, fingers on the triggers of their submachine guns, stood guard in the shadows above the canoes to cover the retreat.

After a tense, silent quarter of an hour the native returned to them. Accompanying him was the native mission teacher, who reported that there were no Japanese between Wide Bay and Palmalmal, confirming the conclusions drawn from aerial photographs. Wright and Figgis entered the village and were invited into a hut where the embers of a fire were blown into cheerful flame. Natives, brought from their beds by news of the strange visitors, crowded around while Simogun stood at the door, watchful for treachery.

The native is usually slow to assimilate a new idea, slower still to determine its implications. Wright waited, watching the reactions of the people gathered around him. They were puzzled and they were torn between a desire to help and fear of reprisals. As he answered their questions, he saw they were slowly swinging his way. The accomplished fact of two Europeans being in the village outweighed the more distant possibility of Japanese action.

When Wright felt the moment was ripe, he announced that all he would require of them was to carry gear away from the coast and after that, silence. The headman of the village was away, but his second nervously agreed to the request. By this time it was too late to do more than hide the canoes. During the day the watchers slept in a hut in the jungle with a local native on guard.

As soon as night fell, Figgis set off in his canoe to find the submarine and guide her to the entrance of the bay for disembarkation of Williams, the two other natives, and supplies. Wright prepared fires on the beach to guide the boats ashore to the accompaniment of nervous protests from the natives that the Japanese had forbidden fires. As the boats approached, the carriers waited restlessly, committed to a course of assistance now but still fearful. Their anxiety spurred them to unload the supplies and carry them to the cover of the jungle with astonishing dispatch. By dawn, everything was hidden, and all marks of the night's activity removed from the beach.

To ensure continuance of native co-operation, Wright gave considerable thought to the position of the villagers. In particular, he wanted to make it possible for them to deny knowledge of his party without compromising themselves. This meant that the Japanese must discover no sign whatever that the denials were false, so Wright carefully chose a campsite in an almost uninhabited area inland.

It took considerable coaxing to persuade the beach natives to carry the supplies further, but at last everything was removed to a jungled valley. Then the beach natives were dismissed except for a few whom Wright particularly trusted, and these moved the supplies still further to a secret site. The few natives who lived in the area chosen had never been disturbed by the Japanese and so were not fearful of lending assistance in setting up the camp.

To keep the location of the camp as secret as possible, the path to it led along a streambed and across bare rocks, then into undisturbed jungle, ending in a climb which needed hands as well as feet and left the chest aching for air. It was 3 miles from the nearest shore and 1,500 feet above sea level.

To carry supplies over the difficult trail and to complete the camp and rig the special aerial required four weeks of hard, anxious work. Trees were left as they stood, so that no sign of the camp could be seen from the air. This security brought its penalty. The sunlight never penetrated to the huts beneath the trees; the camp was forever dark and gloomy. Aircraft often passed over at low altitudes, but the enemy pilots saw nothing except the unbroken leafy canopy.

For an actual lookout, a platform was built in a tall tree from which the coast could be seen to north, east, and south. No craft could pass unseen by the watchers, except on dark nights and during heavy rain.

In case the camp should be discovered, in spite of all his precautions, Wright had a second camp built still further inland and a supply cache hidden there.

When at last the party was ready to come on the air, the charging engine of the teleradio broke down. Williams spent five days working on it, concentrating on the problem to a degree which made the others afraid to speak to him. He got it working finally, and it came on the air just as FERDINAND headquarters was about to abandon hope.

Barges and submarines passed regularly within sight of the lookout post, and were as regularly reported. The submarines at first proceeded openly on the surface, often with cargo lashed to the decks. Guided by the coastwatchers' reports, aircraft attacked this shipping by day and PT boats attacked by night, until the traffic was disrupted.

One day, a small Japanese freighter entered Baien Bay, where the coastwatchers themselves had landed, and anchored between the cliffs to hide from our aircraft. Twenty-five Japanese landed to stretch their legs, completely overawing the timid beach natives. Wright reported the ship immediately and three Mitchell bombers, sent to sink it, flew toward Baien at low altitude. The Japanese leader ashore heard the engines, slapped his chest and said to the natives in a tone of complete confidence, 'Sikorki Japan!' (Japanese aircraft).

A moment later, bombs crashed into the ship. The native appreciates a touch of the dramatic and for months afterwards a call of *Sikorki Japan!* would bring howls of derision.

In addition to reporting barges, submarines, and occasional aircraft, the coastwatchers interviewed natives who had come from Rabaul. Figgis had improved his pidgin to a degree in which he was rarely nonplussed by any expression, however peculiar, and he painstakingly extracted from these natives much information of the Japanese defense system.

Figgis also remembered that to the southwest lived a Luluai, or chief, named Golpak, who had been of considerable help to the retreating soldiers on New Britain in the early days of the war. A meeting with him was arranged in a jungle hamlet near the coastwatchers' camp, and immediately he arrived the watchers knew that in this dignified old man they had a staunch friend. On their part, they could only assure him that the Japanese would one day be driven from the island. But Golpak needed no elaborate assurances, no persuasion. His faith was as strong as theirs and he unreservedly promised his help and support.

Piranis, the principal chief to the north, sent word on his own initiative that he, too, would support the coastwatchers. He was a comparatively young man of strong character, and he had considerable authority in his area, although neither he nor Golpak could impart their resolution to the timid coastal natives. Piranis and Golpak would be forced to obey the Japanese orders but, they made it plain, they would give underground assistance. Dissimulation is second nature to the native, as it is to most subject peoples, and Wright knew that no coaching of the two chiefs was necessary.

The terror of the neighborhood during this period was a Manus native, Eiwei, who was serving the Japanese as a police-boy. He had given the watchers no trouble, which puzzled everyone because it seemed incredible that he had not heard of their presence. One day he drew aside a native who was friendly to the coastwatchers and mentioned that he knew of the party and wanted to assist it. The word was passed on to Wright who sent Eiwei an invitation to visit the post.

Courageously, Eiwei walked into camp, alone, undefended, knowing that if his sentiments were doubted, he would be shot. Tears came to his eyes when he saw Europeans again and met his old friend, Sergeant Simogun. With dignity he told his simple story.

He had been left in Rabaul when it fell and had had to serve the Japanese or starve. Many other ex-police, he said, were in a like position and would come over to our side at the first opportunity. Wright's presence was already common knowledge in their ranks and to their minds disproved Japanese propaganda that Australia was conquered and the war over. His position made clear, Eiwei returned to the Japanese, outwardly to serve them.

The attitude of even the nervous Baien natives was improving under the ministrations of their chief, who had returned from his journey and who was a stalwart, firm man in contrast to his tremulous second.

Among the supplies FERDINAND successfully dropped at night were trade goods with which to pay the natives, so the watchers also stood high in commercial regard. The Japanese paid only grudgingly for labor and seldom for food. They had no goods which the natives desired and some of the Japanese lived at an even lower standard than the natives themselves. Cumulatively, this led the natives in New Britain to despise the Japanese while fearing their force.

Nor did the Japanese provide any native health service. In this they showed a deplorable lack of skill and understanding in administrative problems, for there is nothing the natives appreciate more than medical attention.

Williams, the 'doctor' of the coastwatcher party, was in constant demand to give injections for yaws. His ample supplies of medicine were rapidly exhausted and more had to be dropped by Catalina.

His prize patient was Simogun. Usually a native's teeth are perfect, but Simogun developed an abscess. His face swelled, his head ached, he was unable to eat. Something had to be done. Williams' only 'dental' instrument was a pair of pliers from the radio kit. Sterilizing these, he sat the sick man against the wall of the hut, gave him a good nobbler of brandy, and said a silent prayer. Then, using all force and no skill, he jerked out three back teeth. Poor Simogun was given another stiff snort of brandy which sent him into a drunken sleep.

'What about one for me?' gasped Williams. 'I need it as much as Simogun!' But hard-heartedly, Wright and Figgis made him recuperate on tea.

On another memorable day, Golpak brought in a shot-down Allied airman, captain of a photo-reconnaissance squadron. Golpak had not only guided him but, ironically, had fed him tea, sugar, and milk, which had been one of the rare gifts of the Japanese. With only incidents such as these to break the monotony, the party in true FERDINAND style kept to its post for six months, while it reported seventy submarines, more than a hundred aircraft, and uncounted barges.

But the strain of half a year began to tell. Wright did not smile as often as in the past, Figgis lost some of his airy optimism, and Williams, always quiet, retreated more and more into silence. In their boredom and isolation they were sustained by the knowledge that the Japanese were being driven back elsewhere and that, sooner or later, a time of action, an end to dullness, would reach into the dreary New Britain jungle.

Their opportunity came with FERDINAND's decision to place five more parties for keeping tabs on Rabaul during the Vitiaz Straits offensive. Wright was placed in charge of the landing and was to command the combined parties until they separated to go to their various posts.

On 28 September 1943, after Wright had signaled the coast was clear, the U.S. Submarine Grouper surfaced off Cape Orford with 16 coastwatchers and 27 native helpers aboard. The disembarkation was made in a heavy sea, whipped up by the southeast monsoon, and the first accident occurred before the men had succeeded in struggling into their rubber boats. One of the watchers, a large burly man, fell from a ladder and injured his back so that he had to be left aboard. The others landed in a heavy surf, they and their supplies were drenched, three of the radios totally ruined.

FERDINAND's plans required that all the parties be at their posts by 1 November. This meant that the Gasmata party had barely time to reach its position and the two parties for the north coast had little time to spare. So, these three groups set off at once with the three portable teleradios, while the other two parties remained at Cape Orford until more radios could be dropped. Figgis, with two assistants, was to stay at Cape Orford and maintain the station there.

Wright, Williams, and Simogun, reinforced by two soldiers and a number of natives, made up the party for Nakanai on the north coast east of Talasea. The Gasmata party consisted of Captain J. J. Murphy, a short, energetic former patrol officer; Lieutenant F. A. Barrett, a good soldier with no knowledge of New Guinea; Sergeant L. T. W. Carlson, who had been Noakes' signaler at the Mambare River; and eight natives.

Leading the party for Open Bay, considerably east of Nakanai on the north coast, was Captain R. I. Skinner, a patrol officer who had joined the Army early in the war and served in the Middle East. Lieutenant L. J. Stokie, whose name had been used by his brother-in-law, Mason, for the historic call signals from Bougainville during the battle for Guadalcanal, was his second. A signaler and five natives completed this party.

The three groups set off together, Wright and Skinner having decided to travel along the south coast before crossing the island to reach their posts. Arrangements for carriers and scouts along the route were in the capable hands of Golpak.

At first all went well, in spite of the fact that the men were using a road put in condition and maintained by the Japanese, the only route by which they could hope to make fast enough time. They had traveled twenty miles when word came that Golpak had been arrested. While they pondered their next step, an old Malay named Johannes met them and reported that Golpak's difficulties had been straightened out. This was shortly confirmed by assurances from Golpak himself that the road ahead was clear.

Then, with ten more miles behind them, they received word that an enemy patrol was moving toward them from the permanent Japanese base of Palmalmal. Until the last possible moment the coastwatchers continued along the road, then moved into the jungle nearby and listened silently to the sound of rifle fire as the enemy passed by. The Japanese were firing indiscriminately into the jungle, no one knew why. The coastwatchers could easily have dealt with the eight Japanese in the patrol, but in the interests of secrecy allowed them to pass.

Reaching Golpak's village in Jacquinot Bay, the men found that Golpak himself was in hiding from the Japanese. He risked showing himself, however, to assure them of his support.

A few miles beyond the village and fifty miles from the starting point at Cape Orford, Skinner's party branched off to the north. From this point, a track from village to village would lead him easily to the north coast.

Wright, Murphy, and their men, still headed along the coast, were now reaching an area well-combed by the Japanese. Ten miles to the south was the post of Palmalmal. Therefore Wright led the parties inland and for the next thirty miles they traveled in jungle, parallel to the coast road. This was harder and slower going. There was little drinking water, and the land itself was rough upraised coral, dissected by deep gorges.

Fortunately, Paiaman, chief in this area, helped them with scouts and carriers, much as Golpak had. At one point, in spite of Paiaman's efforts, they experienced a shortage of carriers because all available natives had been called by the Japanese to work on the road. Wright solved this problem by requesting an air attack. Our

Beaufighters strafed the road, giving the natives a sound excuse to desert the Japanese and carry for the Europeans.

At a point about eighty miles from Cape Orford, Wright left Murphy's party and branched off to the northwest. Four days later, after hard going with little food, he and his men reached the territory of the Nakanai people. Wright, one of his two soldiers, and Simogun had all known these people in peacetime and the welcome they received was tumultuous. An enthusiastic carrier line of men, women, and children, frolicking noisily along the track like a holiday crowd, accompanied them to their position twelve miles from the north coast.

After Wright branched off, Murphy's party had fourteen days in which to get into position behind Gasmata, seventy miles farther along the coast. It was a tragedy that Murphy was given this deadline, for as it happened an additional fortnight would have meant everything to him and would satisfactorily have met general military requirements. As it was, however, Murphy was faced with the fact that if he was to reach his post in time he would have to travel by the coast. He, Barrett, and Carlson were all exceptionally courageous and they decided to take the risk.

For thirty miles, they moved without interruption. Then a native, sent to get carriers, brought a Japanese patrol instead. The first intimation the men had of this treachery was a burst of machine-gun fire which killed one of the party's natives. The others crouched and the fire passed over their heads.

After a considerable period of silence, Barrett raised himself to look around. A second burst of fire killed him instantly. Murphy, Carlson, and the natives wormed their way along the ground through the undergrowth until they were clear. Keeping to the jungle, they were shortly seen by more natives, who reported them to the Japanese. This time the enemy patrol rushed them, and, in the melee, Carlson was killed, and Murphy captured, while the natives escaped to make their way back to Figgis.

Something unparalleled in FERDINAND now occurred. The Japanese extracted from Murphy a complete account of the coastwatching parties in New Britain, their composition and location and the workings of the organization which supported them. There can be no doubt that drugs were used to make Murphy talk. Had it been torture, Murphy, who was shrewd as well as brave, would have left out some items on which the enemy could not possibly check. But the information he gave was correct to the last detail.

Among the facts he gave them was information about a promised supply-drop of radio batteries which he never received. Japanese propaganda exploited this incident to intimate that Murphy had talked from pique; utterly ridiculous to those who knew John Murphy.

Naturally, the information the Japanese now held endangered all the parties in New Britain. The five remaining groups were immediately instructed to move to safe positions. Actually all were already as safe as they could make themselves, except Figgis, who moved further inland. The worst immediate result of Murphy's capture was that the Malay, Johannes, who had helped FERDINAND in Golpak's territory, was executed together with his wife and children.

The first year of their occupation in New Britain had given the Japanese no evidence that the Allies were operating on the island, and they had been lulled into a sense of security. It was largely due to this that the original Cape Orford party had been so successful. But now the Japanese swung to the opposite extreme. All police in their employ were ordered to keep a lookout for Europeans, while the Japanese troops busied themselves with patrolling.

Luckily, the attacks on Arawe and Cape Gloucester made soon afterwards, coupled with the heavy Allied air attacks on Rabaul, soon gave the Japanese so much to do that they could not long afford troops or transport for a really full-scale hunt.

At Cape Orford, Figgis, hearing the Japanese intended to establish a post at Baien, encouraged the natives to move from the beach to a place inland. Eventually, five Japanese with a teleradio and a telescope arrived and set themselves up in a hut. As coastwatchers, they had selected a remarkably poor spot, for they could see little from the beach itself. Figgis sent down two natives to work for them so that he might learn whatever plans they concocted. The Japanese also established an air patrol over Baien, but Allied fighters, guided by Figgis' reports, soon forced them to abandon it.

The natives sent by Figgis to Baien had been ordered to commit no sabotage, for Figgis wanted nothing to disturb the enemy watchers' apathy. One day, however, the Japanese decided to move to a new house. Tepsur, one of Figgis' natives, was carrying their radio transmitter when two Beaufighters appeared. The Japanese dropped everything and dived for the jungle. Tepsur took the opportunity to smash the radio against a tree before diving for shelter himself. The Japanese never suspected that its loss was not accidental.

Figgis had managed his move to a safer spot so successfully that friendly natives guiding three shot-down U.S. airmen were unable to find the new camp until Figgis sent down a guide. The Japanese found his old base and destroyed it, but patrols did not even reach the vicinity of the new camp.

Skinner, at Open Bay, was a few miles south of the Japanese post at Ulamoa. His was the best placed of all the parties to report aircraft operating against the Arawe landings, and no enemy raiders escaped his observation.

After disaster had befallen Murphy's party, Skinner heard that twenty canoe loads of natives were on their way from the north to search for him. The natives duly arrived but displayed no enthusiasm in their hunt; one of their boss boys even sent progress reports of the reconnaissance to Skinner. The Japanese followed this attempt with an expedition of troops. Skinner slyly provided their guide, who led them into cruelly rough country, where they of course found nothing although they searched for five weeks.

Meantime, three airmen were brought to Skinner's post. One of them had been found some time previously by natives, who had cared for him with devotion until he was strong enough to travel. The two others had been hidden by Golpak, who himself was still in hiding. The two parties on the neck of land between Wide and Open Bays, one commanded by Captain C. D. Bates and the other by Major A. A. Roberts, both former assistant district officers, were in ideal country for concealment.

From his hideout in rugged, limestone hills, Roberts sent native scouts to the villages near Rabaul to establish an 'underground-railway' system for natives from other areas who had been caught in Rabaul. As these rescued natives drifted out, Roberts extracted information from them and then settled them in a hitherto uninhabited area. Although the Japanese knew there were FERDINAND parties in the vicinity, they apparently did not place any restrictions on information of barge movements, and friendly natives would often report to Roberts when barge arrivals were expected. On one occasion, ten barges were strafed and sunk at one time through reports of this nature.

Bates' post was in flat, but heavily timbered territory, through which indeterminate gullies, scoured by floods, began and ended without apparent rime or reason. It was an area in which a party might conceal itself almost indefinitely. When word was brought to Bates that the Japanese were on his trail, he therefore decided to ambush the enemy patrol rather than to make a hasty move and abandon his supplies.

His and Roberts' natives combined for the attack. They preferred to have no Europeans in the party. They, the natives, could flit silently and swiftly through the jungle, while the more clumsy European might be heard or even seen by the enemy. The guerrilla party stalked close to the enemy patrol's camp in the last light of day and opened fire on the surprised Japanese, killing six. The others hastily retired.

Since the Japanese already knew the coastwatchers were in this area, FERDINAND's usual secrecy and circumspection were not necessary, and Bates' maneuver was all to the good. Before the Japanese could send a stronger force, he shifted camp to a new position.

At Nakanai, Wright was established among loyal and helpful mountain people. The coastal natives nearby were nearly all pro-Japanese, having been won over by Butari, the shrewd, forceful renegade who had headed the mythology-based anti-European movement immediately after Japan entered the war. Butari himself had already reaped his reward from the Japanese; he was in prison and his wife had been forced to become the inmate of a brothel; but his influence lingered on.

One day, a Japanese police-boy accompanied by a pro-Japanese coastal native visited the Nakanai area to get road laborers, and happened to spy a piece of parachute cloth. The two hurried off with it. Wright sent Simogun with a party to intercept them. Simogun missed them, but a native of the mountains, realizing the tribulations a visit of a Japanese patrol would bring on his village, killed the two while they slept.

The Japanese were already aware, through Murphy's information, that coastwatchers were somewhere in the area, but they had been unable to locate them in the interminable, jungle-covered mountains. Their patrols confined their searches chiefly to the flatlands between mountains and coast.

One morning, while one of these patrols was in a flatland village, some of the mountain natives incautiously paid the village a visit. The Japanese promptly imprisoned the mountain men and questioned them. When they denied knowledge of any white men, they were flogged, but not one disclosed a scrap of information. Abruptly the Japanese dropped the inquisition but ordered the mountain men to remain overnight for further instructions.

That afternoon a pro-Japanese native wandering in the hills nearby heard two small mountain boys talking of Simogun. They were brought before the Japanese patrol commander, who thrashed and threatened them until at last they told there was a party in the mountains.

During the uproar that followed, some of the detained mountain men escaped; that night a raid by mountain natives released those still in the village. But meantime the Japanese had taken twelve of the captured natives to the coast, where they were flogged and manhandled. Three were bayonetted to death and then four were more ceremoniously executed. The remaining five managed to escape.

Shortly after this occurrence, a Japanese police-boy who had previously made contact with the coastwatchers informed Wright that the enemy was preparing a search. Wright had just received a drop of three months' supplies. He and his men immediately began transporting them across a wide, deep valley into a new mountain hideout from which the old camp could be seen. On Christmas Day, 1943, they watched the Japanese rifle and burn the old camp.

There had been no time to build good shelters, so for a fortnight the men suffered in continuous rain and cold, then moved back to the old camp. That they could return was owing largely to a ruse of Simogun's. On his own initiative, he had left a letter, addressed to one of the Japanese police-boys, wrapped around some tobacco.

It said that the party had thrown up the sponge and was on its way to join the American forces at Arawe.

The killing of the mountain men in the lowlands meant war between the two tribes. The villages organized themselves for it, placing sentries, digging traps, and keeping all fighting men in a state of readiness. Seeing these preparations, Wright moved his party down into a mountain village. These allies, he knew, could be trusted not to make a separate peace.

Wright and Williams discussed the situation. From the point of view of their own safety, it would be better to resist than to continue evading the Japanese. The natives were ready material for a guerrilla force. The watchers' intelligence role was practically played out, and would not suffer now if they undertook offensive operations.

There was a chance the natives might use arms for internecine warfare rather than against the Japanese, but Wright felt he had sufficient control to prevent this. Weighing these factors, the men came to a decision and sent FERDINAND a signal requesting arms for a hundred natives.

At FERDINAND headquarters, the proposal was carefully discussed. It was a complete reversal of FERDINAND policy, but at length it was decided that the decline of the Japanese forces justified it, and the arms were dropped to Wright.

Wright immediately suffered an embarrassment of too many volunteers. The most suitable were put through a course of musketry, with Simogun and other trained natives acting as instructors. Any native failing to show immediate aptitude was replaced by another, the disappointment of the reject salved by the tact of the native instructors. Before long, each village had its guerrilla section under its own official leader, and the men were sent home to await a call.

All attacks were to be made by lightning ambush and immediate retreat. Speed in the jungle was the guerrilla's strength, against which the Japanese could produce no counterforce. Europeans would only slow the guerrillas down, so all attacks were to be made by natives alone, but only at the direction of Wright or one of his officers. The first affrays were to be defensive, on the mountain men's own borders. When victory here had given them confidence, raids were to be made on the Japanese on the coast.

Defensively, the area was well placed. The coastal flat was less than ten miles wide, with the mountains rising abruptly at its back. Only three tracks led from the coast into the mountains.

News of Wright's preparations traveled and very soon he received requests from Golpak and Paiaman on the south coast that their people be armed too. Wright passed on this request, and our aircraft accordingly made a drop of arms, food, and tobacco to the two chiefs. A group of these south-coast natives was sent to Wright's camp, where they were given a course in musketry and sent back to instruct the others.

Still another group from farther west on the south coast visited Wright and asked for rifles. He had none to spare except a small reserve he preferred to hold, so he told them it was unlikely the Japanese would come their way and that they had no real need for arms.

Two weeks later, they were back with the caps, boots, and water bottles of six Japanese Marines whom they had killed with spears. Their argument was convincing. Wright gave them fifteen rifles and signaled for another consignment. In this drop, he received hand grenades as well, and these of course immediately became a highly favored weapon.

The first guerrilla action was at Umu, just below the mountains, where a party of Japanese had moved into the foothills. There were about twenty of the enemy, and Simogun was watching them with about the same number of guerrillas.

Seeing the Japanese pack their baggage, Simogun realized that he had them at a momentary disadvantage, and he gave the signal to open fire. He himself stepped into the open with his Austen gun spitting. After three shots, suddenly his gun jammed. Quickly changing his magazine, he fired a full burst before the Japanese could take advantage of his plight. Three Japanese were killed and two wounded, while the guerrillas withdrew without loss. The Japanese retired that afternoon, losing one more soldier to a native spearman on their way.

The little action filled the guerrillas with confidence. They had discovered, as others had, that the Japanese was as other men: if cut, he bleeds; if shot, he dies. They knew also that the skirmish would prevent the Japanese from obtaining guides and that the effectiveness of their patrols would be halved.

The Japanese, of course, did not meekly accept this native effrontery. They made a second foray at Umu. At Wright's signal our aircraft bombed and strafed the area, causing no casualties but considerably heartening the guerrillas and disheartening the lowland natives. Then the Japanese dug in and Wright forbade any guerrilla attack. He ordered fires to be lighted only in heavy rain so that the enemy would be given no inkling of the forces around him. The Japanese waited for a week; they had no guides and did not know where to move next.

Then, one night, some Japanese had a bright idea and lighted a large fire as a come-on to the guerrillas. This gave Simogun an idea and he too lighted a fire. As he expected, the Japanese moved out from their strong point next morning and Simogun ambushed them.

After this stratagem, in the middle of February 1944, the Japanese made no further attempt to gain the mountains. Wright's forces, now known as Nakanai Guerrillas, 200 strong, took the war to the Japanese. Their preparations included even the importation of a sorcerer from a village several days' march distant, who blew the ashes of a dead warrior's brain in the direction of the enemy to curse him with blindness.

During this time the remnants of the Japanese forces at Cape Gloucester, battered by the U.S. Marines, had begun their retreat. Their sea communications were constantly raided by sea and air, and their only retreat to Rabaul was along 400 miles of foot track. Rabaul itself was fully occupied by self-defense, and the retreating Japanese could look forward only to being bombed and gunned the whole road east.

When retreating parties, varying in strength from 4 or 5 men to 400, began to reach Wright's territory, he selected a stretch of track which curved inland to avoid swamp and stationed 5 parties of guerrillas, numbering about 30 men each, along it. Each guerrilla section, under a native noncommissioned officer, was housed in huts in the jungle close by. In addition, lone warriors prowled over the area.

The track itself was a clearing five feet wide, over which the branches of the trees closed. It was muddy; trodden to mulch by the feet of those who had gone before, and kept wet by the constant rains.

Where the track crossed a small stream, a guerrilla would sit on his haunches, patient as only a native can be, watching the meandering track to the westward. Behind him, a hundred yards up the creek, would be a guerrilla camp of half a dozen low lean-tos.

The sentry would watch a Japanese soldier come into view, head down, plodding through the mud, his packs covering his back and shoulders, his rifle slung behind the packs. As more soldiers followed, perhaps three together carrying a machine gun, the sentry would count them. Fifteen: not too big for an attack!

He would signal with his hand, and a native boy a few yards away in the jungle, so quiet that he had been invisible, would rise and lope to the guerrilla camp to whisper the news to the non-commissioned officer. No commands would be given, not even signs were necessary, as each guerrilla took his rifle and faded through the jungle to a point farther east along the track. Here, behind the tree trunks around a small, bright clearing halfway up a low hill, the guerrillas would take up their positions.

They had not studied the Manuals of Military Art, but they knew that men walking up a hill in the damp heat naturally stop for a breather at an open space, and that when they stop, they bunch together and lose a little of their vigilance.

The first Japanese would arrive, perhaps stand a little while, then move on a few paces. At this point, the sentry would join the guerrilla party and, with a sign, confirm the fact that not too many Japanese were following. The next few enemy soldiers would reach the open space and stop.

When the guerrilla officer felt the precise favorable moment had arrived, he would raise his rifle and his men would follow suit. Abruptly the silence would be shattered by a ragged volley, followed by the burst of hand grenades. There would be a scream from the Japanese, the screeching of a flight of cockatoos rising from a nearby tree, then silence. Not even a twig could be heard to snap as the guerrillas faded away into the gloom of the jungle.

Sometimes the battles lasted longer. A party of 180 Japanese, ambushed by Simogun early in April, proved alert and returned the fire, even pressing after the guerrillas into the jungle. But as these enemy troops left their camp the next morning, a party of warriors under Sergeant Makelli swept in on the rearguard, wiped it out, and then, holding a ridge, kept the road ahead under fire for an hour. In this action, 37 Japanese were killed.

In two months, Nakanai Guerrillas killed 286 Japanese, as against one guerrilla lost in each of the forces. Credit for a kill was as stringently given as for an enemy shot down by the Air Forces. The top scorer was Sergeant Makelli with 33. Simogun, now a sergeant major, was second with 31.

Nor was publicity neglected. When a force returned, the number of kills was signaled by rifle shots. This, in turn, was taken up by the wooden drums and the news was passed through the mountains. So the Public was told; even though no dinner-jacketed voice said, 'Here is the news.'

Keen as they were for these battles, the natives, just like other fighting men, looked forward to the day when they could hand in their arms and resume work on their neglected houses and gardens.

At the end of February, Skinner left his post on the north coast to take command of guerrillas in the south, leaving Stokie in charge at the old post. As the retreat from Cape Gloucester went on, Stokie, to the east of where Wright's guerrillas were operating, had his scouts keep count of the numbers of Japanese passing by. Whenever a concentration offered a target for aircraft, he passed on a radio signal.

So often was the Japanese post at Ulamoa bombed and strafed that its garrison decided to shift to a position farther northeast, close to the road leading to Stokie's camp. Stokie organized the natives to wipe them out. In a sudden and, to be quite frank, treacherous attack, his guerrillas rushed the enemy post with axes, destroyed it, and then repeated the operation on a Japanese ferry party at a nearby river.

During these operations, Stokie came across three missionaries who had been hiding inland of Ulamoa since the Japanese occupation. He took them under his protection and soon afterwards they were evacuated.

Not so many Japanese retreated along the south coast as along the north. Of these southern parties, many troops were barefooted, without arms, in tattered clothing, and sick, with sores bandaged in dirty rags. They were going, they told the natives, to Rabaul to die. Describing their condition to Figgis, a native said they were worse than the Australians retreating from Rabaul, a figure which Figgis appreciated, as he had been one of the retreating Australians.

Under Skinner's command, guerrilla forces on the southern side of the island killed thirty of these stragglers, after which their score remained stationary for lack of targets.

After their landing at Cape Gloucester, the U.S. Marines had pushed eastward. At the end of February, they decided to bypass the Japanese still west of Talasea by a landing at Volupai, where Harris had kept his lookout during FERDINAND's ill-fated New Britain operations more than a year before. Flight Lieutenant G. H. R. Marsland, engineer on the Paluma, was assigned to forward reconnaissance.

He, a Marine lieutenant, and two natives were landed three miles southwest of Volupai. Although surrounded by Japanese posts, they entered a village and gleaned information on the disposition of the Japanese forces. Marsland was then allotted the duty of piloting in the attackers.

On the night of 5 March 1944, he guided in the leading vessel, then rode ashore on the leading amphibious tank. The landing, made in the first light of dawn, was opposed by heavy machine-gun fire but Marsland, on the top of his tank, was unharmed. In two days, Talasea was taken, although it took considerably longer to root out the Japanese completely.

From Talasea Marsland led patrols toward the east, through country he knew intimately. Once his patrol was fired on, but without casualties. He found many natives who had been employed in peacetime on his plantation and had been taken to Rabaul by the Japanese. From them he learned considerable about the defenses in Rabaul.

With the capture of Talasea, the advance of the armed forces in New Britain ceased. The plan had been to render Rabaul innocuous, while securing Vitiaz Straits, and this had been achieved.

In the south, Skinner's guerrilla forces wiped out the Japanese outpost at Palmalmal. Next morning, a Japanese barge entered the harbor and turned heavy machine-gun fire on the attacking guerrillas. Owing largely to the bravery of a native corporal named Oras, who shot the enemy machine gunner, the barge was destroyed. Although the Japanese later inserted more posts on the south coast, Skinner and his forces were never again cut off by the enemy.

FERDINAND's operations in New Britain had assumed a totally new character. FERDINAND was no longer operating behind the enemy lines. It was actually holding the front line in New Britain.

Communication with the various parties was now easy. The Paluma made trips to the coast whenever she was needed, and the opportunity was taken to relieve all the men who had been a long time in the field. Skinner brought with him Kaole, Golpak's last remaining child, a splendid boy. All his brothers and sisters had been seized by the enemy and taken to Rabaul.

Fairfax-Ross, with a team of 15 watchers, was placed in command on the south coast, while Wobbie Robinson, with 12 watchers, was in charge in the north. Each group had about 200 armed natives.

In the south, the Japanese re-established their post at Baien, and Fairfax-Ross destroyed it. Then the enemy established another post a little farther east. In August, this was bombarded by an Australian naval vessel, piloted to its position by Mackenzie while Fairfax-Ross harried the Japanese from the shore side.

In our wildest dreams, we could hardly have imagined the situation as it now stood. For two years Rabaul, on the Japanese-ridden Gazelle Peninsula, had been a hornet's nest. Rabaul-based planes and ships had won control for the Japanese over much of New Guinea, most of the Solomons. During the Allied advance, Rabaul had been an evil continually to be reckoned with. For a long period, its strength had made even coastwatching impossible on New Britain.

And now 40,000 Japanese were held in that same Gazelle Peninsula by 29 coastwatchers and 400 armed natives. Hemmed in, its command of sea and air lost, the Rabaul garrison could only sit, helpless and ignoble, the limits of its hinterland defined by puny FERDINAND.

21

THE ALLIED FORCES, AFTER TAKING THE ADMIRALTY ISLANDS, decided
to land at Aitape far to the west on the New Guinea border and at
Hollandia in Dutch New Guinea, thereby neutralizing the Japanese
at Madang, Hansa Bay, and Wewak. Headquarters wanted on-the-
spot information of Japanese strength and positions in this area.

Under the Allied Intelligence Bureau system, the Dutch should
have been delegated to provide information from Hollandia. But the
Dutch had so few people that they could not provide a party. Stavermann and his group, who had attempted to reach Hollandia in the
first part of 1943, had been killed before they even crossed the border. In fact, the Dutch had no one in their scant forces who had ever
even been to Hollandia.

So it was decided that FERDINAND should provide a party, to
which the Dutch would add an Indonesian sergeant as interpreter.
And at FERDINAND headquarters, it was decided that here was a job
for 'Blue' Harris.

Harris had been pestering FERDINAND for a real job. He had assisted in the New Britain evacuation, then had sat on the Rai Coast
for about eight months, bickering with the other idling watchers
there while he waited for the war to come his way. At Talasea and
Witu he had escaped the enemy in the nick of time. He had landed
for two nights and two days at Finschafen and had stared into the
eyes of a Japanese there, but nothing more had come of it. He had
been scheduled to land in the Admiralty Islands, but the attack had
taken place without any preliminary reconnaissance and his job had
been cancelled. To 'Blue,' this just didn't add up to enough.

The Hollandia job was just what he wanted. It meant a landing
on an enemy-held coast, among natives who were an unknown
quantity and whose reactions and thoughts would be difficult to
judge.

With the meager information already at our disposal, he prepared as carefully for the job as he could. He painstakingly studied
every chart and air photograph available. His team was already
made up; the one he had prepared for the Admiralty Islands work. It
consisted of Lieutenant R. B. Webber, Sergeant R. J. Cream, and Pri-
vates J. I. Bunning, G. Shortis, and P. C. Jeune, all of the Australian
Army; Julius McNicol, able seaman in the Australian Navy; and Sergeants Yali, Mas, and Buka and Private Mariba of the New Guinea

native police. Webber had been a soldier in the Admiralty Islands when the Japanese had occupied them, and McNicol, Yali, and Mas had all been with Harris on the Rai Coast and at Talasea. To this party, Sergeant Launcelot, the Indonesian interpreter, was added.

The party planned to land from a submarine thirty miles west of Hollandia, then push inland to the mountains, without any contact with local natives if possible. To ensure communication, a party under Captain C. J. Millar, who had been with Bridge in New Guinea, was landed by plane in the Idenburg River, a hundred miles south of Hollandia, where the enemy had not penetrated. If base stations could not receive Harris' signals, owing to the distance, Millar was to relay them on. Harris was to remain ashore for fourteen days and to be picked up at the end of that period by submarine.

The party embarked in the U.S. Submarine Dace on 18 March 1944. Four days later, the submarine was off Cape Tanamerah, the landing point selected. A day was spent examining the shore through the periscope, and a site chosen, but as the submarine surfaced after dark and approached the shore, a powerful light was sighted just where the party was to have landed. So the submarine held off, and next day, after further examination, a small beach on the open coast was decided upon, even though there were several native huts nearby.

With true FERDINAND caution, Harris decided to land with a reconnaissance party before committing the entire coastwatcher group. With him he took Webber, Shortis, Mas, and Launcelot, arms, a walkie-talkie and a flashlight. Code signals were arranged: 'Groggo' to indicate that all was well, and the remainder of the party was to be sent ashore; 'Washout' to indicate that the remainder should stay aboard the sub, which was anchored more than a mile offshore.

The reconnaissance party set off in the rubber boat on the dark, calm sea. Suddenly, before it knew what had happened, it was in trouble. The low groundswell, innocuous in deep water, bunched itself into heavy breakers at the edge of the reef. The reef had not been observed through the periscope, and the rubber boat was against it and tossed by the breakers before the men realized it was there. They tried to shoot across, but the boat struck on the reef and Harris and Shortis, with some of the equipment, were washed overboard. They and the other three struggled to shore, about a hundred yards away, dragging the swamped boat with them. As they reached the sand, tense and shaken, a fire flared up in a nearby hut.

Any attempt at concealment was useless, and a bold front seemed the best move. Harris, Launcelot, and Mas walked to the hut, while Webber and Shortis unpacked the soaked and battered walkie-talkie, to find it completely ruined.

The natives in the hut, questioned by Harris through Launcelot, said that the nearest Japanese were two and a half miles away to the westward. They appeared friendly, on the surface there was no reason for Harris to be suspicious of them, but he was not satisfied. Years of dealing with New Guinea natives had given him an instinct more to be relied on than reason.

On the strength of his hunch, he ordered the signal 'Washout' to be given. Webber flashed the signal with a light, and then sent a further signal asking that the submarine return the following night. No acknowledgment was received from the submarine, so Webber climbed to higher ground to repeat.

From the slight eminence, he was startled to see the other two boats with the remainder of the party just outside the breakers. He watched them repeat the process of overturning and of wading ashore, dragging what equipment they could. On board the submarine, it seemed, some flashes of light not sent by Harris' group had been seen. Imagination had filled in the gaps to make 'Groggo,' the signal that all was well. Only Sergeant Cream, who had had an attack of malaria, had remained aboard.

A worried and sleepless coastwatcher party awaited the dawn. Harris reflected that if the natives were unfriendly, they would report the party in any case. If they were friendly, or in doubt, a show of trust might hold them to him. To his own party he put on a show of confidence. With the morning, he said, they could strike inland and try to reach the Idenburg River.

Dawn showed that the eleven in the party had twelve firearms among them, of which four were submachine guns, two carbines, and the rest pistols and revolvers. A box of hand grenades, some medical kits, the codes and maps, and about one week's rations had been saved.

There had been four natives in the hut. In the morning, they were joined by another, who appeared to have some authority over the others, and who agreed that one of the youths in the hut should guide the party clear of the occupied area.

Hiding their rubber boats as best they could, the party packed up and moved off. They crossed the jungle that fringed the beach, continued inland, and finally made camp in a creek bed. At this point their guide left them, explaining that he would seek a better campsite. When he did not return, the coastwatchers feared he had gone to betray them.

Actually, their landing had been reported to the Japanese as soon as they left the beach. The natives in the hut had waited only until they were out of reach of reprisals from the party. Harris had been right when he signaled 'Washout.'

Next morning, with still no sign of the guide, the party left its camp in the creek bed and followed a path leading through the jungle. It led them up a spur to an open patch of kunai, and they halted at its edge before going into the open. Harris had given his carbine to Yali; perhaps to raise confidence, perhaps because he felt there was trouble ahead and he would give Yali the best chance while he, the leader, took the worst.

As they paused, voices were heard behind them and Webber, dropping his pack, started back to investigate. Dimly he saw a line of Japanese moving forward in the jungle, and he ran to warn Harris, who, meantime, was hurrying the party across the open patch to the shelter of the jungle on the other side. Yali, Mas, Buka, and Mariba were leading, and they had just reached the far jungle when firing broke out.

At the same moment, Webber ran into the open and dropped to earth. McNicol bore to the left and reached the jungle. Harris, Bunning, Shortis, and Launcelot struck to the right under heavy fire, while Jeune, who was last in line, lay still near Webber.

Machine guns and mortars joined in the firing. The position was surrounded, and the Japanese were moving in on the open patch. Mariba, wounded, fell after the first burst of fire. Harris, Bunning, and Shortis, still in the open, kept up an accurate fire, drawing the enemy on themselves. McNicol crawled to the edge of the jungle, at a place where there was no firing, and beckoned Harris to come to him. Harris, wounded in the left shoulder and with his pistol in his right hand, waved McNicol away toward the south.

Sadly, McNicol moved off, seeing that he could do no more for his leader. His movement was seen by the enemy soldiers, two of whom turned to fire at him. Firing in return, he escaped. Then, coming upon two dead Japanese, killed by their own mortar fire, he took the rifle of one. While searching the bodies for cartridges, he heard more Japanese approaching and had to retreat.

Yali and Buka remained hidden on the edge of the jungle, not knowing in which direction to move, while Mas slipped off toward McNicol. Launcelot, uninjured, reached the edge of the jungle, a few yards from Harris, who was still in the open. Jeune crept over to join Webber and the two remained concealed.

The Japanese attack converged on Harris, Bunning, and Shortis. The final phases can only be reconstructed from captured Japanese reports, but these are clear enough. The three men kept up the action for four hours, until at last Bunning and Shortis lay dead and Harris, wounded in three places, faced the enemy alone with an empty pistol. Then they rushed him.

'Blue' Harris faced his captors unflinchingly. The Japanese dragged him to a tree in the open and propped him against it. They questioned him about the party, about the ship that had landed it, about future attacks and movements. But Harris faced them with dumb contempt. He knew his wounds were mortal and that he need fear nothing from their threats or even worry that any weakness of the flesh might betray him. His lips remained closed and his eyes defied them until, exasperated, they bayoneted him and, all of their questions unanswered, gave him the release of death that he desired.

Launcelot lay hidden for four days in the one spot, hardly moving, while the Japanese searched within a few yards of him. He had two tins of emergency rations of which he ate a small portion, and licked the raindrops from leaves.

When at last the enemy seemed to have left, he set off for the beach, keeping to the jungle. A few days later, he met a friendly native who fed and hid him until our forces landed a month later. When he saw the convoy, he paddled out in a canoe and was taken to General Eichelberger, to whom he told his story. Launcelot, at this time, believed himself to be the only survivor.

But five others, also, had managed somehow to five through the massacre. Webber and Jeune had crawled into the jungle, where they remained until dusk the next day. Then, taking stock, they found they had an Owen gun, a pistol, two knives, one tin of emergency rations, five bouillon cubes, some medicines, and a compass. They set out through the jungle, heading first east, then south.

After five days, they realized they had no hope of reaching the Idenburg and that their only chance lay in keeping to deep gullies and trying to survive until our forces landed. Seven foodless days later they found two small caves where they hid for another fourteen days, with only the raw hearts of palmtops as food.

By this time very weak, they heard the air raids and, on 21 April the bombardment that heralded the attack. Next morning, they set out for the beach, and late that afternoon found natives who gave them a hot meal of taro and sweet potatoes, the first real food they had had for four weeks, and sheltered them for the night. Next morning they again set off, guided by two natives. But Jeune was so weak that he could hardly walk, so the natives, by signs, suggested that he be left in a hut while Webber searched for an American patrol. Webber gave his Owen gun to a native to carry, while he supported Jeune, but kept his revolver. Webber tells in his own words what happened next.

When we reached within ten or fifteen feet of the hut, a Jap rushed out and charged us, armed with a sword. I called a warning to Jeune of the presence of the Japanese, released him, and turned to take my gun from the native. I was sure there would be more Japs in the area. The natives were already running. Jeune, somehow, while my back was turned, was closest to the Jap, therefore was attacked first. He fended off a sabre blow and hung onto the blade.

Overestimating my strength, I tried to knock the Jap out with punches to the face and throat rather than use my pistol for fear of bringing more on to the scene. After a struggle, during which the Jap nearly got possession of my pistol, I shot him by forcing the barrel into his stomach, thereby hoping to deaden the sound. This struggle required the combined strength of both Jeune and myself. Jeune told me later he forced his two fingers into the Jap's nostrils and the remaining fingers and hand into his mouth. This caused partial suffocation, thus enabling me to use my pistol effectively. Then, to prevent any outcry he might make, Jeune stabbed him through the heart with his sabre. As it turned out, he was alone, and I could have used my pistol earlier than I did without jeopardizing our safety.

Jeune had suffered cuts on the ear, neck, forearm, and hand, and was still further weakened by the struggle. The two remained hidden awhile, then continued for the beach; Webber scouting ahead and supporting himself on the sabre, while Jeune staggered along, using a long stick for the same purpose. Frequent halts were necessary, but late in the afternoon they met up with American soldiers and were taken to a battalion hospital. Both were evacuated and both recovered, although Jeune's health was permanently affected.

McNicol, who had met up with Mas briefly during the heat of the attack, had lost track of all the members of the party. Late in the afternoon of the day of the ambush, he heard firing near the beach and made his way toward it. He saw about fifteen Japanese, but could not make out at what they were firing, so he hid and worked his way back toward the scene of the ambush. Next day, he searched for survivors and, finding none, set out for the mountains, following Harris' last orders to him.

Next day, he met Mas again, and for thirty-two days the two men lived in the jungle with hardly any food. When they heard the bombardment and reasoned that it must be the landing, Mas was so weak and ill that McNicol set off alone for the beach. He reached an American medical unit and was promptly put in a hospital. All the while, his voice a whisper from a skull, his large eyes pleading, he begged that they go after Mas.

A patrol was sent out almost immediately, but failed to find him. Later another search was made, but with no success.

Yali and Buka had fallen to the ground during the ambush, when Mariba was shot beside them. Buka was unarmed, but Yali fired in the direction of a machine gun that was spitting bullets at Harris. Several of the Japanese wheeled and advanced on them. Yali fired, then he and Buka escaped into the jungle.

The two searched for two days, but could not find any other members of the party, so they struck out for Mandated New Guinea. So far as they knew, the nearest friendly forces were at Saidor, more than 400 miles away, but they faced the journey fearlessly. This is Yali's story:

We had many narrow escapes while walking to Vanimo. As we had no food or matches and could not cook any of the food we stole from native gardens, we grew weaker. When near Vanimo, Buka became ill and weak. One day, we were walking near the beach and heard a launch engine nearby. I decided to investigate as I thought it might be American soldiers.

I left Buka in the bush as he was too weak to come down with me, and then walked down to the beach. Upon arrival at the beach, I ran into some Japanese soldiers who saw me and shouted out to me, asking if I were an Australian police-boy. I then ran into the bush and kept away from the area where Buka was, as I did not want the Japs to follow me back to him.

Later, I returned to the spot where I had left Buka but could find no sign of him. I searched the vicinity for two days and then decided that he had been captured by the Japs. I then decided to push on to Aitape, and after arriving at Vanimo, I received help from the natives and here learned of the American landing at Aitape. I arrived at Aitape where I contacted the Angau officer in charge.

So reported Yali to Lieutenant Ben Hall, planter and labor-recruiter, a man not likely to be sentimental about a native. Hall added to the report that Yali's story, '...does not relate fully the courage and determination displayed by this man in his return to the Allied lines, a journey of a hundred and twenty miles.'

Mariba, he who had been the first wounded by the ambushing Japanese, turned up, incredibly, eight months later. He had been captured and held prisoner, but had escaped and made his way back to our lines. His return gave us some faint hope for Mas and Buka.

Throughout the world there have been foolish arguments on racial virtues. There are those who contend that mixed races inherit the worst traits of both parents, and there are others who hold that complete mixture of races, once stabilized, is best. Others say that all men are creatures of their environment and training. Coastwatchers wouldn't know the erudite points of such matters. They only know that the half-caste Julius McNicol and the full-bred native Yali can have a place in any party where courage and resource are the qualifications.

Among the coastwatchers, the disaster to the Hollandia party spread a gloom which no other casualties had caused. 'Blue' Harris was the most striking personality among a bunch of notable individualists, a man whose vitality was such that his death was, at first, unbelievable. Harris, Shortis, Bunning, Mas, Buka—all had been lost; hearing it, men muttered the meaningless blasphemies and obscenities which had replaced prayer in their vocabularies, while in the far-off Admiralty Islands, Keith McCarthy went to church for the first time since he had been married.

22

AFTER THE EARLY PART OF 1944, the warfare in the Northeast Area passed into a new phase. Cut-off Japanese forces were harried by aircraft and ships, but the Allied offensive pushed north and westward in the Pacific, no longer needing to spend its energies on liberation of the parts of the Northeast Area still occupied by the enemy.

Under these conditions, coastwatching ceased. In New Britain, the coastwatchers had become guerrillas holding no-man's-land. In New Ireland and Bougainville, coastwatcher reconnaissance parties could come and go almost at will, but to little purpose since the Japanese were left to simmer on these islands, their helplessness aggravated by occasional Allied patrols and air attacks.

At Wewak, coastwatcher parties stationed along the enemy's escape route learned that only minor elements of that garrison were attempting to slip away. A major effort of these forces to break through to the west was then foiled by American troops, and the Wewak Japanese, like their fellows in New Britain, New Ireland, and Bougainville, were rendered impotent.

FERDINAND signals, throughout the war in the Northeast Area, had been noted for their reliability, and our radio system had often carried the traffic of larger units. This had not passed unnoticed, and when the offensive passed westward to Biak, Sansapor, and Morotai, a FERDINAND signal unit accompanied the Allied forces to receive and pass on signals from other intelligence organizations.

But coastwatching as a process of obtaining intelligence from enemy-occupied areas was finished. The coastwatchers had done their job and, for their numbers, had made a contribution out of all proportion.

Had FERDINAND not existed, Japan would still have been defeated but victory would have come later and at a higher cost of life. Had Guadalcanal been lost, there would have been no attrition of the Japanese forces. Without FERDINAND it is possible Australia might have been invaded or, at best, would have been able to receive but scant supplies from America, and its value as a base of Pacific operations would have been seriously impaired. Without the coastwatchers, the U.S. Navy would surely have faced still stronger enemy forces when it advanced through the Central Pacific.

For all the help that FERDINAND received from the Allied forces, in a way it owed most to the unwitting help of the enemy. The mistakes made by the Japanese, the fact that they apparently never fully realized what damage was being done them by a few skillful, resolute men, did most to reward FERDINAND's efforts with success.

FERDINAND had been more or less an irregular organization, its men not cast in the conventional military mold. But eventually, as with everything military, formalism gradually infiltrated, until at last, even in FERDINAND, it became more important to know the wording of a financial directive than to know where the Japanese were and what they were up to.

In New Guinea and the Solomons, camps grew where coastwatchers had trodden delicately around the Japanese positions. The camps were organized, set out in orderly rows. Seniority was observed, dress regulations were enforced, the correct form was signed on the appropriate dotted line. Military order prevailed, with a military policeman on the corner to see that it did.

The coastwatchers, like all pioneers, fitted uneasily into the new order they had helped to create. Like the old goldfield prospector, who declaimed that, '...when women and goats come in, it is time for a decent prospector to get out,' the coastwatchers saw that it was time for them too to get out.

So all who could went to the guerrillas and carried on their war in their own way, preferring the silent jungle with its dim, damp twilight to the crowded regimentation of camp and office.

Thus the living. The killed and missing were already part forgotten.

Omaha Beach, 6/6/1944